Inventing Catholic Tradition

Inventing Catholic Tradition

Terrence W. Tilley

ORBIS BOOKS

Maryknoll, New York 10545

The Catholic Foreign Mission Society of America (Maryknoll) recruits and trains people for overseas missionary service. Through Orbis Books, Maryknoll aims to foster the international dialogue that is essential to mission. The books published, however, reflect the opinions of their authors and are not meant to represent the official position of the society. To obtain more information about Maryknoll and Orbis Books, please visit our website at www.maryknoll.org.

Published by Orbis Books, Maryknoll, NY 10545-0308
Manufactured in the United States of America
Manuscript editing and typesetting by Joan Weber Laflamme

Library of Congress Cataloging-in-Publication Data

Tilley, Terrence W.
    Inventing Catholic tradition / Terrence W. Tilley.
      p. cm.
    Includes index.
    ISBN 1-57075-340-7 (pbk.)
      1. Tradition (Theology) 2. Catholic Church—Doctrines. I. Title.

BT90.T55 2000
231'042—dc21

                                     00-032667

Contents

Preface

One of the great joys of writing, at least for me, is that it is a communal practice. Many friends and colleagues have heard or read and constructively criticized part or all of this book. Indeed, without their challenging friendship, this book would not have been written.

As the genesis of this book is an integral part of its story, you can read about its origins in the introduction. Here, I want to acknowledge all those who have made the practice of writing possible for me.

Colleagues at the University of Dayton, Jack McGrath, S.M., and Una Cadegan, first challenged me to begin this work. They, Sandra Yocum Mize, Dennis Doyle, Jim Heft, S.M., M. Therese Lysaught, Maureen Tilley, Mike Barnes, and I have worked on each other's writing for a number of years. The collegiality that makes this possible has improved my thinking and writing immensely. My deepest thanks to them. The students in REL 600, Research Methods in fall 1999 (Mary Brown, Isabel Fernandez, Joe Jacobs, and Vernon Meyer) also helped shaped my thinking in ways that have improved the final form of this book.

Others also deserve many thanks. William Vance Trollinger of the University of Dayton History Department responded to the lecture that was the first public unveiling of ideas incorporated herein, especially those now in chapter 5. I am grateful for his anabaptist eye and his important constructive criticisms. Members of a faculty seminar on religion and the social sciences in the winter and summer terms of 1999, organized by Father Heft and funded by the University and an anonymous foundation, also read and responded to parts of this work as it was in progress.

The College Theology Society and the Society for Philosophy of Religion have heard papers that have incorporated ideas now in this book. Prof. M. Jamie Ferreira of the University of Virginia helpfully responded to a paper that sketched much of the material now in chapters 2 through 4 at the 1998 meeting of the Society for Philosophy of Religion. Other colleagues have also helped improve the argument, including Tom Gaeke, William L. Portier of Mount St. Mary's,

Emmitsburg; Gary Macy, Orlando Espín, and Bernard Cooke of the University of San Diego; Edward Jeremy Miller of Gwynnedd-Mercy College; Vincent J. Miller of Georgetown University; Avery Dulles, S.J., of Fordham University; Tony Godzieba of Villanova University; Bernard Lee, S.M., Loyola Institute for Ministry, Loyola University, New Orleans; and especially Dermot Lane of Mater Dei Institute, Dublin, and Maureen A. Tilley of the University of Dayton, both of whom read the entire manuscript (and parts of it more than once).

Thanks are also due to Sue Perry, my editor, and the staff at Orbis Books who have done much to help clarify and develop the argument in this work.

To all of these and those others whom I have forgotten to include, I owe a real debt, which this preface acknowledges. That they helped me get clearer on *Inventing Catholic Tradition* does not mean, of course, that they endorse the arguments made or the position taken herein.

Introduction

I had never thought, as my theological work developed, that I would write a book on tradition. I did not imagine that I could add anything significant to the fine work by Catholic theologian Yves Congar, O.P., and others on the theology of the Catholic tradition.[1] Congar's work is that of a theological giant. I am not sure that I can stand on his shoulders to see farther than he, but I can offer a different vision of the terrain of "tradition." But since I have now written on tradition, I'd like to say how I came to want to write on it and to highlight the key issues in the line of thought developed here.

The Background for This Writing

A nexus of events has led me to think that I do now have something to add to the fundamental theology of tradition. First, numerous philosophical, historical, and theological developments have created conditions that make it possible to offer a vision different from Congar's. The philosopher Alasdair MacIntyre has construed a tradition as an ongoing argument, one form of conversation.[2] A number of poststructuralist writers, including Michel Foucault and many influ-

---

[1] See Yves Congar, O.P., *Tradition and Traditions: An Historical and a Theological Essay*, trans. Michael Naseby and Thomas Rainborough (New York: Macmillan, 1967; French edition, 1960 [*Essai Historique*] and 1963 [*Essai Théologique*]); for an overview of the modern Catholic theology of tradition, see Georges Boeglin, *La question de la tradition dans la théologie catholique contemporaine* (Paris: Cerf, 1998) and Avery Dulles, S.J., "Tradition as a Theological Source," in *The Craft of Theology: From Symbol to System* (New York: Crossroad, 1996), 87-104. Two landmarks are Josef Geiselmann, *The Meaning of Tradition*, trans. W. J. O'Hara (New York: Herder and Herder, 1966) and Karl Rahner and Joseph Ratzinger, *Revelation and Tradition*, trans. W. J. O'Hara (New York: Herder and Herder, 1966); other works will be cited below.

[2] For the concept of a tradition as an argument, see Alasdair MacIntyre, *After Virtue: A Study in Moral Theory* (Notre Dame, Ind.: University of Notre Dame Press, 1981), 207; also see the discussion in chapters 2 and 3, below.

1

enced by his work, have described the ways in which discourse systems construct and distribute power and knowledge; in fact, once one sees these systems as diachronic rather than punctual, one realizes that Foucault and his fellow travelers are talking about traditions.[3] Emerging discussions in some feminist work and hermeneutical theory have shown the interconnections of tradition and reason.[4] Anthropologists and sociologists have developed more diachronic approaches to their study of culture and thus cast light on the place of tradition in human societies.[5] Historical investigations have shown that what we have often taken to be definitive traditions have been neither constant nor logically developmental.[6] Influenced by James William McClendon Jr., and Robert Schreiter, C.Pp.S, I began to construe a religious tradition as a set of enduring practices.[7] These developments—and numerous others—over the last four decades open up new ways to construe tradition.

These new approaches alone, however, would not have impelled me to think seriously and to write about tradition. Beyond these aca-

---

[3] An example of the creative and insightful theological use of this strand of thought can be found in Vincent J. Miller, "History or Geography? Gadamer, Foucault, and Theologies of Tradition," in *Theology and the New Histories: The Forty-fifth Annual Volume of the College Theology Society,* ed. Gary Macy (Maryknoll, N.Y.: Orbis Books, 1999), 56-85.

[4] Numerous works could be cited here. Beyond the seminal work of Hans-Georg Gadamer, *Truth and Method,* 2d rev. ed., trans. Joel Weinsheimer and Donald G. Marshall (New York: Crossroad, 1989; first German edition, 1960), see the very different works of Catherine Pickstock, *After Writing: On the Liturgical Consummation of Philosophy* (Oxford: Basil Blackwell, 1998); Lorraine Code, *What Can She Know? Feminist Theory and the Construction of Knowledge* (Ithaca, N.Y.: Cornell University Press, 1991); and Rebecca Chopp, *The Power to Speak: Feminism, Language, God* (New York: Crossroad, 1989).

[5] See, for instance, Kathryn Tanner, *Theories of Culture: A New Agenda For Theology* (Philadelphia: Fortress, 1997); Eric Hobsbawm and Terence Ranger, eds., *The Invention of Tradition* (Cambridge: Cambridge University Press, 1983); and Paul Connerton, *How Societies Remember* (Cambridge: Cambridge University Press, 1989).

[6] For instance, see J. Robert Dionne, *The Papacy and the Church: A Study of Praxis and Reception in Ecumenical Perspective* (New York: Philosophical Library, 1987); Gary Macy, *Treasures from the Storehouse* (Collegeville, Minn.: Liturgical Press, 1999).

[7] See Robert Schreiter, *Constructing Local Theologies* (Maryknoll, N.Y.: Orbis Books, 1985); James Wm. McClendon Jr., *Systematic Theology,* vol. 1, *Ethics* and vol. 2, *Doctrine* (Nashville, Tenn.: Abingdon, 1986-94). Also see Terrence W. Tilley, *The Wisdom of Religious Commitment* (Washington, D.C.: Georgetown University Press, 1995), especially chapter 2 and the literature cited there, and also chapter 2 below.

demic developments, a number of events and experiences have convinced me that I might be able to develop a new angle for writing a theology of tradition. The more public academic influences will appear in the course of the book below. However, two more personal experiences were key in convincing me to take up this task.

The first event occurred in the spring of 1995. I was attending a colloquium entitled "The Catholic Intellectual Tradition" at the University of Dayton, (then) my new academic home. Fr. Johann Roten, S.M., read the main paper; the respondents were Professors Sandra Yocum Mize and Joseph Kunkel. Fr. Roten's excellent paper, I thought, might have been construed to limit the Catholic Intellectual Tradition to a set of theological arguments extended over time. I intervened during the discussion period to argue that while formal theological work is done by a small elite among intellectuals (almost exclusively clerics until 1970 or so), the Catholic Intellectual Tradition must be broader than theology, for it clearly includes philosophers, poets, and fiction writers (and others as well). Later in the discussion, a distinguished member of the faculty of the university insisted that in the Catholic tradition, women had never administered the sacraments. That claim, as stated, is simply false. It dismayed me that an educated person could declare in public with an aura of absolute certainty something so blatantly false. So I responded again, this time strenuously. Given the seven sacraments, I suggested that we need to note that women are the co-administrators of matrimony; that they have the duty to baptize in emergencies (and that indeed even non-baptized people can baptize in case of necessity); that women administered the anointing of the sick before the sacrament was clericalized in the ninth or tenth century; that abbesses heard confessions of the nuns in their convents in the Middle Ages and that these practices were indistinguishable from other confessional practices we recognize today as sacramental; and that (arguably and controversially) women presided at orthodox (not heretical or schismatic) Eucharists in early house churches in the first and second centuries. Even the two of the seven sacraments that we would imagine women not to have administered, confirmation and holy orders, may have earlier forms in the history of the development of Catholic ritual that both women and men administered. I also noted that this didn't even consider the other sacraments and sacramentals recognized in the Middle Ages—up to thirty sacraments, according to some orthodox Catholic theologians. The Catholic tradition has not offered a single, consistent answer on either the number or the proper ministers of the sacraments; there is not a "fixed" tradition, as my colleague imagined. And if so in the dry wood of respected academics, what of the green? What of those who never have studied the development of traditions, even of the traditions in which they dwell? It is commonplace, I fear, for people to believe that the eternal truth of a tradition is what they learned in their childhood religious formation, what they heard uttered by a minister, rabbi, or priest the last time they attended services, or what the "common view" relates.

In light of my off-the-cuff comments during that colloquium, I was challenged to stand up—in part so that I would have to take challenges like those I dished out—and give a lecture to a similar colloquium. That lecture was finally given in the fall of 1997. In it I tried to bring together the disparate discussions of tradition into a useful and provocative synthesis. That led to the present book. To respond to the challenge to do that lecture, I found that I had to write a fundamental theology of tradition, even though I had never planned to do so, nor would I have ever thought in the past that it was a task that would fall naturally to me.

The resolution to devote my energy to this work was crystallized by a second event. In the summer of 1997 I attended the fabulous Byzantium exhibition at the Metropolitan Museum of Art in New York. Among the materials on display were a number of icons carved from ivory—something I not only had never seen before but had not even known existed. I was awed by their intricate, thousand-year-old beauty. I was especially struck and deeply moved by a diptych icon, dated to the second half of the tenth century or early eleventh century—an icon now about one thousand years old![8] It portrays twelve scenes from the life of Christ. It is the cover art for this book. The scenes on this diptych and the commentary on them illustrated for me the problems with traditional understandings of tradition.

The four scenes across the top of the diptych are the annunciation of Gabriel to Mary that she would become *theotokos*, the bearer of God; the visitation of Mary to her cousin Elizabeth, when the babe in Elizabeth's womb jumped for joy; the birth of Jesus; and the presentation of Jesus in the Temple. Each of these scenes, as depicted in Luke's gospel, has deep resonances with specific texts in the Hebrew scriptures and form a narrative of the beginning of Jesus' life.

---

[8] The illustration and most of the material in the next few paragraphs are from the catalog of the exhibition, *The Glory of Byzantium: Art and Culture of the Middle Byzantine Era, A.D. 843-1261*, ed. Helen C. Evans and William D. Wixom (New York: Metropolitan Museum of Art, 1997), 144-46.

The middle four scenes form a narrative of Jesus' ministry: his baptism by John in the River Jordan, with the river at the lower left; the transfiguration of Jesus; the triumphal entry into Jerusalem; and the crucifixion. Again, the text of the gospels writes each of these stories with deep associations with the Hebrew scriptures: the baptismal scene in Luke is introduced by a long quotation from Isaiah 40, includes a quotation of Isaiah 42, and is finished with or succeeded by Jesus' genealogy from Adam; in the transfiguration, Moses and Elijah appear; the triumphal entry recalls King David, with allusions to 2 Kings and Psalm 118; the crucifixion text in Luke quotes from Exodus 31 and Psalm 26 and the other gospels make even more references.

The final four scenes are the *Anastasis*, which we translate as the "resurrection," but this event is pictured as Jesus descending into the netherworld to save Adam, Eve, the patriarchs (who stand in for all faithful Jews and others who belong in the heavenly kingdom even though they are outside the explicitly Christian circle—this is also sometimes called the harrowing of hell); the incredulity of Thomas at the resurrection, which we call Doubting Thomas; the ascension into heaven; and the sending of the Spirit to the apostles on the feast of Pentecost.

Although the exhibition catalog doesn't note this, I see a profoundly Trinitarian motif in this diptych. In the upper register, events affect Jesus. In the middle register, the primary agent is Jesus; this is the time of his activity. In the bottom register, the primary agent can be seen as the Spirit (for in each of these Jesus is *not* the primary agent).[9]

The exhibition catalog correctly notes that the twelve scenes of this icon are *not* the traditional twelve great feasts celebrating Christ in the Orthodox Church. This diptych seems to "deviate" from *the* tradition. The catalog suggests that this is because this is not a "public" devotional icon, but an object of personal contemplation. . . . The events illustrated were those of special significance to the patron or the artist."[10] The authors downplay historian Jaroslav Pelikan's suggestion "that the group represents an early example of the evolving

---

[9] That the Spirit's work as portrayed in the last register is vague and hard to see is not really a concern. The Spirit is the Person of the Trinity most difficult to "pin down" and see acting in specific events. Even some feminist proposals to address the Trinity as Creator, Redeemer, and Sanctifier indicate this; the first two actions are specifiable, but the work of sanctification remains necessarily diffuse.

[10] Ibid., 144.

selection of the Great Feasts of the Church."[11] But on this issue Pelikan's view is, in my opinion, much more likely. The tradition of celebrating twelve feasts in the Orthodox tradition is early, but their content is not fixed.[12] In this sense the authors of the catalog evidently presume that since the representations of the diptych icon deviate from the final form of the enumeration of the twelve feasts in the Orthodox Church, that this must be an item of "private devotion" rather than part of a fluid tradition. The authors not only presume that a later form of the tradition is normative for the earlier form of the tradition (a problem of retrojecting later patterns into earlier times, clearly an error in historiography, and, as we shall argue in chapter 4, a serious problem for understanding the Christian tradition), but also introduce an implicit public/private distinction that may well be unwarranted, especially given evolving Orthodox theology and practice, in order to explain how this "deviation" from the norm—the "final form" of the tradition—could have occurred. The authors thus double the confusion: Not only do they retroject a later tradition as a norm for an earlier one, but they retroject a modern dichotomy between public and private practice as the explanation for this "deviation"! If such anachronism is possible in the dry wood of the art historians who deal with religion, what of the green?

Traditions are not fixed but fluid. If we neglect the shifts of tradition or canonize one form as normative, as the catalog authors did, we can misread earlier traditions by taking them merely as parts of definable historical trajectories that issue in a "finished product" that is the "right" tradition. We misread differences in traditions as "deviations," as "errors," or as "private interpretations." A historical theologian like Pelikan knows both the stability and the fluidity of the Orthodox tradition; the art historians make an inference that is based on very limited data, evaluate the earlier fluidity by a later fixed tradition, and introduce a dubious distinction between public religion

---

[11] Ibid., citing Jaroslav Pelikan, *Imago Dei: The Byzantine Apologia for Icons* (Princeton, N.J.: Princeton University Press, 1990), 86-88.

[12] The catalog authors note this, but compare this diptych with other eleventh-century mosaics in other places. Helen Evans says that the others are the "most popular" cycles for the twelve feasts. But the fragmentary archeological data and the difference in locations (and the dating, although that is not as clear) for the comparable works make the claim that one form is "most popular" and the present one is "most unusual" is very odd, although her point that this diptych is unusual in "leaving out" the raising of Lazarus is well taken. I would speculate that it could have been left out because including that scene might have upset the Trinitarian allusions noted above.

and private devotion. Of course, the art historians might be right, but like our distinguished colleague who denied any ministerial role to women in the Catholic tradition, our art historians seem to presuppose erroneously that traditions are fixed and final, at least in a specific stage in their development.[13]

The diptych is a material monument to an ongoing tradition. That tradition extends back not merely to the gospels, but at least to the Hebrew scriptures as well. That tradition is incarnated in the rhythm of the liturgical year, in the devotional life of participants, in the theology that is preached, in texts that are passed on, and in the art that celebrates the life of the tradition. How can we understand the multifaceted concept of tradition and utilize the insights of contemporary scholars to construct an understanding of tradition that recognizes all its manifold facets?

These questions seemed to press on me. As they continued to do so, I realized that to answer them adequately would require more than an occasional lecture.[14] So I found myself writing a book I never imagined I would write, answering questions I never had expected would be mine. How can we formally understand what a tradition is? How can we particularly understand the shape of the Catholic tradition?

The Difficulty of the Concept of Tradition

The concept of tradition is an essentially contested concept. This means that there is substantial, longstanding, ineradicable disagreement about what constitutes a tradition, and, thus, what the concept of tradition is. Clearly, since the Reformation of the sixteenth century, Protestants and Catholics have not only disagreed about the use

---

[13] Dennis Doyle has reminded me of the significant overlap between the scenes of the diptych and the mysteries of the Rosary. Whether there is any historical connection between these devotional items is unknown to me. Eight of the fifteen mysteries of the Rosary are found in the diptych.

[14] Another key event, to be discussed in more detail below, was the remarkable and novel invention of a category of "definitive (but not infallible?)" teachings, promulgated by the Congregation for the Doctrine of the Faith in 1989 and made part of canon law in 1998 by *Ad Tuendam Fidem*. The commentary of Cardinal Ratzinger that accompanied this latter document included a group of "teachings" so diverse that it is difficult to find a nontendentious characterization of what attributes make them members of this specific set of "definitive" teachings that require wholehearted assent.

and the normativity of tradition in the Church but have disagreed about what tradition is.[15] The Orthodox and the Western churches also have different concepts of tradition, with theologians of the former often writing of "Holy Tradition" and using tradition as a norm in a way significantly different from the Western churches. Moreover, social historians have weighed in with important writing about traditions. Their descriptive definitions of what constitute traditions seem both descriptively adequate and to be inscribed in a totally different conceptual universe from that of the theologians and the philosophers concerned with tradition.[16] What this means is that any specific concept of tradition is itself a fluid moment in a larger tradition—the tradition of arguing about what constitutes tradition! It is almost a truism to note that what later ages may come to consider fixed and immutable tradition will be different from what we or our predecessors consider fixed.

For Roman Catholic thinkers, the concept of tradition is theologically very important because it is associated with disputes concerning divine revelation, its sources, and it bearers. Issues including the sufficiency of scripture, the necessity of tradition, and, in general, the relationship of scripture and tradition are always nearby whenever theologians discuss the concept of tradition. Few theologians investigate tradition as anything other than as a major theological category—again, an essentially contested one.[17] This category is deeply shaped by the theologians' view of revelation. Because of this, theologians who attempt to understand the concept of tradition unavoidably take a path that analyzes tradition in a way that is congruent with their understanding of divine revelation. Their sources, moreover, are almost always exclusively theologians, fathers of the Church, official magisterial pronouncements, and Church councils.[18]

---

[15] For evidence for this claim, see the brief, but useful, overview of modern Protestant understandings of tradition written before the Second Vatican Council by Catholic theologian James P. Mackey, *The Modern Theology of Tradition* (London: Darton, Longman & Todd, 1962), chap. 6. Many accounts of the development of tradition have difficulty accommodating some changes in Catholic teaching made at Vatican II, e.g., the support of religious freedom found in *Dignitatis Humanae*.

[16] See Eric Hobsbawm, "Introduction: Inventing Traditions," in Hobsbawm and Ranger, *The Invention of Tradition*, 1-6. I thank Margaret Steinfels for this reference.

[17] See, for instance, Congar, *Tradition and Traditions*, xix: "The word 'tradition'—as understood by Christians—means a variety of distinct, though related things."

[18] See Mackey, *The Modern Theology of Tradition*; and Congar, *Tradition and Traditions*, esp. 233-34.

The approach here does not neglect this work, but utilizes it in a different analytical structure. Because the sociological, historical, and philosophical discussions of tradition that are important for the present work use methodologies that do not attend to revelation, the approach here is significantly different from the usual theological approaches. In the present work, I begin by "bracketing" the theological understanding of the relation of tradition to revelation and discuss tradition in descriptive terms. I leave the connection of this understanding of tradition to the normative issues. In this, my writing of the book and your reading of it follow similar paths: I did no concentrated thinking or substantial writing about the normative issues in the final chapter until the work on the descriptive material in the previous chapters was substantially complete.[19]

As noted above, Yves Congar, O.P., wrote the greatest Catholic theological work on tradition in the second half of the twentieth century. His complex, synthetic position has shaped all subsequent Catholic theological work, including my own. Yet despite its meticulous historical investigations, its constructive theology remains focused at a rather abstract level. Congar concludes that "tradition is not primarily to be defined by a particular material object, but by the act of transmission, and its content is simply *id quod traditum est, id quod traditur*" [what is handed on or over].[20] Congar's basic insight is correct, but it needs development and more concrete specification.

Congar needs well over five hundred pages to say that tradition is not simply content. For *id quod traditur* requires an agent handing something on, something to be handed on, and an agent or agents receiving what is handed on. *Traditio* is a communicative process and a communicative practice. The *tradita* are handed on. Beyond the fact that *tradita* may be a huge variety of things (attitudes, doctrines, visions, skills, practices, virtues, etc.), the item being communicated is not and cannot be the only essential thing. The implications of and nuances in this very important point will be developed in the present text.

But it should be noted that Congar misses something that subsequent French poststructuralists might have noted.[21] In Latin, the word

---

[19] As the notes in chapter 6 make clear, however, I have worked on the issues of truth and authority in other contexts in the past.

[20] Congar, *Tradition and Traditions*, 296.

[21] Consider the brilliant and provocative work of Jacques Derrida, "Plato's Pharmacy," in *Disseminations*, trans. Barbara Johnson (Chicago: University of Chicago Press, 1981), 61-171, as a model for this sort of work.

traditio means not only what was handed on but also *treason*. In fact, early Christian leaders who *handed on* the Sacred Scriptures to the Roman authorities were branded *traditores.* They were traitors. This etymological note is preserved in an Italian motto, *Tradutore, tradditore,* which is usually rendered in English as "The translator is a traitor"—whoever hands on a text from one language to another inevitably is a traitor to the original text. What all this means, of course, is not that those who transmit tradition are traitors, but that attending merely to the barest concept of tradition as *id quod traditur* without close attention to context and particular circumstances of the practice of *traditio* is bound to fail to explicate the rich meanings of the concept of tradition. And while it may seem Derrida-esque or quixotic to do so, I will argue later that it is not only necessary but good that, from one perspective, a *traditor* is a traitor.

The argument of this book begins by clearing some ground. It argues against two dominant views of tradition: that traditions are either fixed, immutable "things," or that they are in some way fictions created out of whole cloth. While both extremes preserve some insights, a more reasonable view lies elsewhere. Chapter 2 introduces an argument about the concept of tradition as a set of enduring practices. Chapter 3 utilizes the concept developed in chapter 2 to examine a specific practice to show how this approach affects our understanding of tradition. Chapter 4 argues that the "grammar" of a practice shapes a tradition, but that the notion of "applying a rule" is much more complex than proponents of "fixed traditions" take it to be. Chapter 5 is a test case: If the previous two chapters have developed a concept of tradition that is basically adequate, using that concept to investigate a tradition should prove illuminating. The test case chosen, especially relevant to current discussions about Catholicism and Catholic studies in contemporary colleges and universities, is to develop the grammatical rules of the Catholic Intellectual Tradition. The sixth chapter turns to that normative problem: How can this constructivist account of tradition be linked with an understanding of truth, revelation, and authority. Here we will harvest insights from the previous chapters, especially contributions from the work of John Henry Newman and the Catholic Intellectual Tradition more generally.

I have here tried to write with a minimum of jargon and "code," a writing practice to which I have been long committed. Nonetheless, some specialized language is unavoidable in constructing a serious theological argument and will be introduced in a way that makes this book accessible both to educated Catholics and interesting to professional scholars. Since I have tried both to approach the concept of tradition in a new way, and in so doing to join what is normally sundered by the walls of administrative departments in academia, there should be something new here for most readers. *Inventing Catholic Tradition* is, then, unabashedly eclectic in that it weaves together threads from many different sources and proudly transverses typical disciplinary boundaries. Yet it also seeks to bring that diversity into a unified, if multicolored cloak.

Two warnings are in order at the beginning. First, because the basic approach in this text is different from many traditional Catholic theological approaches, the usual nomenclature about tradition, ensconced especially by the debates at the Council of Trent (1545-63) and taken for granted as part of the Catholic theological vocabulary since that time, will be conspicuously absent for much of the work. I am not trying to avoid the issues that the use of these terms raises; the key issues are discussed in chapter 6. However, one principal result of the historical and philosophical work of the last four decades—and reflected in the present work—is that terminology can remain constant while the significance of terms changes, sometimes radically. As I will show below, it is simply an empirical fact that key terms in the Christian vocabulary have changed their meanings significantly as the contexts in which they have been used changed. To use the "usual nomenclature" and ask the "usual questions," for example, Is tradition the "bearer" of revelation?, as if these terms and questions had a settled meaning, is incompatible with both the method of investigation and the results of the investigation. For those who are "old hands" in working on tradition, this book offers a new conceptual map of the terrain. I ask you to take this approach on its own terms to see if it indeed is useful.[22] After all, the comparison of one

---

[22] The present approach, with its focus on practices as primary, parallels in some respects the work of some U.S. Latino/a theologians. See Roberto S. Goizueta, *Caminemos con Jesús: Toward a Hispanic/Latino Theology of Accompaniment* (Maryknoll, N.Y.: Orbis Books, 1995), especially 78-100, 119-31; Orlando O. Espín, "Tradition and Popular Religion: An Understanding of the *Sensus Fidelium*," in *The Faith of the People: Theological Reflections on Popular Catholicism* (Maryknoll, N.Y.: Orbis Books, 1997) 63-90; and María Pilar Aquino, "Theological Method in U.S. Latino/a Theology: Toward an Intercultural Theology for the Third Millennium," in *From the Heart of Our People: Latino/a Explorations in Catholic Systematic Theology*, ed. Orlando O. Espín and Miguel H. Díaz (Maryknoll, N.Y.: Orbis Books, 1999), 6-48. For better or worse, the present approach differs in that it is a more generalized analysis, that is, one not centered in the practice/praxis of a specific set of communities, whereas U.S. Latino/a theologians focus especially on the practice/praxis of Cuban-American, Mexican-American, and Puerto Rican communities in the United States.

sort of map to another can take place, in practice, only after one has tried to navigate using each independently of the other and then comparing the results.

Second, this text does not undertake the task of offering a "grammar" of the Catholic tradition. In one sense, our basic grammar is already defined in the *regula fidei*, the Creed. To write such a grammar is either to write a commentary on the Creed[23] or to show how that grammar shapes Catholic life in practice.[24] There are many excellent examples of such grammars, from simple expositions, to systematic theologies, to the *Catechism of the Catholic Church*. There is no reason to offer, at this time, another entry in one of those fields, even if I could. The latter is a project worth undertaking but is not merely "another book"; rather, it is another wide-ranging research program that would result in a set of books.

If the understanding of tradition developed here is accurate, it has two major implications. First, the *sensus fidelium* is passed on in the practices of the faithful. Second, if this faith is to be kept alive, it requires that the faithful of every place and order in the enduring community that is the Church Militant engage in inventing Catholic tradition.

---

[23] One fine example is Nicholas Lash, *Believing Three Ways in One God: A Reading of the Apostles' Creed* (London: SCM Press, 1992; Notre Dame, Ind.: University of Notre Dame Press, 1993).

[24] A quartet of books by Lawrence S. Cunningham suggests the direction such a theology might take. See *The Catholic Heritage* (New York: Crossroad, 1983), *The Catholic Experience* (New York: Crossroad, 1985), *The Catholic Faith* (New York: Paulist Press, 1987), *Catholic Prayer* (New York: Crossroad, 1989); my own earlier work, *Story Theology* (Wilmington, Del.: Michael Glazier, 1985; reprint, Collegeville, Minn.: Liturgical Press, 1991) is also an initial exploration of one way such a theology might be developed.

ONE

Traditions:
Made or Given?

Exploring the concept of tradition raises a host of problems. The first and foremost is a conflict between basic stances of those who study traditions and those who dwell in them. This conflict has become acute in the last two centuries: Historians who study traditions have shown that those components of traditions that participants take to be invariant have shifted remarkably over time. Historical investigations have undermined some participants' belief in the stability of traditions. Perhaps the most difficult issues raised by this emergence of historical consciousness are those associated with the higher criticism of the biblical texts.

Historical-critical investigation of the Bible has profoundly affected the ways in which we interpret the biblical texts. Debates about the biblical texts and their meanings have occupied theologians and Church leaders from the beginning. However, it is only during the last two centuries that ordinary Christians have had to face the challenge of reconciling their traditional faith in the Bible as the word of God with the results of historical investigation.[1] Believers' faith presumes that the Bible is in some sense *given* by God to humanity. Historical research seems to show that the Bible is *made* by human processes. Not only are books in the Bible composites of earlier traditions,

---

[1] This story has been told in various ways. See, among others, Hans Frei, *The Eclipse of the Biblical Narrative: A Study in Eighteenth and Nineteenth Century Hermeneutics* (New Haven, Conn.: Yale University Press, 1974); Robert M. Grant and David Tracy, *A Short History of the Interpretation of the Bible,* 2d ed. (Philadelphia: Fortress, 1984); Van A. Harvey, *The Historian and the Believer* (New York: Macmillan, 1966).

but also evident inconsistencies can be found within and between its books.[2]

In response to challenges from historians—many of them committed Christian academics—Christians have reconciled the *givenness* of the Bible with the *madeness* of its texts in numerous ways. Some evangelicals have engaged in various forms of perspective-reversals. Whereas historical investigation presumes an academic perspective that takes the subject of its study as a human construction, and thus gives the subject of its study no privileged status, some evangelicals first recognize the Bible as God's inerrant word to humanity and then accept only the methods and the results of higher criticism that are compatible with this religious perspective. Some evangelicals reject higher criticism altogether. Others reject forms of investigation that require practical atheism about the origins of the text. Some liberals accept the most challenging results of higher criticism that deny much (or all) historical reliability of the texts and accommodate their religious beliefs to these radical conclusions. Between (and even beyond) these extreme responses are numerous patterns in which committed Christians accommodate history with tradition.[3]

Yet such accommodations are not without cost. As the history of the "warfare of science with religion" has taught us, a typical argument about the status of tradition typically poses the question in antithetical terms.[4] Do we support "creation" or "evolution"? Must we only "read" the Bible or can we "interpret" it? In terms relevant to the present chapter, we ask, Are traditions "made" or found, constructed

---

[2] Of course, people also find conflicts between the Bible and the results of philosophical or scientific investigations. The nineteenth- and twentieth-century conflicts between forms of evolutionism and creationism are one form of this sort of conflict. Insofar as this is a conflict *between* traditions, rather than *over* tradition, it is not a central issue for the present investigation.

[3] Robert Schreiter, *Constructing Local Theologies* (Maryknoll, N.Y.: Orbis Books, 1985), 117, suggests that when scriptures are read *normatively*, believers read them to provide guidance for the community in the *present;* and that when they are interpreted *critically*, scholars interpret them to ascertain how they were constructed and what they meant in the *past*. Obviously, the latter can influence the former readings, but neither way of reading can be reduced to the other.

[4] A classic text in this area is Andrew Dickson White, *A History of the Warfare of Science with Theology in Christendom* (Gloucester, Mass.: Peter Smith, 1978; reprint of original edition of 1896). Ian G. Barbour, *Issues in Science and Religion* (New York: Harper & Row, 1971; first published, 1966) and John F. Haught, *Science and Religion: From Conflict to Conversation* (Mahwah, N.J.: Paulist Press, 1995) provide recent, accessible discussions of these issues.

or given? This chapter argues that a better way to understand tradition is to show a better alternative to such dichotomies. My argument is that *traditions are neither made nor found, yet both constructed and given.*

Scholars and/or Participants?

Scholars of and participants in some traditions often presume that if those who live in a tradition in some way make up that tradition, it cannot be authentic. Many participants, especially in religious traditions, assume that the tradition is, in some sense, originated and guided by the supernatural. In having that status, the tradition is a bedrock of stability in a world often hostile and baffling. The supernatural roots of the tradition may be beyond the realm of human understanding. Indeed, some participants seem to make that very claim so as to put the foundations of a tradition outside the purview of scholarly criticism. More important, participants testify to the bearings that the traditions give them in their paths in life. Whether it is the invariant yearly cycle of ritual found in many religions, the life-cycle rituals that the religions provide, or the beliefs that underlie or are ingredient in them, traditions inculcate a sense of stability in an unstable world, a beacon that can give one reliable bearings in the voyage of life, especially in the modern world.[5] They even give a person an identity. As Catherine Bell put it with regard to specific rites, "The invariant routines of Alcoholics Anonymous or Zen monasticism are understood to be necessary to the reshaping of the individuals."[6] Stability in tradition is seen as necessary to shape and reshape lives; insofar as traditions do this work effectively, the stability must be there for them to function as participants find them to do.

The position that traditions are "found" is practically ubiquitous among people who dwell in strong traditions. The shape of a tradition—whether expressed in the patriotism of a nationalist, the devotion of a religious believer, or the ethnic pride of an identifiable

---

[5] The study of ritual has been a staple of the modern project of the academic study of religion. For a brief overview, see James C. Livingston, *The Anatomy of the Sacred: An Introduction to Religion*, 3d ed. (Upper Saddle River, N.J.: Prentice-Hall, 1998). For a more comprehensive overview of the theories of ritual study and richer analyses of specific rituals, see Catherine Bell, *Ritual: Perspectives and Dimensions* (New York and Oxford: Oxford University Press, 1997), especially 91-169.

[6] Bell, *Ritual*, 151.

minority (e.g., Welsh)—is taken for granted as immutable, as *given*.[7] For traditions to be worthwhile, they must connect us with our for-bears, assure us that we carry on their contributions, and assure us too that our successors will continue on the tradition we have had passed on to us and then faithfully preserved to pass on to them. We cannot "make up" traditions. Traditions must be given us by God or the Church or history or some other process independent of human creativity—a creativity all too easily prone to fictionalization.

Traditions expressed and embodied in ritual practice are typically taken as "found," not made. In summarizing some work of anthro-pologist Roy Rappaport, Nathan Mitchell writes that ritual's "deepest and most stable messages are canonical (consisting of messages con-cerned with ultimate realities not visibly present but conveyed through symbols). Canonical messages are never invented or encoded by par-ticipants; they are 'found' or 'discovered' as already given in and by the rite."[8] If Rappaport is correct, then, to be effective, ritual prac-tices must carry meaning that is "symbolic, enduring, invariable, and ultimately independent of human agents."[9] While some superficial aspects of ritual may change, participants and scholars see those vary-ing aspects as not essential to the tradition that the ritual carries. The tradition and the ritual remain essentially invariant, given or found, not made. In sum, not only participants in strong traditions carried in rituals but also some scholars of ritual practice support the claim that traditions, especially ritual traditions, must be given, not made.

Yet scholars typically find that all traditions are in some ways con-structed by those who participate in them, and are "all too human" indeed. There is no need for a "supernatural" explanation for a process explainable by natural historical factors. The obvious conclusion,

---

[7] Throughout this book, I take up examples from many traditions. As my goal is to focus on Catholic traditions, many of the examples are Catholic. How-ever, the issues concerning tradition and traditions are not unique to the Catho-lic tradition. The other examples show that analogous issues, problems, and resolutions can be found in many traditions. Most of the claims I make can apply not only to one tradition but at least analogously to many. Chapter 3 shows how using multiple examples shapes a general understanding of the nature of tradition. Chapters 5 and 6 turn to specifically Catholic issues.

[8] Nathan D. Mitchell, *Liturgy and the Social Sciences* (Collegeville, Minn.: Li-turgical Press, 1999), 33, commenting on Roy A. Rappaport, "The Obvious As-pects of Ritual," in *Ecology, Meaning and Religion* (Richmond, Calif.: North Atlan-tic Books, 1979).

[9] Ibid., commenting on Aidan Kavanagh, *Elements of Rite: A Handbook of Litur-gical Style* (New York: Pueblo, 1982; Collegeville, Minn.: Liturgical Press, 1990), 55. Mitchell points out Kavanagh's dependence on Rappaport.

then, is that those scholars and participants alike who accept a dichotomy between either malleable "human construction" or stable "divine givenness" of a tradition, and who also come to accept that traditions are humanly constructed, would have to find that participating wholeheartedly in such a humanly given tradition, especially a religious tradition, would not be possible without some form of self-deception.

The view that traditions are all "made up" is almost ubiquitous among academics who study traditions. Rituals are human creations that have become ossified and thus seen as sacred. Not only are the "peripheral" adaptations human constructs, but the very traditions the rituals carry are human made. They find the answer to the question that titles this chapter so obvious as to be not worth discussing.[10] Some scholars find that *tradition* is a social control mechanism invoked to camouflage power plays by a political, ecclesiastical, or cultural elite—and is made up by the elites as they go along.[11] Academic historians, like sociologists, political scientists, and anthropologists, have the professional duty of *analyzing* and *explaining* human behavior and so should be much more aware of the constructed nature of traditions than participants. Yet the presumption that this vantage point is somehow the *true* view or necessarily *better* than the participants' is usually only assumed, not argued for. One needs to ask *what* the analytical vantage point is better *for*. It is not clear that analysis of traditions is better than living in traditions if humans are to flourish.

When academics study traditions, they often seek to discover how a tradition has changed. Scholars' analysis of the shaping and reshaping of a tradition and the significance of elements in a tradition through time tends to focus on change in the tradition studied. Highlighting such change also can have the effect of undermining the acceptance of a tradition by its participants, just as historical-critical study of the Bible can serve to undermine what participants take as the "plain

---

[10] William Vance Trollinger Jr., in his response to the lecture from which this book grew, reported the following: "'Traditions: Made or Found?' . . . for historians the answer to this question is obvious. A few weeks ago a colleague of mine in the history department . . . came into my office waving in her hand one of the sheets announcing Prof. Tilley's talk. Before I had the chance to say anything, she said, 'Well, they should have just asked us. There's nothing difficult about this question [whether traditions are made or found]. *We* know the answer, don't we, Bill?' Knowing what she would say, I asked her anyway: 'What *is* the answer?' Her emphatic reply: 'Traditions are made, of course!'"

[11] See the early works of Michel Foucault, who works out these issues in great detail.

sense" of scripture. Yet such scholarship can be unbalanced, as Paul Connerton notes. He finds that some social theories are "defective because they are unable to treat adequately the fact of social persistence,"[12] that is, the enduring power of a tradition. Indeed, Connerton suggests that the critical vantage point typical of academics may even obscure the continuities in traditions and the significance of such stability.

Academics also often tend to discount heavily the perceptions of those who dwell in strong traditions, except when considering participants' reports of how the ritual and tradition shape them. But what reasons are there for presuming that the academics' analytical (or deconstructive or archeological or genealogical) stories about "making up" traditions convey more of the truth about the human condition—or the condition of a thriving community—than the participants' testimony? What reasons are there for presuming that critical analysis of a life-world is always "liberating"? Even to ask questions such as these can perplex scholars. For it is to ask the fundamental question: Is there good reason to engage in critical scholarship that may undermine traditions? The utility or goodness of academic work is so much taken for granted that the question rarely arises as a serious, academic question.[13]

Academics participate in a tradition that began in earnest in the Enlightenment. It is a tradition of doubting all traditions, of not accepting any personal trait, social arrangement, or intellectual claim as "given," and of searching systematically for the causes of each of these. The purpose of such scholarship is often construed as the liberation of individuals and communities from traditions that necessarily shackle their minds and imaginations. Participants assume in practice that this critical work is far better than participating in the traditions—and so tend to devote their time to analysis rather than to participation in the traditions analyzed. Their goals are to understand traditions, often in order to undermine them, rather than to dwell in them. The tradition

---

[12] Paul Connerton, *How Societies Remember* (Cambridge: Cambridge University Press, 1989), 39-40.

[13] In my experience, this sort of question more often arises as a *vocational* question: Am I called to be a scholar or a practitioner, a priest/rabbi/minister/doctor/lawyer/accountant/teacher, or a teacher/researcher in a university/medical school/law school/seminary? But this issue is one of a person's capacity to participate in one of those forms of life, not whether the form of life itself is good to participate in. Also, this is not a question about scholarship in general but about the specific practices of analyzing traditions.

of critical inquiry assumes that this search is not only good for the scholars but also (at least potentially) liberating for all. Critical scholarship is to be done because it benefits the common good.

Why should we accept the claim that participating in the Enlightenment tradition of critical scholarship of tradition is a good and truly liberating activity? Why should we assume that criticism of tradition is a force to free human minds? Of course, one can take it as a matter of faith that liberation from any and all tradition is ipso facto a very good thing. But this sort of "faith" is just what the analysts seem to argue *against*!

Moreover, it is hard to see what *arguments* there could be (at least arguments that are not self-referentially incoherent) not merely to sustain a claim that we *can* be free from tradition, but to show that we *should* be free from tradition. For example, Nicholas Wolterstorff has argued that even though some traditions are "still a source of benightedness, chicanery, hostility, and oppression," the Enlightenment project of attempting to think outside any and all traditions cannot be sustained. Wolterstorff claims that "we shall have to acknowledge what the thinkers of the Enlightenment would have found appallingly unpalatable; namely, that examination of tradition can take place only in the context of unexamined tradition, and that in our examination, our convictions as to the facts are schooled by our traditions."[14] For Wolterstorff, tradition is inescapable. While one might participate in one tradition rather than another, to take a position beyond all traditions is incoherent.

---

[14] Nicholas Wolterstorff, *John Locke and the Ethics of Belief* (Cambridge: Cambridge University Press, 1996), 246. Wolterstorff's argument, focused primarily on Anglo-American philosophy, is paralleled by Hans-Georg Gadamer, *Truth and Method*, 2d rev. ed., trans. Joel Weinsheimer and Donald G. Marshall (New York: Crossroad, 1989; first German edition, 1960; revised translation based on the fifth German edition, 1986). Gadamer analyzes the "prejudice against prejudices" of the Enlightenment (271-77; quotation at 272). What he writes about authority applies to the authority of tradition, with which we are concerned here: "The Enlightenment's distinction between faith in authority and using one's own reason is, in itself, legitimate. If the prestige of authority displaces one's own judgment, the authority is in fact a source of prejudices. But this does not preclude its being a source of truth, and that is what the Enlightenment failed to see when it denigrated all authority" (279). One wonders, however, if the distinction between faith and reason can ever be found "in itself," that is, without considering particular exercises of faith and reason, and perhaps even faith *in* reason. For an early and influential account that even science has "fiduciary foundations," see Michael Polanyi, *Personal Knowledge: Towards a Post-Critical Philosophy* (Chicago: University of Chicago Press, 1958).

Wolterstorff has extended an insight associated with, among others, the philosopher Ludwig Wittgenstein. Wittgenstein once wrote, "The *questions* that we raise and our *doubts* depend on the fact that some propositions are exempt from doubt. . . . It belongs to the logic of our scientific investigations that certain things are *in deed* not doubted."[15] We cannot engage in inquiry without presuming as given that into which we are not inquiring. "If you tried to doubt everything you would not get as far as doubting anything. The practice of doubting itself presupposes certainty."[16] Whenever we raise questions, we question particular claims; but when we do so, we leave all other claims unquestioned. Just as one can, in theory, replace every plank of a wooden boat while underway, so one can, in theory, question everything one believes. But just as one, in practice, can only replace those planks one or a few at a time (for one would have no place from which to make the repairs if one tried to replace all of them at once) and rely on the planks not under repair, so one can question one's beliefs or propositions or hypotheses one or a few at a time, while relying on the unquestioned to give one a place from which to raise questions.

Wolterstorff extends this commonplace by noting that working within traditions gives us the beliefs that we hold. To attempt to analyze, inquire, doubt, or question a given item in a tradition requires participating in *some* tradition (perhaps not the tradition under inquiry). To use the illustration mentioned earlier, to raise historical-critical questions about the Bible presumes a tradition of critical historical inquiry sufficiently developed to give one a place to stand to raise questions about a biblical text. While questioning the Bible, one does not—and practically cannot—raise questions about the practice of questioning the Bible. That practice necessarily is taken for granted while one exercises it.

Wolterstorff's point is that the Enlightenment thinker's commitment to rationality arises within a tradition. Numerous contemporary philosophers have even argued that such a commitment is a faith commitment, in the sense that it is not founded on argument

---

[15] Ludwig Wittgenstein, *On Certainty*, ed. G. E. M. Anscombe and G. H. von Wright, trans. Denis Paul and G. E. M. Anscombe (Oxford: Basil Blackwell, 1969), §§341, 342.

[16] Ibid., §115 (I have altered the translation slightly from the literal rendering of "Das Spiel" as "game," to rendering it as "practice." See the discussion of "practice" in chapter 2 below.)

but is grounded in hope and sustained and supported by fellow practitioners. This is not to say that such a commitment is unwarranted or silly or arbitrary or even religious. Rather, it is merely to note that this commitment makes sense within the context of a tradition.[17] Whether one ought to participate in the practices of a tradition, including the traditions of critical inquiry and rationality, is another question.[18]

Critical inquiry is also often skeptical inquiry.[19] This leads to a more personalized dichotomy: Those who analyze and explain traditions cannot simultaneously accept them so as to be able to dwell in them authentically. One has to choose to be either an insider or an outsider, a participant or an analyst. For an academic, it would surely seem better to be an analyst, to participate in the liberating tradition of rational inquiry rather than in the all-too-often benighted practices of nonacademic traditions, especially religious ones. An academic would of course support that commitment to the tradition of critical analysis.

However, one has to choose between the two if and only if the dilemma were unavoidable, if and only if one had to occupy one role or the other, if and only if critical inquiry had to be skeptical. But the

---

[17] Many radical "postmodern" contemporary theorists have "deconstructed" traditions by construing them as discourse systems that create subject positions ("places"—social, economic, psychological, and physical—for people to inhabit). For critical discussions of these more radical theories that are profoundly suspicious of anything like traditions, see Vincent J. Miller, "History or Geography? Gadamer, Foucault and Theologies of Tradition," in *Theology and the New Histories*, ed. Gary Macy, The Forty-fourth Annual Volume of the College Theology Society (Maryknoll, N.Y.: Orbis Books, 1999), 56-85; Terrence W. Tilley et al., *Postmodern Theologies: The Challenge of Religious Diversity* (Maryknoll, N.Y.: Orbis Books, 1995), 41-88, 110-13, and Catherine Pickstock, *After Writing: On the Liturgical Consummation of Philosophy* (Oxford: Basil Blackwell, 1998).

[18] See Terrence W. Tilley, *The Wisdom of Religious Commitment* (Washington, D.C.: Georgetown University Press, 1995). Although my focus in that text is on commitment to religious traditions, I argue in chapter 5 and the epilogue that the analysis can be applied *mutatis mutandis* for commitment to and in other types of tradition as well.

[19] See the analysis of the evolution of the study of religion in J. Samuel Preus, *Explaining Religion: Criticism and Theory from Bodin to Freud* (New Haven, Conn.: Yale University Press, 1987); for a critical appraisal of Preus's work (on which some material in the next few paragraphs is based), see Terrence W. Tilley, "Polemics and Politics in Explaining Religion," *The Journal of Religion* 71/2 (April 1991): 242-54; for an argument against my view, see Donald Wiebe, *The Politics of Religious Studies: The Continuing Conflict with Theology in the Academy* (New York: St. Martin's Press, 1999), 132-35.

dilemma is avoidable, and the choice between participation and analysis is not forced.

It is possible for a person to be both a participant and an analyst. One striking illustration of this is a comment contained in a letter from the Roman Catholic modernist theologian George Tyrrell to an Anglican sympathizer, A. L. Lilley, dated 14 August 1908. Tyrrell is reporting a conversation he has had with Baron Friedrich von Hügel (who held very advanced historical-critical views, yet would later seem to repent of his own modernism) and Henri Bremond (a French priest and sympathizer who would later be reprimanded by ecclesial authorities for his attendance at Tyrrell's deathbed): "The Baron has just gone. Wonderful man! Nothing is true; but the sum total of nothings is sublime! Christ was not merely ignorant but a *tête brulé* [*sic*]; Mary was not merely not a virgin, but an unbeliever and a rather unnatural mother; the Eucharist was a Pauline invention—yet he makes his daily visit to the Blessed Sacrament and for all I know tells his beads devoutly. Bremond's French logic finds it all very perplexing."[20] Von Hügel evidently did say the Rosary daily, as Tyrrell suggests.

Some might conclude that someone like von Hügel must be a master of duplicity or self-deception. Yet a better explanation is that von Hügel worked with two very different "explanations" of religion, one "naturalistic" (based in the emerging tradition of historical-critical analysis of religion) and the other "supernaturalistic" (or "transcendent," as von Hügel would say, based in his philosophical idealism and the deep and enduring spirituality developed in his beloved Catholic tradition). It is not psychologically or logically impossible to have two sufficient explanations for the same phenomenon, and not even unusual for someone who believes in God as a transcendent cause to hold two such incommensurable, but compatible, explanations, both of which may be sufficient, but neither necessary, to explain the phenomenon. Von Hügel is perhaps an extreme case, but he illustrates that a scholar can both explain and dwell in a religious tradition—a position occupied by many scholars in political science, economics, and other disciplines that examine the scholars' own polity, economy, or society. Chapter 6 develops an account of one way of understanding

---

[20] Alec R. Vidler, *A Variety of Catholic Modernists* (Cambridge: Cambridge University Press, 1970), 117-18, citing the papers of A. L. Lilley (then in a private archive, now in St. Andrews University Library). Vidler draws a different moral from this story than I do.

just how this is possible for someone who has developed an "analogical imagination."[21]

What makes the dichotomy seem plausible is that it is typically presented in the context of religious traditions. Would we argue that an analyst of democracy or capitalism should not or cannot reasonably participate in the practices of democracy or capitalism? Why then do we presume that an analyst of a religious tradition should not or cannot reasonably also participate in the practices of the tradition? Hence, the option between participation and analysis is not a forced option, and the view that one must choose one or the other (and ought to choose analysis) is unwarranted. One does not have to choose to be an insider or outsider, a participant or an analyst. What applies to the analysis of and participation in other traditions also applies to religious traditions.

Of course, one might argue that a religious tradition is sufficiently unlike other traditions so the analogy fails to apply and that a person cannot really live coherently in both religious and analytical-critical intellectual traditions. One might argue, as Freud did, that there is a radical difference between the two types of tradition. When challenged to recognize that his own faith in science is merely the substitution of an emotionally unsatisfying illusion for the satisfying illusion of religion, he responds:

> You will not find me inaccessible to your criticism. I know how difficult it is to avoid illusions; perhaps the hopes I have confessed to are of an illusory nature, too. But I hold fast to one distinction. Apart from the fact that no penalty is imposed for not sharing them, my illusions are not, like religious ones, delusion. If experience should show—not to me, but to others after me, who think as I do—that we have been mistaken, we will give up our expectations.[22]

The two differences Freud finds are that one can refuse to participate in scientists' practices but not in religion's, and that science is self-correcting but religion is not. Whatever may have been the case in certain locales in Freud's time, the advent of religious freedom and

---

[21] This important concept was explored by David Tracy, *The Analogical Imagination* (New York: Crossroad, 1981).

[22] Sigmund Freud, *The Future of an Illusion*, trans. James Strachey (New York: W. W. Norton and Co., 1961), 53.

widespread religious indifference, even in countries in which the human rights tradition recognizing the rights of conscience is weak, undermines the claim that penalties attend for refusing to be religious. Of course, the nonreligious person may "cut himself off forever from his only opportunity of making the gods' acquaintances," as William James once put it.[23] But persons who refuse to be scientific also cut themselves off from participating in the practices of science and developing the habits of mind that scientific practices develop. Hence, there are prices to be paid for *not* participating in either the traditions of science or the traditions of religion, just as there are prices to be paid *for* participating in each of those practices. That leaves us with the claim that science and religion are essentially different in that the former is self-correcting and that the latter is not. In the terms we are using here, Freud's position claims that religious traditions are, for their adherents, so strongly "found" that they cannot be "remade." While this view of Freud's may seem plausible, the question is whether it is true.

While Freud's account might be true of some isolated community, it is certainly not true of religious traditions overall.[24] Traditions worth dwelling in are neither simply "made up" by con artists, power-hungry elites, or do-gooders, as some scholars suggest, nor "found" or "given," that is, created in some way independent of human contribution. The dichotomy between "made" and "found" traditions is as false a dichotomy as the dichotomy of scholarship and participation. Some scholars are, and some are not, participants. Some participants are, and some are not, scholars.

The problem that generates the dichotomy can be called the reification of tradition. Some scholars and some participants treat tradition as a "thing" with a definite "essence." Any change—other than a superficial one—in that "thing" means an essential loss of the tradition. But does it make sense to construe a tradition as a "thing" passed down? My claim is that it does not account for what we know about actual traditions.

---

[23] William James, "The Will to Believe," *The Will to Believe and Other Essays in Popular Philosophy* (New York: Longmans, Green & Co., 1897; reprint edition, New York: Dover Publications, 1956), 28.

[24] See, for example, Michael Horace Barnes, *Stages of Thought: The Co-Evolution of Religious Thought and Science* (New York: Oxford University Press, 2000). Barnes shows that both scientific thought and the theology of the living faith traditions are not static but self-correcting.

Faithfully Remaking Religious Traditions

The most common belief among religious folk, especially those who participate in strong traditions—for example, Catholicism—seems to be that tradition is a heavy gold rock. It is a weighty object mined in the past that is passed unchanged from one generation to the next.[25] Or it is a folded cloak that is unfolded over time. Or it is a growing tree, essentially the same from sprouting acorn to mature oak. Or *id quod traditur* is an ancient family heirloom, passed on from generation to generation, so fragile as to need the protection of heavily padded cages of law. These root metaphors for tradition preserve the centrality of the *tradita*, that which is passed down. But they so profoundly obscure the crucial role of *traditio,* the actual process or practice of passing on the tradition, that many problems, both historical and theoretical, arise. To treat tradition as merely *tradita*, as these metaphors encourage people to do, is to fail to understand the ways traditions develop in general, and, more particularly, the history of Christianity; the teaching of the Catholic Church in the Second Vatican Council; the historical evolution of Catholic consciousness; and the insights of recent communication theory.

Historically, traditions change significantly. It has been said that it is *the* Catholic tradition that the pope appoints bishops. But newspapers, popular books, and magazines report without qualm that while the pope has often, since the Middle Ages, invested kings and bishops with their offices, the actual selection of who is to be a bishop has been fully in Roman hands for only a century. St. Ambrose of Milan was acclaimed bishop by the people of Milan despite his desire not to hold that office, as it would ruin his civil service career. Medieval and modern European bishops were typically elected by the cathedral chapter and/or nominated by the ruler. Bishops were selected locally but invested with their offices by the central authority.

---

[25] In one way, this seems remarkable insofar as the Second Vatican Council has a much more flexible and nuanced view of tradition, apparently based in large part on the work of Congar. For a brief summary, see George H. Tavard, s.v. "Tradition," *The New Dictionary of Theology,* ed. Joseph A. Komonchak, Mary Collins, and Dermot Lane (Wilmington, Del.: Michael Glazier, 1987), esp. 1040-41.

The practices varied widely, but the present universal practice of Rome selecting bishops is a modern, novel invention.[26]

Many Catholics support the practice of defining seven rituals as sacraments with the claim that Jesus established seven and only seven sacraments and that the Catholic Church has always taught this. But this number is contingent. Historians note that the number of sacraments varied from theologian to theologian in the Middle Ages; some found as many as thirty and some as few as two. It was only during the Council of Trent (1545-63) that the number was officially fixed at seven. Yet even the Second Vatican Council speaks more freely when it talks of the Church as sacrament.[27] Some Catholics believe that the only Catholic account of the Real Presence of Christ in the Eucharist is *transubstantiation.* But in the two centuries before St. Thomas Aquinas came up with a definitive meaning for that term influenced by the retrieval of Aristotle, other accounts, including symbolic ones not at all conformable to an Aristotelian approach, were taken as orthodox teaching. Moreover, for three centuries after St. Thomas Aquinas came up with a specific meaning for that term, there were theological debates about the Eucharist in which the opponents of *transubstantiation,* as Thomas understood that term, were in the majority.[28] More mundanely, in the United States, popular belief has

---

[26] John R. Quinn put it this way: "Until roughly 1800, Rome's intervention in the appointment of bishops in dioceses outside the Papal States was rare. Until 1829, it was the policy of the Holy See to leave the appointment of bishops to the local Church where possible. At the death of Pope Leo XII in 1829, there were 646 diocesan bishops in the Latin Church. Of this number, excluding those in the Papal States, only twenty-four were directly appointed by Rome" (see "The Exercise of the Primacy and the Costly Call to Unity," in *The Exercise of the Primacy: Continuing the Dialogue,* ed. Phyllis Zagano and Terrence W. Tilley [New York: Crossroad, 1998], 21). Quinn refers to Garrett Sweeney, *Bishops and Writers: Aspects of the Evolution of Modern English Catholicism* (Wheathampstead: Anthony Clarke Books, 1977), 199-200, 207-31. Theologian Michael Buckley, S.J., has called for a reexamination of the process of naming bishops: Would "papal restoration of ancient legislation on the [local] selection of bishops and their stability within their sees . . . contribute significantly to the strengthening of the episcopate and local churches today?" (*Papal Primacy and the Episcopate: Towards a Relational Understanding* [New York: Crossroad, 1998], 94). This is an example of a major modern shift in tradition, one that is still being debated.

[27] See the beginning of the decree on the Church's missionary activity, *Ad Gentes:* "The Church has been divinely sent to the nations of the world that she might be 'the universal sacrament of salvation'" (Walter M. Abbott, S.J., ed., *The Documents of Vatican II* [New York: Guild Press, America Press, Association Press, 1966], 584).

[28] See Gary Macy, *Treasures from the Storeroom* (Collegeville, Minn.: Liturgical Press, 1999).

been that people have always knelt during the canon of the Mass. But this was, like the Christmas tree, an adaptation of German customs by the Church.[29]

This acceptance of tradition as somehow permanently given does not apply only to religion. People tend to believe that the traditional symbols of the nation, the flag and the anthem, are sacred from time immemorial. Yet the earliest national anthem is evidently the British anthem. The earliest national flag is apparently the French Revolution's tricolor. Such symbols of national identity are actually products of the eighteenth century. The use of flags and anthems as national symbols is not from time immemorial at all.[30]

Examples could be multiplied, but my point is this: Historical investigations have shown that there have been marked shifts in the content of practices and beliefs we accept as "given" on the basis of tradition. Historians have also shown that many beliefs and practices we currently or recently have rejected as "not found" in the tradition are legitimate options in fluid and developing traditions. Some of these traditions, especially liturgical ones in the Roman Catholic Church, changed dramatically in the second half of the twentieth century. These changes have been absorbed into the common beliefs and practices of Catholics.[31] If that which is passed on as a tradition has to be passed on "unchanged and uncorrupted" over long periods of time, then there are no concrete traditions that will pass the test. Appeals to warrant contemporary beliefs on the grounds that they are traditional are always subject to overturning by historical research—and

[29] I owe this point to Fr. Thomas Gaeke, pastor of St. Mary Catholic Church, Dayton. Liturgical postures are important for understanding a tradition and one's place in it. See Connerton, *How Societies Remember*, 73-74, and the comments in chapter 2 below. Until the thirteenth century, laity normally stood during Mass (see Joseph A. Jungmann, S.J., *The Mass of the Roman Rite: Its Origins and Development*, trans. Francis A. Brunner, C.SS.R. [New York: Benziger Brothers, 1951], 1:239-40). Canon 20 of the Council of Nicea (325) ordains standing as the mode for prayer, reinforced by canon 90 of the Council of Quinisext (also called the Council in Trullo; 692), which forbid kneeling in prayer on Sunday (see Philip Schaff and Henry Wace, eds., *Nicene and Post-Nicene Fathers* (New York: Charles Scribner's Sons, 1900], XIV:42, 403).

[30] Eric L. Hobsbawm, "Introduction: Inventing Traditions," in *The Invention of Tradition*, ed. Eric Hobsbawm and Terence Ranger (Cambridge: Cambridge University Press, 1983), 7.

[31] This does not imply there is no resistance to change. For an investigation of some of the organized forms of opposition in the United States and Canada to recent changes in Catholic practices, see Michael W. Cuneo, *The Smoke of Satan: Conservative and Traditionalist Dissent in Contemporary American Catholicism* (New York and Oxford: Oxford University Press, 1997).

that frequently happens. The fact that religions can evolve in ways profoundly affecting their adherents is known not only to historians and scholars but to religious participants as well. Freud's overarching point about religions is wrong, considering both historians' perspectives and believers' actual practices.

In terms of communication theory the point is more subtle, yet its basis is simple. As noted earlier, the process of tradition requires at least three distinct components: the agent doing the handing over, that which is handed over, and the agent that receives what is handed over. The introduction noted the Italian witticism, *Tradutore, tradditore* (The translator is a traitor). But this does not and cannot apply only to translators. It applies to everyone who transmits a tradition to someone in a different context, however minimally different. In short, the reception of the tradition involves changing the tradition *if* the tradition is a narrative, belief, practice, or attitude that is to endure.

One remarkable example of this is the Christian doctrine of the universal need for redemption. A primary way this doctrine is expressed in Western Christianity comes from reading Genesis 2–3 as a story of "original sin," which Jesus Christ overcomes in his cross and resurrection. Yet this reading, almost second nature to Christians, is not the only "natural" reading of the story. As Robert Schreiter puts it:

> When the story was read to some Ipili elders in the New Guinea highlands, they thought it must be a Christian initiation-rite story, describing what it is like to grow from childhood to adulthood. Among the Sherenti in Brazil, local people changed the man-wife relationship to brother-sister in the story; for why should man and wife be ashamed of appearing naked before one another? When the story was told to a people in East Africa, they missed the point of the Fall altogether. They were fascinated with how God walked with the couple in the cool of the evening.[32]

Given that the usual Western Christian reading of the story is, to put it mildly, not obvious in these different cultural contexts, the question is how one can construe the need for redemption in such contexts. My point is not to answer that question but simply to note that one cannot simply pass on the story of Genesis 2–3 as if "original sin," the

---

[32] Schreiter, *Constructing Local Theologies*, 96-97, citing Philip Gibbs, "Kaunala Tape: Toward a Theological Reflection on a New Guinea Initiation Myth" (M.A. thesis, Catholic Theological Union, 1977); Pierre Maranda, ed., *Mythology* (Harmondsworth, England: Penguin Books, 1972), 7; and a communication from Spiritan missionaries working in Kenya and Tanzania.

"canonical" interpretation of that story, will evoke an understanding of the universal need for redemption in one's hearers. To be faithful to the tradition may require extensive reworking of the *tradita* if the tradition is to be received in a new context.

While this example may seem extreme, it highlights the fact that *tradita* alone do not carry the tradition. Further, it illustrates the practical point that the greater the difference between the context in which the *traditor* learned the tradition and the context in which the tradition is transmitted, the greater the possibility that a shift in *tradita* may be necessary to communicate the tradition. Paradoxically, fidelity to a tradition may sometimes involve extensive reworking of the *tradita*. In the perspective of communication theory, then, it is naive to think that *tradita* alone can carry the tradition.

In sum, the general claim that religious traditions are so unlike other traditions that one could not be a participant and an analyst, exemplified by Freud's critique, cannot be sustained. This is not to say that Freud's point never applies to any traditions. There may be traditions that propagate delusions. There may be communities or institutions that are so authoritarian—that is, controlled by elites so absolutely—that there are no places in which possible changes in the traditions those communities or institutions carry can be proposed and developed. However, such institutions cannot endure indefinitely. While they can remain stable by rigid policing of their members, that stability is fragile. Even the Catholic Church, often caricatured as such an unchangingly authoritarian institution, cannot endure indefinitely without change. For instance, the Church became an institution whose tradition necessarily included *ultramontanism* (finding authority "over the mountains" [that is, over the Alps in Papal Rome]) only in the nineteenth century. Yet that tradition did not extend without significant change in its acceptance and effect beyond the pontificate of John XXIII (1958-63). Even in an institution like the Catholic Church, stable traditions cannot be guaranteed indefinitely by the power of ruling elites, even the tradition that the ruling elites have the only valid authority in the tradition. Whether intentionally or not, traditions, to endure, seem to require reconstruction, revision, and reinvention as circumstances change.

The Contexts for Traditions

Traditions are necessarily historically embodied and inculturated. It is those concrete, historic practices, beliefs, and attitudes that are open for our study. If traditions are like anything in the natural world, they are more like bacteria or viruses, which adapt themselves to their hosts and their environments. Staphylococcus Aureus today is the "same" bacterium it was fifty years ago, but it has evolved from being vulnerable to eradication by penicillin then, to being resistant now (in some strains) to every antibiotic humans have invented. Common cold viruses and human immunodeficiency viruses mutate even more rapidly.

Traditions mutate, sometimes radically, as they are passed on. The environments in which traditional beliefs, practices, and attitudes are transmitted and the items from other traditions that their holders encounter change their significance. One can ask, "Is staph the same bacterium as it was fifty years ago?" In terms of its genetic heritage, and basic biological identification, the answer may be yes, just as Homo sapiens is "the same" today as Homo sapiens was when the species first appeared. But for human purposes, especially for treatment of infection, staph is *not* the same bacterium it was fifty years ago; its evolution has changed its relationships to other agents (like antibiotics) so that it can arguably be said to have changed its nature, even if it is in some way the same species. Is it the same or not? Homo sapiens today may be genetically the same as Homo sapiens was fifty thousand years ago. But as humans are social by nature (say Aristotle and Aquinas, among others), insofar as human social interactions have changed, Homo sapiens has changed. Is the species the same or not? Similar questions about the identity and difference of traditions yield answers that are not merely perplexing but highly disputed.

Oral traditions mutate rapidly. Perhaps the most obvious example of such mutation is in the oral (and possibly some written) traditions behind the passion narratives in the gospels. Without an extensive excursion into higher biblical criticism, we can say that mutation in traditions passed down orally and/or in writing must have happened. There are many technical disputes about this, but two interesting and obvious mutations must have occurred regarding the day of crucifixion: Did Jesus die on the fifteenth day of the month of Nisan, as Matthew, Mark, and Luke have it, or on the fourteenth day of the month of Nisan, as John has it?[33] Did Simon of Cyrene help Jesus carry his cross, as the synoptics have it, or did Jesus carry his own

---

[33] See Hans Küng, *On Being a Christian*, trans. Edward Quinn (Garden City, N.Y.: Doubleday, 1976), 150. Küng reflects here a consensus in modern biblical scholarship.

cross, as John 19:17 insists? There are numerous differences in the gospels which indicate that while there certainly was constancy in the stories told, there was also change in those stories as they were passed on and received before the books of the New Testament were written.[34] And even after the texts were completed, they evidently underwent some changes and additions (e.g., the longer ending of Mark).

Sometimes even written traditions mutate so rapidly that even very recent events are obscured. In a brilliant and humorous article, Patrick Henry, whose usual field is early Christianity, shows how American historians who have written on "American civil religion" have butchered a quotation taken from a speech of President Dwight David Eisenhower given on 22 December 1952. Eisenhower said (roughly), "In other words, our form of government has no sense unless it is founded in a deeply felt religious faith, and I don't care what it is."[35] Many scholars of American religion have typically taken Eisenhower to be exemplifying the "civil religion" at the basis of American life or supporting a vague religiosity as a foundation for our government or democracy. But what they did was to misinterpret this quotation by taking it out of its context. Supporting the "civil religion" was not, as Patrick Henry shows, Eisenhower's meaning at all. Henry's summary of the history of the transmission of this proof-text is worth quoting:

> It begins to look as if the tradition of what Eisenhower said on December 22, 1952 . . . is materially shaped by the polemical/rhetorical concerns of those who pass the tradition on. The statement can be treated as tragic, comic, ludicrous, fatuous, naive, sincere, traditional, innovative. It can be made to refer to government, society, church and state, the American Way of Life. And in its most recent manifestation, the tradition has undergone a change that suddenly makes the Synoptic problem not so unmanageable after all.[36]

---

[34] It is not my intention to canvass the proposed *solutions* to problems Bible study raises. My only point is that the best account of the changes requires mutation in the tradition at minimum.

[35] Patrick Henry, "'And I Don't Care What It Is': The Tradition-History of a Civil Religion Proof-Text," *Journal of the American Academy of Religion* 49/1 (March 1981): 35-49; Eisenhower quotation, as reconstructed by Henry after his analyses, at 46.

[36] Ibid., 44.

Eisenhower probably meant to note that *all* political systems are founded in faith-like basic commitments—or so I would interpret him in the context of the speech as cited by Henry. But what Henry has shown is that not only do ancient traditions become transformed, but that in less than three years in a period that some of us still remember, scholars subjected Eisenhower's remarks to wild distortion in reporting and interpretation and "created" a tradition that construes those remarks in ways Eisenhower might not have recognized, much less condoned.

Now it may be that those who believe traditions are *found* and *stable* can concede that from both historians' and participants' perspectives traditions may have *some* diversity and perhaps even instability. But what has not been shown is that traditions change at their core. An objector might claim, "Christians have always affirmed, for instance, the dogmas of Christology and the Trinity. They have always—at least until recently—proclaimed that salvation comes through Christ alone. We can concede that tradition can change in accidentals, but you haven't shown it changes in essentials."

These are certainly issues which need to be addressed, but to do so in a fully adequate way would take us far afield. Nonetheless, I can make a basic response to this sort of objection. First, in the Catholic tradition there is a presumption of the question that some parts of the tradition are more central than others. Theologians, as the Second Vatican Council put it, "should remember that in Catholic doctrine there exists a 'hierarchy' of truths, since they vary in their relation to the fundamental Christian faith."[37] However, it is not clear how one would establish what is "higher" and "lower" in the hierarchy descriptively without a circular argument using criteria drawn from the tradition.[38] Moreover, with regard to the Catholic tradition, it has been difficult, if not impossible, to indicate concretely how that hierarchy is shaped. Second, it is not the case that Christians have had one definitive Christology. The gospels and Paul certainly have different Christologies. The Church has had numerous Christologies operative in particular times and places. The introduction of the definitive

---

[37] *Unitatis Redintegratio*, no. 11, in Abbott, *The Documents of Vatican II*, 354.

[38] In addressing this issue, in terms of primary and secondary truths, Avery Dulles, S.J., found seven different ways in the literature to make this distinction. There is certainly no consensus (see *The Resilient Church* [Garden City, N.Y.: Doubleday, 1977], 55-56). At the time of writing, Dulles supported an approach borrowed from Lutheran theologian George Lindbeck, which he labeled "historical situationism." Chapter 4 argues for a version of this view but argues for rejection of a key element in Lindbeck's rule theory of *doctrine*. Chapter 6 extends this understanding to the concept of revelation.

homoousios to define Jesus' relation to the Father is not only unscriptural (as opponents of the definition pointed out in the disputes leading up to the Ecumenical Council of Nicea in 325) but also problematical for theories of salvation, as it was unclear how someone "one in being" with the Father could indeed be like enough to humanity to be the savior of humanity. Third, not all Christians believe in the Trinity, but even those who do are faced with radical linguistic changes in the meaning of the terms used to define the dogma. Between the Councils of Nicea (325) and Chalcedon (451), *hypostasis,* a key term in Trinitarian theology, mutated significantly. Prosopon-persona-person (three Persons) and ousia-substantia-being (in one God) are *not* two sets of perfect synonyms. Even the two basic models of the Trinity accepted widely in Christianity, the personal model (which stresses the unity of God as person-like) and the social model (which stresses the sociality of the three-personed God), however the linguistic terms are taken, are as incompatible with each other as wave *vs.* particle theories of light.[39] As anyone who has tried to involve students in the subtleties of early Christological and Trinitarian controversies knows, the Greek and Latin terms have much slippage and are not semantically equivalent to our modern English terms—a fact that frustrates students and faculty alike in the classroom. Fourth, salvation is necessarily saving of some individual or group, by some agent, from some evil, and for some good. Salvation as a bare concept is semantically empty without these specifications. For instance, one of the evils humans are saved from, according to modern and contemporary tradition, is original sin. But original sin emerges as a concept only with Augustine in the fifth century, and we need to "avoid the anachronistic tendency to read Augustine's position back into biblical texts (principally Genesis 3 and Romans 5)."[40] Moreover, Gabriel Daly notes that current debates over original sin have changed the issues—and even the concept of what constitutes original sin. Daly writes that the

---

[39] Much recent writing on Trinitarian theology has tried to provide ways for reconciling these two approaches. See, for instance, Catherine M. LaCugna, *God for Us: The Trinity and Christian Life* (San Francisco: HarperSanFrancisco, 1991); and Joseph A. Bracken, S.J., *The Divine Matrix Creativity as Link between East and West* (Maryknoll, N.Y.: Orbis Books, 1995), and *The Triune Symbol: Persons, Process and Community* (Lanham, Md.: University Press of America, 1985).

[40] Gabriel Daly, O.S.A., s.v. "Original Sin," in Komonchak et al., *New Dictionary of Catholic Theology,* 727. For examples of ways in which the story of Genesis 2–3 can be heard rather differently in different cultures, see Schreiter, *Constructing Local Theologies,* 96-97. Schreiter reminds us that the Augustinian reading of that story as one of a "fall" is merely one reading of the story.

context of the debate over original sin is no longer that of classical Pelagianism (which presupposed moral earnestness, the practice of asceticism, and an elitist approach to christian life) but rather that of a complacent acceptance of the world as it is, coupled with a post-Freudian and post-Darwinian tendency to reduce phenomena which were formerly described as sin to the physical and psychological determinism of human nature.[41]

In each of these examples regarding "central" doctrines of Christianity, there is substantial fluidity, flexibility, or variation in the meaning of the doctrines.

The point is this: A verbal token, translated from language to language and historical context to historical context, connected with different concepts to get its significance, and embodied in different cultures and practices, cannot simply "mean the same thing." A constancy in verbal tokens cannot guarantee a continuity of tradition; insisting on the use of a specific phrase or formula is no guarantee of continuity, but may indeed gloss over lack of continuity in a tradition.[42] Even the Second Vatican Council recognized that the language in which Christian doctrines are formulated can shift and require restatement, and thus identical linguistic reiteration cannot be either a necessary or sufficient condition of identity in what the formulation expresses, the "deposit of faith." As the Council put it, "Therefore, if the influence of events or of the times has led to deficiencies in conduct, in Church discipline, or even in the formulation of doctrine (which must be carefully distinguished from the deposit of faith), these should be appropriately rectified at the proper moment."[43]

---

[41] Daly, "Original Sin," 730. Although Daly does not use semiotic theory as Schreiter does, they make much the same point.

[42] The pliability of the Roman Catholic tradition is an important component in Francis A. Sullivan, S.J., "Recent Theological Observations on Magisterial Documents and Public Dissent," *Theological Studies* 58/3 (September 1997). Sullivan argues that "the history of Catholic doctrine suggests the need of great caution in claiming that something has been taught infallibly by the ordinary universal magisterium, if there is reason to judge that a position on which there was consensus in the past no longer enjoys such consensus" (515). Sullivan cites several issues on which dissent from common teaching in one era became doctrine in another: "the Church's judgment on the morality of owning and using human persons as slaves, on the taking of interest on loans, on religious liberty, and on non-Christian religions." Sullivan also cites John Paul II's encyclical *Evangelium vitae,* which fails to mention the classic Catholic view that unbaptized children go to limbo.

[43] *Unitatis Redintegratio,* no. 6, in Abbott, *The Documents of Vatican II,* 350. The editor commented, "It is remarkable, indeed, for an Ecumenical Council to admit possible deficiency of previous doctrinal formulations."

In short, my response to the objection is that even if there were clear verbal continuity in formulating "essential" concepts and propositions of the tradition, there is great difficulty in determining the meanings of those concepts. In fact, there is reason to believe there may be real instability in whatever formulations one might choose as expressing the "core" of a tradition such as the "deposit of faith," the "core" of the Catholic tradition.[44] The contexts in which that "core" is expressed radically affect the expression; and if there is a "deposit of faith" or other "core" of a tradition, there can be no direct access to that "core." All communicable expressions are necessarily contextualized expressions.

Another objection would be that this view ignores the organic development of tradition proposed by John Henry Newman in his *Essay on the Development of Doctrine*. But the problem with Newman's account of development is that what doesn't change is the *idea* of Christianity, an idea that is beyond every expression of it.[45] The issue

---

[44] Although the two are often elided, some Catholic theologians try to make a clear distinction between dogma and doctrine. Dogma is the revealed truth; doctrine says how that truth should be understood. But, considered from the point of view of semantics, this distinction won't hold; it would mean dogma was incomprehensible. Dogma without doctrine would be *literally* incomprehensible or meaningless. In this view, dogma could not develop because it was empty! A story told about the late biblical scholar Fr. John McKenzie illustrates this point. When asked if he believed in the assumption of Mary into heaven, he replied that of course he did, since it was infallibly defined, but that he had no idea what it meant. Could one ever have a conviction, a life-guiding and character-constituting belief, if one has no idea what that belief meant? The pragmatic effect of the dogma/doctrine distinction would make dogma irrelevant to life.

[45] In the *Essay on the Development of Christian Doctrine* (London: James Toovey, 1846; reprint of the 1845 edition). Newman writes: "Creeds and dogmas live in the one idea which they are designed to express, and which alone is substantive; and are necessary only because the human mind cannot reflect upon it, except piecemeal, cannot use it in its oneness and entireness, or without resolving it into a series of aspects and relations. And in matter of fact, these expressions are never equivalent to it. We are able, indeed, to define the creations of our minds, for they are what we make them and nothing else; but it were as easy to create what is real as to define it. And thus the Catholic dogmas are, after all, but symbols of a divine fact, which far from being compassed by those very propositions, would not be exhausted, not fathomed, by a thousand" (56-57). This passage is a quotation that Newman took from his *University Sermons* (*Fifteen sermons preached before the University of Oxford: between A.D. 1826 and 1843*), preached and published when Newman was an Anglican. He converted to Roman Catholicism while the *Essay* was in press. In the 1878 edition of the *Essay*, published when Newman had been a Roman Catholic for over thirty years, this passage is severely truncated; the notable omission is the last sentence. Despite a wealth of scholarship on Newman, it remains unclear to me whether the changes in the *Essay* are due more to intellectual reconsideration or to avoiding publishing works that would be offensive to pious (Roman Catholic) ears.

for Newman was not so much determining whether doctrine developed in the tradition as discerning what are the notes or tests of authentic development. Newman's work has more a normative than a descriptive orientation, and I shall reserve consideration of it until we raise the issues of *legitimate* change in traditions in chapter 4.

Having noted some likely objections and replied to them, we can return to the main point: Traditions are simply not found. They cannot be found because they are not content alone. *Traditio* is a communicative praxis. Its particular *content* may be the traditional material communicated, but that content is subject to a process of communication, including transmission and reception.[46] For anyone to take *id quod traditur* as the total of tradition separable from the contexts and processes of communication and from the forms of life in which those traditions have their life cannot offer an account of tradition but only of a malleable part of the tradition.[47] These forms of life must, at minimum, be pliable. If they are perfectly rigid, they either die as contexts change because that elite can no longer maintain the identity of the tradition or become the possession of an esoteric elite who "keep the old traditions alive" as a compartmentalized practice or set of practices and beliefs.

Inventing Traditions

So far, the argument sounds as though it is supporting the claim that all traditions are "made." Alas, this is only part of the story. Traditions

---

[46] Schreiter, *Constructing Local Theologies*, 110-12, claims that an insider ordinarily does not have to be aware of the process of *traditio* but is normally only aware of the *tradita*, that which is passed on. In his view, it is the outsider who raises claims about the process. However, in some sense, insofar as a person is constituted not within one tradition alone but in several, a person comes to take this "outsider" perspective while remaining an "insider." Schreiter recognizes this for times of crisis, but this has become practically normative in Western society. Moreover, it is surely arguable that people have never been formed solely in "the Christian tradition," but necessarily in an inculturated version of that tradition with the admixture of political, social, and economic patterns that are distinguishable from the Christian tradition. Writing from a radically different perspective, Presbyterian feminist theologian Mary McClintock Fulkerson has persuasively argued that there cannot be a theological discourse free from any "contemporary signifying practices" (*Changing the Subject: Women's Discourses and Feminist Theology* [Minneapolis: Fortress, 1994], 368).

[47] In *The Wisdom of Religious Commitment*, I describe a "presumption of substitutability" for philosophers of religion who substitute debate over the rationality of holding religious propositions for the wisdom of being a member of a religious tradition (27, 55, 58). Similarly, reducing *traditio* to *tradita* is useful for some purposes, but such reduction ought not blind one to the other components of tradition.

can literally be deliberately invented. As suggested above, some critics would claim that we make up traditions as we go along. We pick from the past what we want for present purposes. Traditions are entirely constructs, mere fictions developed for purposes of claiming power and constructing identities. Their apparent constancies are merely screens for hiding people from harsh realities. Traditions are devices intended to deceive. Either they deceive subjugated people and keep them from noticing that the power elites create traditions that legitimate their power, or they deceive all of us into thinking that there is some meaning in the eternal cacophony of random events that constitutes human life.

For instance, Eric Hobsbawm has persuasively argued that the period from 1870 to 1914 was one in which new traditions were deliberately invented almost wholesale in Europe for the purposes of reinforcing and reinvigorating political and social power and identity.[48] In a paper on the deliberate invention of a particularly Welsh tradition in Wales in the late eighteenth and early nineteenth centuries, Prys Morgan writes:

> In Wales the movement of revival and myth-making grew out of a crisis in Welsh life. . . . It required a superhuman effort by a small number of patriots to force their fellow-countrymen to appreciate their heritage, to value what was their own. They felt that the only way to bring this about was to *ransack the past and transform it with imagination*, to create a new Welshness which would instruct, entertain, amuse and educate the people.[49]

If we were to generalize Morgan's point, we'd say that we deliberately invent traditions, mining the past for its gold, and use those traditions to establish an identity. Those who claim that *all* traditions are made in the sense that they are "deliberately invented" would take the invention of modern "Welshness" as a paradigm for understanding every cultural or religious tradition that endures.

It is rare for postmodern theorists to write about traditions as constructs. For them, the concept of tradition is subsumed, as far as I can tell, into the concepts of epistemes, discourse systems, regimes of knowledge, and other clever constructs. For them, the concept of

---

[48] Hobsbawm, "Mass-Producing Traditions: Europe, 1879-1914" in Hobsbawm and Ranger, *The Invention of Tradition,* 263-307.

[49] Prys Morgan, "From Death to a View," in Hobsbawm and Ranger, *The Invention of Tradition*, 99, emphasis added.

identity, whether "Welshness" or "Catholicity" in particular or "identity" in general, would refer to constructs. Identities, many would say, are pure fictions that we create. Some feminists would say that the valorization of tradition and the construction of traditional identities for members of a community are constituents of a pure power-play designed to ensure the continued hegemony of those who dwell in the higher realms of patriarchal structures. Some genealogical masters of suspicion would analyze traditions embodied in cultures and institutions as constitutive of power relations; we all collude in the maintenance of these power relations unless we revolutionarily seek to establish a form of power more favorable to our own interests. Nonetheless, implicit in their works, as much as in most historians' work, is a claim that traditions are constructed.

But we don't have to look to the eighteenth or nineteenth century for such deliberate inventions of identity and power by power elites. They are common much closer to our own time. What has struck me is how people in power perceived as defenders of tradition are, in fact, inventors, creators, or violators of tradition. My primary example is the Roman Catholic Church's Congregation for the Doctrine of the Faith (CDF).

Under the guise of preserving the Catholic tradition, the CDF has introduced innovations that can be enforced not by the intellectual power of the theological argument in support of them, but by the ecclesial power of this office as guarantor of orthodoxy. Although various issues could be cited as possible misuses of evidence, including the misuse of patristic evidence against the ordination of women to the priesthood in *Inter Insignores*,[50] an obvious recent one is the debate over the lectionary, the book of readings used for Mass.[51]

In 1990, the U.S. Catholic bishops overwhelmingly (84%) approved criteria for the evaluation of inclusive language translations of the scriptures for use in the liturgy. In 1991 they approved the New Revised Standard Version for use along with the revised psalter of the New American Bible, both of which use inclusive language rather than *man* or *men* for human beings. The CDF approved this in 1992. Although the NRSV is still (at the time of writing) approved for use in

---

[50] See John Hickey Wright, S.J., "Patristic Testimony on Women's Ordination in *Inter Insignores*," *Theological Studies* 58/3 (September 1997): 516-26.

[51] This section depends in large part on Richard J. Clifford, "The Rocky Road to a New Lectionary," *America* 177/4 (16 August 1997): 18-22, who not only summarized well various news stories but also published the "secret" Vatican norms (which also can be found in *The National Catholic Reporter* for 4 July 1997) and analyzed the situation well.

Canada, the Congregation for the Doctrine of the Faith withdrew its permission for the United States in 1992. A "moderately inclusive" lectionary was proposed and accepted with evident great reluctance and much disagreement on a temporary basis by the U.S. bishops at their meeting in June 1997. Only a very rare scholar (and perhaps even a few bishops) finds this lectionary in the least inclusive by contemporary standards, even by the standards of contemporary evangelical Protestants who have developed inclusive language translations.

The CDF rejected the translations previously approved, based on secret norms published "illicitly" in *The National Catholic Reporter* in July 1997. That these norms are out of touch not only with contemporary scholarship but also with the Catholic tradition is made clear by biblical scholar Richard J. Clifford, S.J.:

> These norms are without precedent among modern pronouncements of the Magisterium on the Bible. All the church documents I have examined . . . direct scholars to the original biblical text, which they are to translate and explain in accord with sound modern scholarship. This is not the route the norms take. It is very significant, I think, that the norms *cite no church document* (except for a general citation, under Norm 2, of Chapters 3 and 4 of the "Constitution on Divine Revelation"); for the norms depart from the tradition.
>
> To sum up, the norms are a defensive measure, an ad hoc device to prevent inclusive language translations in the United States, an attempt to resolve specific translation problems from the lofty height of principles. Based on an inadequate theory of translation, they are carelessly composed, ecumenically retrograde, self-contradictory and without precedent in recent pronouncements of the Magisterium on the Bible.[52]

In his excellent article, Fr. Clifford details the inadequacy of many of the specific norms proposed. One of them is patently absurd: the blanket prohibition of changing singulars to plurals in certain circumstances. Even the Septuagint, the Greek translation of the Hebrew scriptures that was the Bible for Paul, the earliest Christians, and Christians to the Reformation, "*normally* changes the Hebrew

---

[52] Ibid., 22.

singular . . . to the plural" in its translation of the book of Proverbs.[53] The CDF claims that it is trying to preserve the "original meaning" of the text, but what it is actually doing is ordering the use of word-for-word translations of ancient texts. Given the fact that linguistic tokens can and do shift their meanings as the context in which they are used shifts, this simplistic approach which pretends, frankly, to preserve the original meaning cannot work—even if there is a single, determinable "original meaning," a point hotly debated among contemporary biblical scholars.

These norms are not consistent with but rather in violation of the tradition. They (apparently deliberately) invent a new tradition. They then use administrative power to enforce adherence to this novel innovation. They make one form of the content of the tradition, a noninclusive biblical translation, an absolute. This is a clear example of a power elite inventing a novel (pseudo) tradition to reinforce its own power over an institution. What Hobsbawm writes about other invented traditions applies here: "However, insofar as there is such a reverence to a historic past, the peculiarity of 'invented' traditions is that the continuity with it is largely fictitious. In short, they are responses to novel situations which take the form of reference to old situations, or which establish their own past by quasi-obligatory repetition."[54] The norms of the CDF respond to a novel situation by saying we can't do what the bishops have encouraged as appropriate in the U.S. context because that would violate norms of translation that have produced noninclusive translations. They appeal to a dubious or nonexistent tradition as authoritative when the authority of that tradition is at issue! This is hardly a convincing argument.

The process of deliberately inventing traditions in this way is clearly a social control mechanism. But like every social control mechanism, it can provoke resistance when it is imposed.[55] This stimulation of communities and individuals to resist such imposition suggests that a tradition is being not merely invented but deliberately invented and even imposed upon an unwilling community. In the present case, the resistance of the American bishops and the Catholic Biblical Association to the translation norms and the "moderately inclusive" text *on the basis of the tradition* is a clear indicator that this novel tradition is being invented and imposed.

---

[53] Ibid.

[54] Hobsbawm, "Introduction: Inventing Traditions," 2.

[55] Robert Schreiter makes a similar point about local resistance to the "global hyper-culture" of consumerism in *The New Catholicity: Theology between the Global and the Local* (Maryknoll, N.Y.: Orbis Books, 1997).

Some distinctions need to be made here. First, not all deliberately invented traditions are resisted. If Prys Morgan's research is accurate, then the deliberate invention of Welshness was not resisted. As chapter 2 claims, an individual cannot directly intend to invent a tradition, but some clever individuals can deliberately initiate practices that they hope and even expect will flourish and become a tradition. Second, not all resistance is to unwanted invention. The widespread dissatisfaction among U.S. Catholics with the limitation of priestly ordination to celibate males can be seen as issuing in resistance. But what provokes that resistance is not an invented tradition, but the perceived refusal of authorities to consider seriously arguments that the tradition needs to be reshaped in order to respond to the sacramental needs of the faithful, and to respond credibly to those arguments. Third, traditions can be made and remade without being deliberately invented. Traditions thrive just because they adapt with integrity to changing circumstances; below we shall describe some of these changes as inventions (for they *are* inventions). However, such changes are not *deliberate* inventions of novel traditions as described here. This sort of change, reinvigoration, or reinfection is reflected in an adage applied to the churches that carry the Christian tradition: *Ecclesia semper reformanda*. The Church is always to be renewed—neither to be rigidly fixed nor to be deliberately invented or resuscitated. Fourth, the present issue is about a specific *act* of an authority with true legitimacy in the Catholic tradition. That some find the specific act infelicitous does not mean that they are attacking "the authority of the magisterium" in some wholesale manner—a point made clear in chapter 6.

Hobsbawm has observed that "when the old ways are alive, traditions need be neither revived nor invented."[56] I would add to that another adage: When a person or group in authority fears the old ways may be moribund, it may seek to revive traditions and actually have the effect of inventing novel traditions. It is one of the tasks of the historian to show us just how traditions have endured or have been deliberately invented. In fact, the historian, by destabilizing a present "received tradition" through showing it rather recent—as the examples mentioned above illustrate—can contribute to the development of other versions of the tradition. The historian's work, if it becomes received in the community, then, may become a constituent of a new story, a new tradition, in which the community can live.

---

[56] Hobsbawm, "Introduction: Inventing Traditions," 8.

Certainly the work of historians of the liturgy in the twentieth century, for example, Jungmann, was a necessary condition for the reformation of the Tridentine liturgy, which had become the universal standard in the Catholic Church.

Perhaps it is obvious, but traditions are not always imposed on a community, whether deliberately invented or enduring. In many ways they provide support for individuals and groups and are willingly accepted despite the problems they seem to embody.[57] Whether they are recently, deliberately invented or more ancient, insofar as they help create identities and do not meet debilitating resistance, traditions, even those less than ideal by their supporting regimes of domination, may nonetheless be cherished by people who would face losing their identity and (relatively) stable subject positions if they abandoned them.

In sum, feminist and constructivist arguments that traditions are made, not found, do have some evidence in their favor. The proponents of these views note that traditions are deliberately invented for purposes of social control. But that is certainly not the only function, effect, or purpose of a tradition, nor is social control a predominantly or exclusively negative characteristic of all traditions, nor are all emergent traditions "made" in the same way. Even when traditions are reinvented by authorities or practitioners, their purpose may or may not be one of social control. What we must learn from those who take traditions as necessarily made is that there cannot be a "theological discourse free from contemporary signifying practices."[58] Every tradition is necessarily mutated, invented, and reinvented as it is

---

[57] Two recent books don't make precisely this claim, but they do illustrate and support it. In *Changing the Subject*, especially 282-87, Fulkerson illustrates how the religious discourse of Appalachian women provides resources for both oppression and liberation. These women rely on God the Father to help them through their lives, including abusive situations, despite the fact that a patriarchal discourse system keeps them in bondage. In *Thank You, Saint Jude: Women's Devotion to the Patron Saint of Hopeless Causes* (New Haven, Conn: Yale University Press, 1996), Robert A. Orsi shows how the traditional practice of the devotion enables women to cope with difficult circumstances that they cannot leave. (By the way, the St. Jude devotion, as Orsi demonstrates, is clearly a "deliberately invented tradition" in the sense used here. In 1929, a new practice was initiated in the hope that it would "take" in a religious community; it did and thus became a tradition. Today people unfamiliar with Orsi's work find it hard to believe that the broad acceptance of Jude as the patron of impossible causes is of such recent invention.)

[58] Fulkerson, *Changing the Subject*, 368.

inculturated.[59] No verbal formula, no matter how cherished, can guarantee continuity of tradition.

Conclusion

What we cannot neglect, and what those who cling to traditions as found or given can and must teach us, is that traditions are *perceived as* stable, continuous, and certain. As such, traditions serve to confer identity on a community or people.[60] Traditions delineate that path that a community has taken. By conveying a worldview and by discriminating "our" path from other paths, traditions distinguish our community from other communities. Traditions are "communication systems" that provide both relative stability and relative flexibility to cope with novel situations or data. However much instability and innovation scholars may notice in traditions, people generally dwell in them as though they were stable and find such scholarship disturbing, at best.

Traditions provide a sense of stability, a communal space in which people can dwell, and a set of practices that shape how the participants live in the world, even though many people who dwell in those traditions realize that they have evolved from what they were when they were founded. Clearly, the arguments supporting the deliberate construction and invention of tradition apply to some traditions, and perhaps even to some aspects of many traditions. What the critics have shown us is that traditions not only are, but must be, malleable

---

[59] Fulkerson, ibid., makes the even stronger claim that "'theological' or faith discourses and those of 'culture' come into being at the same time." In this she is arguing that neither the traditions passed on nor the already realized cultural and social locations of those receiving the traditions have a priority over each other. Descriptively, this is indeed correct as an analysis of the emergence of local theologies (and *all* theologies are local!). Normatively, however, for theologians like Schreiter, there is a need to give some form of priority to the tradition and some criteria for discerning appropriate from inappropriate inculturations (see *Constructing Local Theologies*, 117-21). Nonetheless, the tradition cannot be a sufficient ground or warrant for such judgments. Both Schreiter and Fulkerson would agree on that point.

[60] See Schreiter, *Constructing Local Theologies*, 105-7, 117-21; and Morgan, "From a Death to a View," 99-100, for two very different perspectives on the function of tradition in bringing about a communal identity. The present paragraph for the most part follows Schreiter's analysis.

if they are to thrive in times and places different from the ones in which they originated.

However, the critics have also not satisfactorily accounted for the sense of stability traditions provide. Rather, they have simply tended to dismiss this stability as an illusion. But it is a logical fallacy to infer that because the stability of some traditions is an illusion, that the stability of all traditions is an illusion. The question is whether appropriate malleability is compatible with stability, whether traditions can be both constructed and given. The critics have given evidence to support the constructedness of traditions; participants experiencing the tradition as something to which they must conform, rather than something they create, give evidence to support their givenness.

Living traditions are neither perfectly rigid nor purely malleable. Neither side has the whole story. But this negative characterization leaves us with a more important question: How then can they be characterized constructively? We can now proceed to the virtuous task of charting a middle course in characterizing traditions between the vicious extremes of "madeness" and "foundness": Traditions are not "things," but socially embodied, interwoven, enduring practices. Chapter 2 explores this mediating approach.

The Concept of Tradition

This chapter argues for an approach to understanding tradition different from those that lead to the oppositions (made *vs.* found, participant *vs.* analyst) enumerated in the previous chapter. It seeks to show that a religious tradition is best understood as an enduring practice or set of practices including a vision (belief), attitudes (dispositions, affections), and patterns of action. To put the strength of the present approach briefly: other concepts of traditions have presumed that the key is to know *what* a tradition is. The present approach presumes that knowing a tradition is much more fundamentally a knowing *how* to live in and live out a tradition. If traditions are recognized to be networks of enduring practices, then one knows them when one knows how to participate in them. Traditions are not reified "things" that can be known apart from practice, any more than languages are "things" that can be known apart from linguistic performance and competence.

A Practical Approach to "Making" and "Finding" Traditions

To get beyond the dichotomy of construing traditions as made or found, we can begin by focusing on how traditions function. Robert Schreiter writes that a "tradition presents a way of life, providing pathways on *how* to behave and *how* to think."[1] A tradition gives a community and its members ways to communicate and patterns to develop both collective and individual identity. Participating in a tradition shapes communities and persons by shaping their practice and their

---

[1] Robert Schreiter, *Constructing Local Theologies* (Maryknoll, N.Y.: Orbis Books, 1985), 107, emphasis added.

thought, but communities and persons do nonetheless reshape traditions in the ways they receive and enact them. The patterns of shaping and being shaped in and by a tradition need to be briefly explored.

First, people are shaped by traditions. In what has become a commonplace in ritual studies, rituals discipline and shape not only the "mind" and speech of the participant but also the participant's body.[2] We learn practices, including traditional practices, that become part of our bodily memory and thus of our identity. We learn *how* to behave in a vast number of social situations.[3] We learn these practices of a tradition as we learn skills: by apprenticeship, if not to a "master" of the tradition, then by simply learning how to live in the tradition itself. We learn *how* to speak, to read, to write; we learn *how* to act in various situations (manners and morals); we learn *how* to run, to swim, to teach, to rear children, to use concepts, to tell jokes. In each of these we participate in practices that show or teach us *how* to do these things, including how to communicate. We engage in each of these practices more or less well, more or less creatively, more or less effectively. The variety of practices in which people are shaped in their learning suggests both the variety of traditions that shape them and the different levels and kinds of abilities they develop. This diversity is, in part, what makes the individuals who participate in traditions distinctive.

Second, people can and do reshape traditions as they receive them by enacting them. Adapting religious rituals from the "old world" in a "new world," changing patterns in architecture because of the availability of new materials for construction, raising the standards of excellence in sports, and reinterpreting the Constitution as new awareness of human rights emerges are all ways in which a community (or sometimes, creative individuals) reshapes a tradition. Such creative reshaping requires that elusive quality called imagination. Both an agent (one who can imagine new ways of enacting the old paths) and a community (which can also originate, share in, and develop imaginative ideas) need this quality if their practices are to be fresh. Without imagination—even in stable contexts—practices can become stale. Those who support the rigidity of traditions usually find that *some* changes in traditional practices are necessary, some imagination

---

[2] See, for example, Talal Asad, *Genealogies of Religion: Disciplines and Reasons of Power in Christianity and Islam* (Baltimore: Johns Hopkins University Press, 1993), 251.

[3] Paul Connerton, *How Societies Remember* (Cambridge: Cambridge University Press, 1989), esp. 72-79.

needed—even if the changes are superficial and the imagination minimal—in order for traditions to make necessary accommodations to new host cultures or to changing cultural circumstances.[4]

Schreiter suggests that imaginative transgressions of boundaries may reshape traditions: "Thus, when Jesus rearranged the boundaries concerning who would have a place in the kingdom of God, who would have the first place and the last, a distinctively different image of what it meant to be a part of the chosen people arose."[5] This image became part of the memory of him that his followers inscribed in the gospels. For such transgressions to bring about changes in a tradition, the transgressor has to know how to violate boundaries in ways that others can understand and incorporate into their own practices.[6] Such creative transgression, then, reshapes the tradition by resetting its boundaries. In this instance, some people who were "outside" become included as the boundaries are effectively redrawn to incorporate them.

Nonetheless, we don't make up traditions out of whole cloth. Even though someone may want to create a tradition, creating a tradition is not an act one can perform. This is not because in some sense people may not want to create traditions, just as some middle-aged people want to be young again (they may succeed, for a time, at *looking* young, but *being* young is no longer a possibility for them). Like becoming young again, creating a tradition is ordinarily not something that an individual or a group can coherently *intend* to do, even if it wishes to, wants to, or hopes to. To show why this is so, we need to borrow some distinctions from the philosophy of action.

A general point in theories of human action is that some acts simply cannot be intended. One illustration of this general point can be seen if one considers, for example, a woman playing golf.[7] She cannot *intend* to hit the ball into the cup from a tee 150 yards away. She may wish for or want or need or hope for or pray for a hole-in-one to win a match. But, as any golfer can attest, getting a hole-in-one is *not* within the golfer's control; it is not an act she can plan or intend to

---

[4] See Aidan Kavanagh, *Elements of Rite: A Handbook of Liturgical Style* (New York: Pueblo, 1982; Collegeville, Minn.: Liturgical Press, 1990), 55.

[5] Schreiter, *Constructing Local Theologies,* 66. Schreiter makes this point about social change, but it also applies here.

[6] Transgressors may not be able to say *what* they did that was so effective. Agents may not be able to describe discursively or demonstrate on demand their "know how."

[7] For this illustration I am indebted to Peter Dalton of the philosophy department of Florida State University.

perform. A hole-in-one results from a combination of a well-hit (usually) golf shot (an act some people *can* intend to perform and can perform successfully), and a number of other uncontrollable factors that lead golfers to attribute a hole-in-one to an act of God or a lot of luck. What one *can* do is to learn how to hit golf shots well; one can expect to hit some chips and many putts into the cup, and the better the golfer one is, the more difficult are the shots one is likely to hit closer to the pin or even to hole out successfully (but even professionals miss putts from two feet away). Yet one cannot intend to make a hole-in-one, because a hole-in-one is not an act one can intend to perform; rather, it is a *result* of an act one can intend to perform if one has the skill (to hit a tee shot well) plus other factors. The principle is this: One cannot *intend* to perform an act-with-results that one cannot, in ordinary circumstances, make occur.[8] In contrast, for a golf professional, in ordinary circumstances, *not* to hit the green from 150 yards is either bad luck or a bad shot, a failure in executing an act (a good golf shot) for which one has the skill. If one has the skill, one clearly *can* intend to hit a ball on the green and have a reasonable chance of performing just that act. In sum, some of us can intend and execute some acts (hitting the ball on the green), but none of us can intend some other acts (hitting a hole-in-one) because the results of those acts are beyond the possibility of our determining them.

Analogously, one cannot intend to perform the act of creating a tradition. One can certainly engage in an act that one hopes or wishes would be a model for other acts, and thus the beginning of a tradition. But whether what one does becomes a tradition depends on factors beyond one's own control. It was not within Dwight Eisenhower's control to determine how his saying about faith would become part of the consciousness of Americans. Like making a hole-in-one, too many factors beyond an agent's control are needed for a tradition to develop to make it coherent for an agent to intend to perform an act that initiates a tradition.

---

[8] Philosophers will recognize the slipperiness of "ordinary circumstances." They will especially note cases of entrapment, wherein a person works to set the circumstances in such a way so that another person in those circumstances cannot but act in a certain way. There are various ways of handling this sort of case to acknowledge the responsibility of the person who entraps over the one who is trapped, but these need not concern us here. The point is to note that when one *intends* to complete an act, one presumes ordinary circumstances obtain, without regard for truly extraordinary circumstances (acknowledging that one may sometimes set the circumstances as well as perform the act).

This is not to deny that a shrewd person may be able to understand that conditions in a community are ripe for a certain sort of act to take root and to become a tradition, and then take action to inaugurate that pattern of action (a practice). Perhaps this is what Jesus did. But less controversial examples of this abound in contemporary sports and entertainment. Consider the NFL-AFL championship game, now known as the Super Bowl. Late January was something of a spectator-sport desert for television in the United States when the game between the two rival football leagues began. That the game has become a national holiday with numerous traditions (incessant television coverage, large parties, inauguration of advertising campaigns, and so on) is obvious, but it was not the action of Pete Rozelle in working to inaugurate it that made it a tradition, but the fact that the contest took place in conditions in which the practices associated with Super Bowl Sunday were lucky enough to become an indubitable and (so far) enduring American tradition. Mr. Rozelle could not have determined that his idea would "take" and become a tradition. As with the hole-in-one, whether an act one performs starts a tradition, even if one wants one's action to do so, is not something one can determine.[9]

The obvious exception to this seems to be some deliberately invented traditions. But even in the case of the CDF constraining the lectionary, there is sufficient resistance that the response to the CDF is not uniform. Moreover, it should be noted that an individual did not invent the tradition. It took a curial body, acting officially in the context of established canonical structures, to invent the tradition. Authorities within a community can control the ways people engage in practices. Yet like the authoritative prohibition of "artificial" contraception, even such an imposition may be ineffective in shaping the practices of all the members of the community. Authorities who regulate or deliberately invent traditions cannot always control whether their rules or inventions "take" in the community.

In contrast, an individual or community in certain circumstances can perhaps act to destroy a tradition by taking away the conditions

---

[9] One exception to this is the deliberate invention of novel traditions, especially as noted in chapter 1. In these cases, special circumstances obtain—patterns of authority, a cultural "need," and so on—that make it possible for traditions to be deliberately invented. While the Super Bowl may be an invented tradition, it is hard to imagine that its present pattern of being a midwinter holiday was deliberately intended by the originator. Such a holiday might even have been described as beyond Pete Rozelle's wildest dreams. And with the case of deliberately invented traditions that are imposed on a populace, the important phenomenon of resistance must be noted (see chapter 1, 40-43).

necessary for it to thrive. For example, some colleges and universities have begun always to schedule spring break in the week in which St. Patrick's Day occurs in order to eliminate the tradition of heavy drinking that has grown up on their campuses. With large numbers of residential students excluded from campus housing, a condition necessary for heavy "partying" (large numbers of people present on the feast day) is eliminated and thus the tradition is eliminated. By taking away the conditions in which a tradition thrives, one can undermine a tradition.

These preliminary reflections on "making" traditions balance the arguments in the first chapter, where those who would find that traditions are "found" received little support. Insofar as traditions are made, they cannot ordinarily be intentionally made or made by individuals. The participants' intuitions that made traditions are not *traditions* at all is right at least in this: Save for manipulation, overbearing authority, and other similar circumstances that enable one person or a small group to have extraordinary power to shape a culture, traditions cannot be *intentionally* made.

In sum, any adequate theory of tradition must account for both the fact that traditions shape individuals' and communities' identities and the fact that individuals and communities can reshape traditions but cannot intentionally make traditions completely *de novo*.

A Practical Theory of Tradition

Theologian Yves Congar has offered a simple definition of a tradition: "Tradition means, in itself, a transmission from person to person. . . . Tradition is not primarily to be defined by a particular material object, but by the act of transmission, and its content is simply *id quod traditum est, id quod traditur*."[10] Congar nuances and develops this definition when he comes to discuss the Christian tradition. But essential to a tradition, as Congar's definition highlights, is the fact that it is the process of the communication of tradition, what Congar calls transmission. We learn how to communicate a tradition. Such communication is a practice we learn by engaging in acts of "transmitting" and "receiving" what is communicated. While Congar was

---

[10] Yves Congar, O.P., *Tradition and Traditions: An Historical and Theological Essay*, trans. Michael Naseby and Thomas Rainborough (New York: Macmillan, 1967), 296.

working almost exclusively within the history of the Christian tradition, his basic understanding of tradition suggests that the heart of a tradition—any tradition—is a communicative practice.

Philosopher Alasdair MacIntyre's definition of a living tradition also centers on communication: "A living tradition then is an historically extended, socially embodied argument, and an argument precisely in part about the goods which constitute that tradition."[11] To engage in an argument, one party has to understand the others. Each must be willing to change his or her own view in light of the considerations the other proposes, and each has the right to expect the same of the other. MacIntyre's account of a tradition is also a practical account. However, MacIntyre's theory applies primarily to intellectual traditions in general, and philosophical traditions in particular. The primary ability requisite for participating in a MacIntyrean tradition is knowing how to argue. The theory is too limited to apply to broader cultural traditions, liturgical traditions (worship is hardly argument), religious traditions, and other "softer" traditions in which "argument" is not the central mode of discourse and knowing how to argue the most important ability for a participant to have. It is also easy to assume that the contents of the arguments, the *tradita*, are more crucial than the arguing, the *traditio*.

Historian Eric Hobsbawm's definition of invented traditions actually covers all traditions: "a set of practices, normally governed by overtly or tacitly accepted rules and of a ritual or symbolic nature, which seek to inculcate certain values and norms of behaviour by repetition, which automatically implies continuity with the past."[12] While using terms different from those of MacIntyre or Congar, Hobsbawm also focuses on tradition as a communicative practice. From the examples Hobsbawm gives, it is clear that he does *not* take "repetition" to be "mindless repetition," but repetition for the sake of continuity with the past. However, Hobsbawm tends to give rules a status that is, at best, problematical. It is not clear that rules govern a tradition. One may (and often does) begin to *learn* a tradition by learning how to follow the rules one is taught, but that practice, as shown in chapter 4 below, does not warrant the claim that rules therefore

---

[11] Alasdair MacIntyre, *After Virtue: A Study in Moral Theory* (Notre Dame, Ind.: University of Notre Dame Press, 1981), 207.

[12] Eric Hobsbawm, "Introduction: Inventing Traditions," in *The Invention of Tradition*, ed. Eric Hobsbawm and Terence Ranger (Cambridge: Cambridge University Press, 1983), 1.

govern a tradition, as if they were something logically or ontologically prior to the practice or performance of the tradition.

Robert Schreiter explicitly draws an analogy between a religious tradition and a language system.[13] Schreiter's notion of language is that it can be seen as a semiotic system comprising semantic components (such as meaning and values of linguistic terms), syntax (structural or grammatical rules that relate semantic components and shape or reshape their meaning), and pragmatics (the possible linguistic performances a speaker can engage in—performances always shaped by context and never "words alone"). Faith is like linguistic competence, the ability to speak the language, to "perform" it. Intellectual, ritual, and other practices are like linguistic performances, the practices that shape and express the competence. The "loci of orthodoxy" are like the grammar, the syntax of the linguistic system. But as Schreiter notes, competency in a language (faith) and the grammatical rules of the language (doctrine) are always *inferred* from the performances of individuals and communities as they engage in the practices of speaking the language (or of living the faith). To reduce the tradition to any of its elements (syntax, semantics, pragmatics) is to miss the significance of the tradition. However important performance is for Schreiter's work, his larger concerns about theology leave him little room to focus on the significance of the performances of practitioners.

Religious traditions have also been helpfully understood as "cultural-symbolic systems" (Clifford Geertz)[14] and "discourse practices" (Kathleen Boone).[15] All these various approaches to tradition in general and religious traditions in particular have in common an explicit focus on the practices of communication and identity formation. In various ways they all show that because there are such tight connections among actions, beliefs, and attitudes in a tradition, one cannot understand beliefs without understanding the actions and attitudes with which they are linked in a practice or set of practices. They differ in the philosophical accounts of language-in-practice that they use and the factors they highlight. For instance, anthropologist Clifford Geertz depends on the work of Ludwig Wittgenstein, critical theorist Kathleen Boone on the work of Michel Foucault, and theologian

---

[13] Schreiter, *Constructing Local Theologies,* 115ff.

[14] See Clifford Geertz, *The Interpretation of Cultures* (New York: Basic Books, 1973).

[15] Kathleen C. Boone, *The Bible Tells Them So: The Discourse of Protestant Fundamentalism* (Albany, N.Y.: SUNY Press, 1989).

Robert Schreiter on the work of C. S. Peirce and Noam Chomsky. MacIntyre develops his account in the process of developing a theory of virtue, Hobsbawm in the service of an almost iconoclastic approach to tradition, and Boone in an exposition of the practices of American Protestant fundamentalism. In general, however, these expositions focus more on the *communication system* that structures a tradition or on the *identity* developed, rather than on the *practices* that are their basis.

Nonetheless, practice is central for each of them to detail what a tradition does. What Schreiter, for example, calls pragmatics is a description or theory of performance or practice.[16] Yet the term *practice* has become a term of the art in contemporary philosophy (epistemology, philosophy of religion, ethics) and in Christian theology. If we are to develop a practical theory of tradition, the concept of a practice requires clarification. I find that the descriptive definition of James Wm. McClendon Jr. is a clear and useful starting point for exploring the concept of practice. Adapting Alasdair MacIntyre's understanding, McClendon writes:

> Social practices, like games, strive for some *end* beyond themselves (health for the practice of medicine, livable space for architecture), require intentional participation on the part of *practitioners,* employ determinate *means,* and proceed according to *rules.* So a "practice" . . . is a complex series of human actions involving definite practitioners who by these means and in accordance with these rules together seek the understood end.[17]

This basic definition needs to be developed in three ways.

First, the process of seeking the goal or end of the practice can involve the practitioners having a shared vision, that is, a web of convictions expressing the goal of the practice sufficient to define that goal and its relation to the goal(s) of human life and to additional supporting beliefs, especially with regard to how such goal(s) can be

---

[16] One approach to language that takes pragmatics as central is "speech act theory." For one account of this approach, see Terrence W. Tilley, *The Evils of Theodicy* (Washington, D.C.: Georgetown University Press, 1991), chaps. 1-3.

[17] James Wm. McClendon Jr., *Systematic Theology,* vol. 2, *Doctrine* (Nashville, Tenn.: Abingdon Press, 1994), 28. Some material below expands material first published in Terrence W. Tilley, *The Wisdom of Religious Commitment* (Washington, D.C.: Georgetown University Press, 1995), chap. 2.

reached. I will argue below that *vision* is a key characteristic of religious traditions. Second, engaging in the practice develops dispositions appropriate for persons involved in the practice (especially those that support seeking the goal and that incline people who participate to use the appropriate means). McClendon's work does not ignore the affective component in practices, but it is not highlighted sufficiently in the above working definition. Paul Connerton highlights this aspect of a tradition in a discussion of postures: We learn that a person is of a higher social rank because we bow or curtsey to them; these "manners" are practices that shape our attitudes—a point whose importance appears in chapter 3.[18] Third, a practitioner learns the "grammar" of the practice, a set of inferred rules that show how means (material means and skills) and ends are connected in the patterns of actions that constitute the practice. I have argued elsewhere that this is the real contribution and importance of Pascal's "wager argument."[19]

Practices come in many varieties. Consider piloting an airplane as a practice. It is learned not merely by learning a theory or set of rules, but by showing in practice that one has the skills that those rules guide one to learn. If one has acquired the skills, mastered the practice, one receives a license to fly.[20] Additionally, there are other unwritten rules that guide a pilot in developing the proper attitudes and dispositions, or at least the proper demeanor. Commercial pilots, for instance, learn how to talk to passengers in the "Chuck Yeager style" of unflappable, quiet confidence; pilots display this attitude by using a minimum of calm, drawled words to the passengers, no matter what problems affect the flight. The practice employs determinate means such as airplanes (rather than dirigibles), airports, the air traffic control system, and so forth, and learned skills. It requires intentional participation by definite practitioners, that is, the licensed pilots. The goals or purposes range from enjoying the pleasure of flying to getting people and cargo from place to place safely.[21] The

---

[18] Connerton, *How Societies Remember,* 73-74.

[19] See Tilley, *The Wisdom of Religious Commitment,* 19-26, which analyzes the wager as a practical argument.

[20] Pilots are licensed for certain types of aircraft, in certain conditions, for certain purposes. There are a variety of pilots' and instructors' licenses, but that variety need not concern us here.

[21] Some might consider flying an airplane not a practice but rather a skill in which rules are followed strictly. But as we shall see in chapter 4, following a rule requires creativity. For aircraft piloting, a prime example of this creativity can be found in the story of Air Canada Flight 143. Both engines failed, and yet the pilot brought the plane down safely. See William Hoffer and Marilyn Mona Hoffer, *Freefall* (New York: St. Martin's Press, 1989).

practice is cooperative and involves more people who are not pilots than who are pilots to make air travel successful. When such cooperation fails, accidents can occur. Piloting provides one example of a practice, specifically a professional practice.

Another practice is that of pastoring a religious community. Here the rules may not always be as clear as in piloting, but there are rules usually established by congregations and other governing bodies to guide pastoral practice. The means involved are as extensive and various as in all kinds of human interactions, but specific skills—such as those for religious education, leadership in ritual, and so on—that may go beyond technical skills are required. The practitioners are set off from the congregation in various ways, for example, by election, ordination, installation, and thus form a defined (however loose or permeable) group. The ends of pastoral practice are conceived variously depending on the community involved; in Roman Catholicism, one purpose of pastoral practice can be construed as empowering the community to live a life of discipleship, to be for the world the body of Christ.

One factor that tends to distinguish a religious practice from other types of practices is a shared vision.[22] As noted above, a vision is a web of convictions. It expresses the goal of a practice. It links those particular goals to the more general goals of human life. A vision also integrates the means used in a practice to those goals. In this context, convictions also function as a technical term: convictions are not all the beliefs an individual or community holds, but those persistent beliefs that are not easily given up; if they *are* given up, then the character of the community or person is significantly changed.[23] One can be a member of the company of pilots without having a web of convictions that express a shared vision of what piloting is or what an airline should be or what the system of air traffic should be or is. One can be a good, practicing pilot whatever one's economic, political, or religious convictions might be. Similar claims can be made about many professional practices, for example, architecture and medicine. One can be a good practitioner without

---

[22] This is not to claim that a religious vision is *the* defining characteristic of a religious tradition. Other traditions and practices may also require such ideological commitment or a shared vision, for example, political traditions, educational traditions. However, a tradition without some sense of a shared vision cannot be religious. Vision is a necessary component of a religious tradition, but is not sufficient to distinguish religious traditions from all other traditions.

[23] Compare McClendon, *Doctrine*, 29, and the works cited therein.

sharing a vision (as understood herein) with one's fellow practitioners.[24] However, one cannot participate in a religious practice fully without sharing a vision with one's fellow practitioners. One cannot be a Christian pastoral minister unless one shares a sense of purpose informed by a vision of human life as created, redeemed, and sustained by the God present and revealed in and through Jesus the Christ. That religious visions are difficult to detail should not be surprising; they are complex and their specific lineaments are often controverted even among participants. They are the subject of arguments among participants in the practices. While pastoring is a professional practice as much as piloting is, it is also a religious or ideological practice. It is the presence of an ideology expressed as a vision that characterizes religious (and some other) practices and sets of practices.

Insofar as they are enduring, practices like piloting and pastoring go far to constitute traditions. To become a pilot or a pastor one learns the practice. In so doing, one learns a tradition that has grown up over time and been instantiated in a community that carries it. For both sorts of practices, institutions have grown up (for example, the Federal Aviation Administration, the American Baptist Convention, the American Medical Association) that grow out of the communities of practitioners and that work to preserve and adapt the practices for subsequent practitioners. Practices can often be analyzed without paying much attention to institutions, but institutions (even ones with minimal authority in a practice) are necessary for practices to endure beyond a generation and become traditions.[25]

Practices are not private. Although individuals acting alone can engage in practices idiosyncratically and even unsocially, that does

---

[24] This presumes the existence of "anideological" practices and traditions, those in which participants do not have to have a shared ideology or vision (see note 28 below). The presumption seems obvious for practices like piloting, but it is not so clear for the professional practices of medicine and law. Insofar as such practices require that their practitioners do have a shared vision (as vision is described herein) to be able to engage "authentically" or "fully" in the practice, then these, too, would be more assimilable to ideological practices and traditions (such as religious ones) than to anideological practices and traditions. M. Therese Lysaught has helped me to see this point more clearly.

[25] This point is adapted from Max Weber's analysis of charismatic, traditional, and institutional authority (see *Max Weber on Charisma and Institution Building*, ed. S. N. Eisenstadt [Chicago: University of Chicago Press, 1968]). For an argument that argues for the necessity of institutions even for religious experience to occur, see Terrence W. Tilley, "The Institutional Element in Religious Experience," *Modern Theology* 10/2 (April 1994): 185-212.

not make that person's practice something so separable from a community that it could be deemed private. To engage in a practice, an individual has to learn how to act. Even biological processes like eating, drinking, and elimination have social components that supervene on biological necessities (at least in the human species). Hence, practices are first practices of communities of practitioners, and derivatively the practices of individuals. As noted above with regard to traditions, individuals are shaped by practices and shape and reshape them as they engage in those practices.

Each practice requires its practitioners to develop skills in order to engage in the practice. Some skills are technical and limited to one practice or set of practices. However, there are other abilities that persons develop and carry into many, perhaps all, of their practices. Many of these skills are virtues, character traits that may be developed in one practical context or role but become part of one's character. A person of true virtue can carry that ability from one practice to another and be recognized as courageous or wise or just in many practices.[26]

Given the understanding of tradition as communicative and identity-shaping, and given that practices as understood herein serve to constitute communicative competence and shape identity, we can construe a *tradition* as an enduring practice or set of linked practices.[27]

---

[26] In *The Wisdom of Religious Commitment*, 101-18, I sketch the contexts in which practical wisdom might be developed and recognized and argue that truly wise (prudent) persons are those who *can* carry this ability into all their practices.

[27] As in the previous chapter, a religious or quasi-religious tradition can be understood as one form of a tradition. Many of the practices in a tradition are "doxastic practices," that is, practices that form beliefs for practitioners (see William P. Alston, "A 'Doxastic Practice' Approach to Epistemology," in *Knowledge and Skepticism*, ed. M. Clay and K. Lehrer [Boulder, Colo.: Westview, 1989]; idem, *Perceiving God: The Epistemology of Religious Experience* [Ithaca, N.Y.: Cornell University Press, 1991]; Nicholas Wolterstorff, *Locke and the Ethics of Belief* [Cambridge: Cambridge University Press, 1996], xvii-xix: and Terrence W. Tilley, "Religious Pluralism as a Problem for 'Practical' Religious Epistemology," *Religious Studies* 30/2 [June 1994]: 161-69). The *purpose* of some practices is belief formation; for others, belief formation may be a *component* of the practice. Many religious practices may be of the latter type in that their practitioners form beliefs as a constituent of their seeking other goals; for example, one may form beliefs about sin and grace as a constituent of attempting to live a life pleasing to God. In those cases, belief formation is not a purpose of a practice but a component of it. In either case, however, it is confused to treat religious beliefs as if they were independent of religious practices. Religious belief is the result of engaging in religious practices, a component of engaging in religious practices, or can itself be a religious practice, as McClendon suggests (see *Doctrine*, 28-29).

A specific ideological tradition will be constituted by a (roughly) definable set of practices. Ingredient in these traditions will be specific beliefs that are generated by or implicit in the practices, especially beliefs that articulate the vision that the tradition carries. For present purposes, I shall ignore other forms of ideological and anideological[28] traditions to focus primarily on religious traditions (although some examples from both ideological and anideological traditions will be considered).

For example, we can consider the Catholic tradition. It can be very formally construed as that set of enduring practices in which the members of the Church (however understood, but especially as the body of Christ and the people of God) strive for the sanctity of life characterized by authentic discipleship. One becomes a disciple, a member of the body of Christ, by participating in ritual (devotional and sacramental) practices; developing with the help of God's grace a moral life (moral practices); learning how to participate in the life of the Church, which anticipates the full realization of the reign of God (ecclesial practices, especially the practices that constitute working for social justice); and doing all this according to the "grammar" of the tradition (for example, scripture, creeds, confessional statements, magisterial pronouncements, catechisms). The Catholic tradition, then, can be seen primarily as a set of practices that, when engaged in properly, shape people into a communion of saints.[29]

---

[28] By *anideological* practices and traditions I mean to pick out those practices and traditions without a component vision, such as piloting an airplane. This does not imply that a person can be anideological; rather, I want to point out that persons with different ideologies, and hence different visions, can participate fully in some practices. Ideology factors out when considering some practices as practices even though some principles and virtues may be necessary for participating in a given practice. The inverse of this is the recognized fact that some virtues and principles may be developed in different kinds of practices. Not all virtues and principles are necessarily linked to a specific ideology, even if all people have ideologies of some kind.

[29] This very quick account admittedly sounds monolithic. However, it is *not* intended that way. *Sanctity* is a polyvalent term, with many different instantiations. The point adapted from Charlesworth below applies to this account: even if it is "universal," it is not uniform for it presumes that all of the practices that constitute the Catholic tradition are inculturated variously in different times and places (Max Charlesworth, "Universal and Local Elements in Religion," in *Religious Inventions: Four Essays* [Cambridge: Cambridge University Press, 1997]). Sanctity in the contemporary city is not identical in practice to sanctity in the medieval monastery, although there are clear analogies between such sanctity and some real similarities in practice. Moreover, the saintly practices typical of the community imaged as "the Body of Christ," "the pilgrim people of God," or

Similar accounts could be given for other religious traditions. A similar, but somewhat vaguer, construal could be given for the Christian tradition generally. Different Christian traditions would construe devotional and ritual practices differently, may not highlight the church as the body of Christ, and would include different confessional statements and catechetical manuals.

Seeking to lead a life of holiness appropriate to one's context involves Catholics in having a shared vision of a sacramental universe, a key element in the Catholic Intellectual Tradition (as chapter 5 shows). God's unfailing divine grace permeates and perfects the personal, interpersonal, social, political, and natural realms.[30] Although we may reject divine grace, it is always available for us if we would but accept it. God's grace enables people to pattern their actions to goodness and holiness. Ingredient in the practices of the Catholic tradition, there are specific forms of doctrine or creedal beliefs, such as those about grace, that Catholics learn as they participate in the practices that constitute the tradition.

Engaging in specific practices learned in local communities is the way in which even universal claims are learned. The universal necessarily is inculturated and learned in and through the particular. As philosopher Max Charlesworth put it, "Religious truths ([many of] which are implicitly or explicitly universal) have to be lived out in local contexts or traditions."[31] Even though many religious believers claim universality for some of their beliefs, those claims are located and thus local. We humans simply cannot get in position to take a universal, God's-eye view. However it may be for God or the angels, *we* live in specifiable locations for a specifiable time. This is *not* to claim that concepts cannot "travel" to other locations or be expanded across cultures, or that concepts developed in one place and time

----

the "perfect society" (all drawn from Vatican II's *Dogmatic Constitution on the Church, Lumen Gentium*) may not be totally harmonizable. The description of such similarities and analogies, as well as such differences and diversities, goes far beyond the points I seek to make in this book. Elizabeth A. Johnson develops an account of the communion of saints as one that promotes a "solidarity in difference" (see *Friends of God and Prophets: A Feminist Theological Reading of the Communion of Saints* [New York: Continuum, 1998], 3).

[30] A theological approach that ignores or underestimates one or more of these realms will be seriously incomplete. For an example of such a criticism, see Thomas G. Dalzell, S.M., "Lack of Social Drama in Balthasar's Theological Dramatics," *Theological Studies* 60/3 (September 1999): 457-75, which analyzes the roots of Balthasar's strong focus on the interpersonal and his neglect of the social and political realms beyond the interpersonal.

[31] Charlesworth, "Universal and Local Elements in Religion," 81.

cannot be useful, illuminating, or appropriate in another place and time. Rather, it is to claim that *translation* of terms and persons will be involved. That one might have the same concept in different contexts is not based on the necessary translatability that a universal language would seem to warrant, but on contingent circumstances. We cannot speak a universal language. We do not live, move, and have our being everywhere. We do not have universal experience, though some of us claim to have at certain specific times and places experiences of the Universal—but even these are always in and through particular experiences at particular times and places, experiences that might have analogues at other times and places. Hence, universal claims must be "adapted and interpreted in the light of local needs, exigencies and experience,"[32] because they necessarily grow out of specific locations and in response to specific issues. But that origin does not determine that the only destiny for the use of such concepts must be that specific time and place.

Universal claims are often expressed in rather abstract propositions. Yet if these claims are to have the status of convictions in the life of a community or an individual, they must be life-shaping. Their significance can be determined not by their meaning as abstracted from every context (what could that mean?), but how they function in the life of a person or community. An example of this is the concept of universal human rights. Proponents of a human right, such as the "right to life," shape that right in various ways. Some find no limits whatsoever to that right, even repudiating self-defense in the face of violence. Others find that there may be circumstances in which a human "forfeits" that right (for instance, if one is convicted of a capital crime). Others question whether those who are not in some way "fully human" have that right. Many would proclaim this a "universal right" but would nonetheless limit its applicability in practice. The life-shaping and concrete significance is not the universal claim but its actual use. Like other abstract "universal claims," there are multiple ways to incarnate the "right to life" in the concrete worlds of human life—and no appeal to the abstract claim is sufficient (and may not be necessary) to adjudicate among competing concrete and practical uses of the claim.

If a universal truth is something that exists independent of any and every time and place and is not ingredient in the actual religious life of a community (a tradition) or an individual (a personal conviction),

---

[32] Ibid., 82.

then human beings—necessarily bound, at least in this life, to specific times and places—cannot have direct access to or unqualified understanding of such truths.[33] Participants in religious communities may claim universal validity for (some of) their convictions. However, such universal claims must arise and be transmitted in particular times and places and, as I shall argue below, through particular practices. If they are not, they are practically irrelevant. Their true significance is their use in practice.

In light of the discussions of *traditio* in chapter 1, I would argue that this practical approach to understanding tradition avoids the problem of equating tradition with *tradita*, that which is passed along. The danger seems to be in reducing some *tradita*, for example, specific religious beliefs, to no importance whatsoever. By focusing on practices, does this practical approach to tradition underplay belief? My claim is that this analysis properly "places" religious beliefs as integral to religious practice. The best way to argue for this view, however, is indirect: If the analysis is illuminating of the concept of tradition—specifically, if it can account for problems in understanding tradition that plague the "content-oriented" accounts without losing what those accounts portray well—then that is good evidence in favor of this "practical" approach.

Practice and Praxis

However, before we can understand practices, a clarification is needed. Many recent philosophers and theologians have written not of "practice" but of "praxis."[34] Varying uses of the term *praxis*, a Greek word usually translated "action," are rooted in two different philosophical traditions.[35] First, there is a classic tradition rooted in

---

[33] For an application of this point to revelation in the Christian tradition, see chapter 6.

[34] For some classic examples, see philosopher Richard Bernstein, *Praxis and Action: Contemporary Philosophies of Human Activity* (Philadelphia: University of Pennsylvania Press, 1971), and theologian Gustavo Gutiérrez, *A Theology of Liberation: History, Politics, and Salvation*, trans. and ed. Sister Caridad Inda and John Eagleson (Maryknoll, N.Y.: Orbis Books, 1973).

[35] In what follows, I am indebted to the succinct and clear summary of Dermot Lane, "David Tracy and the Debate about Praxis," in *Radical Pluralism and Truth: David Tracy and the Hermeneutics of Religion*, ed. Werner G. Jeanrond and Jennifer L. Rike (New York: Crossroad, 1991), 18-37. For a succinct summary of Tracy's view, see David Tracy, *Plurality and Ambiguity: Hermeneutics, Religion, Hope* (San Francisco: Harper & Row, 1987), 10.

Aristotle, which links *praxis* to *theoria*. In this tradition *praxis* is creative and self-creative activity (actions done for the sake of doing them). Praxis is typically distinguished from *theoria* (the activity of the mind) and from *poesis* (usually translated from the Greek as "production," meaning roughly actions done as means to a goal that might be reached other ways) and from *techne* (simply making things).[36] Theologically, this strand of understanding praxis appears in the work of David Tracy, where *praxis* is the intellectual activity that is distinctive to human beings or human action that emerges from theoretical reflection *(theoria)*. Second, there is a tradition that emerges from a Hegelian and Marxist strand that construes *praxis* as the distinctive human activity that transforms both self and society in response to structural patterns of injustice. Some Marxists have preferred the term *revolutionary praxis* to designate this transformative activity. Theologically, this strand appears especially in the work of liberation theologians like Gustavo Gutiérrez. In the former strand, *praxis* is a "second order" activity, the result of reflection; in the latter, it is a first-order, pre-reflective pattern of action "of solidarity [whose source] is the prereflective, intuitive commitment of faith to liberation."[37]

The problem is that *praxis* (in both senses) has been contrasted with *practice,* especially religious practice. Praxis is taken to be intrinsically worthwhile, while practice is simply "repetitive exercises," both physical and intellectual. Praxis is seen as intrinsically creative or liberating, while practice, especially religious practice, is denigrated because in practices people are supposedly dominated by an external rule in which mere repetition constitutes the practice.

However *practice* may be used in some contexts, to reduce practice in all contexts to mere repetition is an error. Of course, a practice, as in a novice musician practicing the violin, a devotee practicing a ritual, or a competitive diver practicing a dive, may begin by being repetitive. It may be repetitive work to develop one's techniques. Such forms of repetition should be understood more as *techne,* as the acquisition of a *skill,* than as any kind of practice or praxis. Such rudimentary practitioners are trying to get the basics of a practice; they are apprentices in the practice, learning the skills needed to engage in the practice. However, to limit the use of the term *practice* to such

---

[36] See J. L. Ackrill, "Aristotle on Action," in *Essays on Aristotle's Ethics*, ed. Amélie Oksenberg Rorty (Berkeley and Los Angeles: University of California Press, 1980), 93-101.

[37] Lane, "David Tracy and the Debate about Praxis," 33.

activity is an error. Such a limited use of *practice* is certainly not always, and probably hardly ever, relevant to *practice* as used herein.

Nonetheless, it is important not to neglect the acquisition of a skill.[38] Skills are often internal constituents of practice (and praxis). One can, perhaps, learn a skill without becoming a participant in a practice. But if one did not have the requisite technical skills (ability to operate the controls of an airplane and to follow the commands of an air traffic controller for piloting, to understand the rubrics for a ritual for pastoring), then that person simply could not engage in the practice or in authentic and effective praxis, however praxis is understood. Such a person may have a vision, but it is one detached from practice, a dream that one does not know how to turn into deeds. An unskilled dreamer is not a practitioner.

Conversely, a person with skills may or may not engage in a practice like pastoring. For instance, someone who knows all the tricks of the trade for successfully sustaining or increasing membership in a church may or may not be a person who has the wisdom to build a community for the reign of God (what one might call the praxis of the Church). Yet a pastor must have the skills requisite to be able to sustain membership and enthusiasm, and so on. This is, finally, a technical skill, even though it is a very complex and subtle one, a necessary means in the practice of pastoring. Without this skill, the community to sustain the practice can wither.

Having technical skills does not make a person a good practitioner. But the absence of a technical skill—such as the inability to "fabricate" a community—is an indicator of the absence of a person's ability to engage in a practice well. To engage fully in a practice does not mean engaging in mere repetition at the novice level or mere development of technical skills any more than engaging in exercises means performing repetitive behavior without development. One need only think of Ignatius of Loyola's *Spiritual Exercises* to remember that there are sophisticated forms of exercise that may involve repetition, but real exercises for the body and soul—however much repetitive activity contributes to them—are far more than repetitive activity. They are practices that one participates in. Their purpose is to shape and reshape the body and soul and make it possible for practitioners to do things they could not have done without the discipline of the practice.

---

[38] I owe this point to discussions with Bernard Lee, S.M., Loyola Institute for Ministry, Loyola University, New Orleans, concerning the relationship of praxis and its associated virtue, phronesis (practical wisdom).

The pianist's finger exercises, the singer's vocal exercises, and the weightlifter's repetitions are not the point of the practices, but they build the foundational skills needed—perhaps only occasionally—to excel in the practice. To participate fully in a practice, to master it, is to go far beyond mere repetition and skill acquisition. Among other things, it requires that elusive ability called imagination.

Beyond the problem of presuming that a practice can be understood as mere repetition, the major theological and philosophical objections to the use of *practice* is that practicing really is reducible to following a rule. These objections are rooted in fundamental misunderstandings of the concept of following a rule, a concept explored in the next two chapters. In brief, it may be true that some practices may begin with the requirement that a participant learn to follow a rule "mindlessly." But it is hard to imagine how one could understand practices as we do here ("a complex series of human actions involving definite practitioners who by these means and in accordance with these rules together seek the understood end") and also call them "mindless."

Part of the confusion comes from the fact that the concept of practice used herein is found in yet another strand of the philosophical tradition, that of the later work of Ludwig Wittgenstein. For Wittgenstein, praxis and practice were not clearly differentiated.[39] To try to resolve these terminological and conceptual problems, one can take Aristotelian praxis and Marxist praxis as species of Wittgensteinian practices. Praxis—in either sense—is not to be contrasted with practice, but to be contrasted with those basic rudiments and technical skills that competent practitioners must learn in order to be able to engage in a practice reasonably well. One cannot simply start to engage in either Aristotelian or Marxist praxis *de novo* any more than one can sit at a piano for the first time in one's life and play a concerto. To be able to engage in authentic praxis of either Aristotelian or Marxist varieties, one must prepare by learning appropriate skills and practice(s)—or, perhaps better, be prepared by friends and teachers working in the appropriate circumstances. Neither form of praxis is a solitary activity. Nor are they possible for pure novices.

---

[39] See Ludwig Wittgenstein, *Philosophical Investigations*, 3d ed., trans. G. E. M. Anscombe (New York: Macmillan, 1958 <1953>). Wittgenstein wrote in German and used the term *praxis,* as in "Darum ist 'der regel folgen' eine Praxis" (202), which has come into the English translation as "practice."

One can, however, come to recognize bad practice. When the piano is out of tune or the concerto poorly played, one can (unless one is tone deaf or otherwise unqualified to judge) hear the need for change, even though one cannot play a concerto. One may not have the skills or the training to minister to a community, but one can (at least sometimes) recognize when the word is not rightly preached, the sacrament not rightly administered, the life of faith not rightly lived. Practices and traditions can degenerate. However, the issues involved with evaluating practices must be deferred to chapter 4.

Conclusion

This chapter has developed a basic practical concept of tradition. As Robert Schreiter put it with regard to the study of language, "We really have only performances of the language before us."[40] As with a language, so with a tradition; we really only have performances of the faith before us. Whether those performances are speech acts or other types of acts, we cannot but begin with performances and their patterns, that is, practices. Chapter 3 puts this approach into practices by starting with specific practices and by showing their significance. Practices carry the traditions that shape people, and people shape the practices and the traditions they carry.

---

[40] Schreiter, *Constructing Local Theologies*, 115.

THREE

Practices as Tradition

This chapter uses the concept of tradition developed in the previous chapter to explore the ways in which practices carry a tradition and shape beliefs. The primary examples will be religious practices that are in flux. This is not to suggest that practices are always malleable or always changing in important ways. Examining practices undergoing transformation, however, can highlight elements in a tradition ordinarily taken for granted by participants. If we have only performances of and in the faith before us (as claimed in chapter 2), then changes in performance practice and resistance to those changes may reflect changes in faith. Examining such a possibility and its significance is essential for an account of tradition.

Moreover, as elements in practices change visibly and quickly, the distinction between participants and outsiders becomes irrelevant. Participants are forced to take the position of analyzing scholars. They may be partisans or advocate changes in practice. In either case, they have to summon up reasons for their "take" on the matter when challenged. Participants have to try to figure out what is changing in the practice, why it is changing, and whether that change is good. "External" scholars' work, then, becomes internalized as participants attempt to understand what they are doing and what is happening to them. Save for dismissive and reductionist scholars who would reduce religious practice and belief to delusion, like Freud, participants may even welcome scholars' help when practices are in flux.

After focusing on a particular practice and showing how understanding it enables us to understand a tradition, the chapter addresses objections to the practical theory of tradition. Chapter 4 will take up the trickiest aspect of this account, the status of rules in a practice and in a tradition.

Understanding Practices: Eucharistic Practice and Belief

To begin understanding practices, especially in light of the basic view of the primacy of particularity and the vagueness of universal claims discussed in chapter 2, we begin with particular practices. As they are obvious examples of practices, we can first consider ritual practices.

Rituals are invented. As Barbara Myerhoff has noted, "Our ceremonies, our most precious conceptions and convictions—*all are mere invention*, not inevitable understandings about the world at all but the results of mortals' imaginings."[1] That our conceptions and convictions, however contingent and constructed, can nonetheless be construed as true is a point argued in chapter 6. Here we merely note that rituals which seem "given" to us are invented and contingent: they might have been otherwise.

In ritual we find interconnected patterns of acting, of believing, and of feeling. The elements of such practices have become so woven together that they can be distinguished analytically but not separated practically. Specific beliefs can function as presumptions of, rules for, or constituents of ritual practices, as when Roman Catholics believe in the Real Presence of Christ in the bread and wine of the Eucharist. Such a belief shapes the properly devout Catholic's attitudes and behavior not only toward the Eucharist and the way the eucharistic elements are to be handled in a ritual setting, but also toward himself or herself as a participant in the ritual. The ritual behavior can function to reinforce beliefs and attitudes, as when during the Mass the priest engages in gestures highlighting the consecration of the bread and wine so as to reinforce the belief in the Real Presence and evoke an attitude of reverence. The attitudes the participant has can shape the participant's beliefs—and the "participant" may be an isolated individual, a member of a group, or the group as a whole—and they may be necessary for a proper participation in a

---

[1] Barbara Myerhoff, *Number Our Days* (New York: Simon and Schuster, 1978), cited in Nathan D. Mitchell, *Liturgy and the Social Sciences* (Collegeville, Minn.: Liturgical Press, 1999), 42. Mitchell evidently approves of Myerhoff's view and of the similar view of Ronald Grimes, "Reinventing Ritual," *Soundings* 75:1 (1992): 21, which makes similar claims and extends them to the notion that language is invented in its performance. While this is similar to what we note about following a rule in chapter 4, that way of putting the matter may overstate the creativity of most ritual or linguistic performances.

ritual.[2] The fact that rituals are "invented" and contingent does not mean that one can separate their constituents to understand their meaning apart from their place in the ritual practice. One cannot substitute *in vitro* dissection for *in vivo* understanding.[3]

Theologians, trained in conceptual analysis and synthesis, often overlook the significance of posture and position. Paul Connerton, however, recognizes that position and posture are important for preserving community memory, that is, tradition. "Power and rank are commonly expressed through certain postures relative to others; from the way in which people group themselves and from the disposition of their bodies relative to the bodies of others, we can deduce the degree of authority which each is thought to enjoy or to which they lay claim."[4] A change, then, in postures or positions may well invoke a change in other aspects of the tradition incorporated into the ritual.

But behaviors—including posture and position—alone do not constitute actions, and patterns of behaviors alone do not constitute practices.[5] Behaviors alone are incomprehensible and even pointless unless they are connected appropriately with beliefs and attitudes that together constitute the practice. Without there being such connections, a person cannot undertake intentional actions and an observer cannot understand the behaviors observed as human actions, rather than as random behavioral events. Without such connections, making

---

[2] Yves Congar, O.P., *Tradition and Traditions: An Historical and a Theological Essay*, trans. Michael Naseby and Thomas Rainborough (New York: Macmillan, 1967) lists the liturgy as the first principal monument or witness to tradition (427-31). Congar tends to rely on ritual as a "fixed thing"(428), yet notices how rituals have shifted (428-30). The present essay focuses on the shifts visible to all who study ritual; to see the actual constancies requires a trained eye, a point Congar undervalues.

[3] I make a similar point with regard to the practices of philosophers of religion in *The Wisdom of Religious Commitment* (Washington, D.C.: Georgetown University Press, 1995), 93-101. For that discipline to be possible in its classic forms, philosophers must presume that they can substitute the examination of propositions derived from religious practice and belief for the examination of practice and belief itself. I argue that this approach is not fully satisfactory as a concrete philosophy of religion, rather than as an abstract natural theology.

[4] Paul Connerton, *How Societies Remember* (Cambridge: Cambridge University Press, 1989), 73.

[5] Of course, it may be possible for people to engage in some practices, especially ritual practices, mindlessly or by rote. This is the truth in the rejection of ritualism. But my point is that the folk who participate in practices mindlessly are *not* participating in practices but merely going through the motions. At best, they are novices in the practice, at worst deluded by thinking that their repetitive behavior is the meaning of the practice. That sort of behavior is not full participation in a practice.

the sign of the cross could not be distinguished from the twitching of arms, genuflecting from the buckling of the knee, or a handshake from an involuntary grab. Behaviors make sense because they are parts of practices.

To develop this point we can explore a specific belief, the Catholic doctrine of the Real Presence of Christ in the Eucharist. The significance or meaning of the doctrine of the Real Presence can be paraphrased or summarized theologically, but it cannot be fully understood except when it is connected with the ritual practices of the community that holds the doctrine. As Schreiter has pointed out, changes in the celebration of the Roman Catholic Mass, such as use of the vernacular with the presider facing the people, rather than Latin with the priest "facing the wall" or "leading the people," significantly affected the belief in the Real Presence for Catholics. With changes in action come changes in belief; the Eucharist comes to signify a communal meal more than a sacrifice. The significance of the altar changes; it more signifies the meal table than the place of sacrifice where the human confronts the divine. No longer do only priests touch the consecrated bread; lay ministers also distribute the hosts into people's hands.[6] As the doctrine of the Real Presence is intimately connected with the topography of the ritual space and behavior, the doctrine changes its significance, especially when the sacrifice motif is substantially muted in the ritual.

Changes in behavior may signify changes in other parts of the performed tradition. For instance, as an altar boy in the mid-fifties, I was not permitted to touch the sacred vessels (the chalices and ciboria) that held the consecrated wine and bread without having a cloth between my hand and the vessel, even when carrying them to or from the altar before or after Mass. While this may have been the policy of the local sister sacristan enacted in order to save polishing the gold vessels, it created an attitude of reverence among sometimes unruly altar boys. That this practice is no longer common—and seems almost laughable to younger Catholics today—suggests that the tradition has shifted so that such behaviors are no longer appropriate. Shifts in what Connerton calls "bodily practices" may indicate other shifts in "shared memory" as well.

Some Church leaders lament that the worshiping community has lost the true concept of the Real Presence. Charles R. Morris, in the

---

[6] Robert J. Schreiter, *Constructing Local* Theologies (Maryknoll, N.Y.: Orbis Books, 1985), 67-68.

context of a discussion comparing and contrasting contemporary ways of celebrating Eucharist, summarizes a point made by many:

> One of the primary worries of conservative theologians . . . is that thirty years of post-Vatican II progressive "communal meal" liturgies have undermined the Catholic belief in the Real Presence. Survey data suggest that they may be right. The majority of Catholic weekly church-attenders, the most faithful Catholics of all, believe that the consecrated host is only a symbolic representation of Christ, rather than Christ himself.[7]

However, Morris also reports (without citation of source) a very appropriate concern that he attributes to theologian Fr. Avery Dulles: that such surveys are so theologically unnuanced as to be practically meaningless. He also neglects to note that the survey to which he alludes is only one of many. Others suggest that different ways of asking the question about the Real Presence will get rather different answers. Sociologist Andrew Greeley has reached rather different conclusions from survey data collected and analyzed by the National Opinion Research Center. He has written numerous articles on this, cogently summarized in a letter to the editor of *America*:

> On major matters of faith—God, Jesus, the Resurrection, life after death, the Real Presence—the overwhelming majority of American Catholics are resolutely orthodox. Moreover, there is little sign of erosion of orthodoxy among the young. Finally, the religious orientation of Catholics continues to be both sacramental and communal and sharply different from that of American Protestants. Dissent, for most American Catholics, focuses on matters of sex and gender.[8]

Surveys asking believers to choose between theologically loaded phrases may not surface the actual beliefs people hold. Moreover,

---

[7] Charles R. Morris, *American Catholic: The Saints and Sinners Who Built America's Most Powerful Church* (New York: Random House, 1997), 393.

[8] *America* 179/1 [4 July 1998], 29. Responses to questions about beliefs developed in the NCR-Gallup Survey support this claim (see William V. D'Antonio, et al., "The American Catholic Laity in 1999," *National Catholic Reporter* 29 October 1999, 12, esp. chart 2).

their beliefs may not be very precise. Hence, a survey asking ordinary believers to make distinctions among precise theological terms or propositions may easily distort the picture of belief patterns it snaps.

It is not clear that participants have lost or must lose their sense of the Real Presence as the ritual practice of Eucharist changes from emphasizing the sacrifice to emphasizing the meal. However, the precise linguistic sense of the doctrine of the Real Presence may well have shifted as these behaviors have shifted. In this, Morris's view cannot be fully discounted. If beliefs are indeed shaped by participation in practices, then as practices shift, beliefs will be likely to shift, too. Some theologians still working with the same theological concepts and doctrinal abstractions verbally unchanged from those developed when one style of practice was dominant may deplore the loss of the concept of Real Presence among the laity. But these theologians may not have noticed that the ritual practice no longer so clearly connects belief in the Real Presence as they have understood it with the belief that the Mass is the reenactment of the sacrifice made once for all on the cross.

Morris also reports that Dulles said that Pope John Paul II, in confirming the traditional formula of transubstantiation for describing what happens to the eucharistic elements in the celebration, is "imposing a justifiable 'language discipline'" on the community. But if such a formulation, developed in the medieval era and having multiple meanings, many of which did not rely on Aristotelian categories, is alien to the liturgical practices on which it is to be imposed, it simply can't make sense of the Real Presence of Christ in those liturgical practices. The doctrine may be inconsistent with the semiotics of the practice that constitute the Mass as it is actually celebrated following the rubrics. Transubstantiation is developed in the popular ecclesial cultures of the Middle Ages with linguistic practices that no longer exist as popular practices. It is not that "the elements are transubstantiated into the Body and Blood of Christ" is false, but that the concept is out of place, just as theoretical discussions of hermeneutics are out of place in sermons. Perhaps the concept no longer fits into the discursive ritual practices of celebrating the Eucharist. Because the culture in which transubstantiation made sense is so distant from our present practice and our ordinary ways of thinking, it may be that that specific linguistic token understood as implicating Aristotelian distinctions between substance and accident cannot be connected sensibly with the actual practice in which people participate. Transubstantiation may be a "linguistic discipline" to be imposed.

But it may well remain *practically* meaningless as a theology for and of eucharistic practice.[9] It may even acquire a new meaning hardly connected to the traditional sense, for example, that transubstantiation refers to the transformation of the worshiping assembly into the body of Christ in and through reception of the Eucharist. The point is that once the term *transubstantiation* is no longer connected with the ritual as traditionally performed, the meaning of the term becomes indeterminate and its significance for the community that uses it cannot simply be imposed, even if the term itself is imposed by an institutional authority on a community.

It is not that such a terminological imposition is an inappropriate exercise of authority, or that John Paul II does not recognize the importance of practices for determining meanings. Rather, the problem is that such imposed "language disciplines" may no longer have the capacity or intelligibility to be part of the language of the practice because the participants—presider and congregation alike—do not or cannot see a natural (rather than an artificial or forced or merely nominal) connection of such technical language to the liturgical and other language they use in engaging in the practices, including worship, that shape their lives. Because the discourse practice or semiotic system of the people engaging in worship has changed significantly since the thirteenth century, other theological accounts of the Lord's presence in the Eucharist may be more suitable than one at home in the intellectual culture that flourished some seven hundred years ago. Hence, the meaning of the term comes loose from its traditional ritual mooring and floats free to be captured by the next wave of semantic enthusiasm. The imposition of the linguistic discipline of using a specific linguistic token like *transubstantiation* simply cannot

---

[9] Gary Macy, "The Eucharist and Popular Religiosity," *Proceedings of the Annual Convention of the Catholic Theological Society of America* 52 (1997): 39-58, has shown that multiple theologies of the Eucharist in the Middle Ages were accepted as properly Catholic. That does not mean that because Aquinas's theology was not widely accepted in the late-thirteenth and fourteenth centuries that one of the other theologies current at that time should be substituted today. Rather, the multiplicity of authentically Catholic theologies suggests that no one set of theological words can be the necessary and sufficient expression of the presence of Christ—especially given the rich and multiple Catholic vision that we live in a sacramental universe, a point to which I return below. Also see Gary Macy, *Treasures from the Storeroom: Medieval Religion and the Eucharist* (Collegeville, Minn.: Liturgical Press, 1999), which reprints the essay cited above along with other research on these topics.

guarantee of itself what that token means for the people celebrating the Eucharist, clergy and laity.

But the problem, if there is one, is not the laity. The problem is that Church leaders and theologians who call for such linguistic discipline have not noticed that the concept of the Real Presence *as it is received and understood in the community* shifts its meaning as the ritual shifts. Concepts receive their significance from their place in a semiotic system. As the other constituents in the system shift, especially ritual behaviors, so the meaning of the concept must also shift. The significance of the Real Presence and thus the doctrine of the Real Presence shift meaning as the actions and attitudes shift, despite the apparent continuity of the linguistic token Real Presence and its "equivalents" in other languages and contexts, much less its explanation as the result of transubstantiation.

The shift in liturgical practice does not mean that the concept or the doctrine of the Real Presence is lost, even though its significance may change for participants in the practice. In his discussion of contemporary eucharistic practice, Morris points out that liturgies which seem more communal than sacral are offered in parishes where the same Real Presence doctrine is taught. Morris also notes, "In most Catholic parishes . . . parishioners receive communion quite reverently."[10] What some conservatives may see as a loss of devotion may simply be a change in liturgical style that calls for new forms of catechesis to keep a healthy and connected concept of Real Presence part of the traditions that shape participants' consciousness.

Another factor that cannot be ignored is the culture in which the practice is to be undertaken. The distinction between substance and accident, which is presumed by the traditional concept of transubstantiation, is not one that makes sense in contemporary culture. This renders *transubstantiation* a culturally anomalous term. In translating Catholic doctrine for catechizing the Great Lakes area Native Americans, Fr. Jean de Brébeuf, S.J. (1593-1649), one of the North American martyrs canonized in 1930, faced the problem of explicating the Eucharist without reinforcing ritual cannibalism, which had rather different religious overtones than the Eucharist. Cornelius J. Jaenen put the point clearly: "'Brébeuf translated the Eucharist into Huron as *Atonesta*, which signified an act of gratitude and thanksgiving in the sense of a memorial or purely symbolic ceremony.'

---

[10] Morris, *American Catholic*, 392, 393.

European theologians would have hardly approved."[11] Brébeuf realized that attempting to utilize a linguistic token that might have won the approval of more "orthodox" European theologians would have been religious disaster in the missionary context in which he labored. In this case, *Tradutore, tradditore* may characterize his theology, but remaining literalistically "faithful" to the traditional concept by repeating the linguistic tokens canonized in the tradition would have been even more treacherous to the Christian faith in that situation. The ways in which even doctrines thought to be necessary to the tradition are inculturated may require radical shifts in formulations because of wildly different linguistic and other practices in a recipient culture. If the tradition of the Church is necessarily inculturated in many cultures, this means that theological formulations may have to be textually inconsistent with each other in order to be effective tokens for passing on the tradition in different cultural contexts. In sum, beliefs co-inhere with and get their significance from a web of prescribed and proscribed patterns of actions and attitudes in their cultural setting.

Another factor is simply the way words change meaning as time goes by. A relevant example is the term *transubstantiation*. As Gary Macy has pointed out, when this term was used in the Fourth Lateran Council in 1215, it could cover three types of theories of the eucharistic change. One was *coexistence*: that the bread and wine remained along with the Body and Blood. A second was *substitution*: the substance of the bread and wine was annihilated and the substance of the Body and Blood remained. A third was *transmutation*: the substance of the bread and wine was changed into the substance of the Body and Blood.[12] Orthodox theologians held theories of all three types even into the fifteenth century, at which point coexistence seems to have been excluded. The view that an Aristotelian-Thomistic understanding of

---

[11] Jay P. Dolan, *The American Catholic Experience: A History from Colonial Times to the Present* (Garden City, N.Y.: Doubleday, 1985), 58. The embedded quotation is from Cornelius J. Jaenen, *Friend and Foe: Aspects of French-Amerindian Cultural Contact in the Sixteenth and Seventeenth Centuries* (New York: Columbia University Press, 1976), 145. For our purposes, the point here is not how to resolve the problem, but that the problem arises. The dilemma such a missionary faces illustrates the point that an item of tradition, like a doctrine, may have significantly different religious meanings, determined by the different places it takes in (religious and nonreligious) practices, especially when these practices vary widely between the initiating culture (French Catholicism) and the target culture (Iroquois and Huron tribes).

[12] Gary Macy, "The 'Dogma of Transubstantiation' in the Middle Ages," in *Treasures from the Storeroom*, 82-83.

transubstantiation as transmutation was *the* medieval doctrine is not warranted. Macy concludes: "Despite a surprisingly tenacious belief that a 'dogma of transubstantiation' was promulgated by the Fourth Lateran Council and enforced by the medieval Church, the evidence suggests this was never the case, especially if by this one equates transubstantiation with transmutation."[13] The same verbal token shifted its meaning substantially: the word remained the same and the meaning changed—a point often misunderstood in writing on medieval theology.

If we can generalize this point, and I think we can, this makes it clear that the significance of a doctrine in a tradition can undergo a major semantic shift while the verbal token expressing it (in the present case, *transubstantiation*) has remained unchanged. And as the eucharistic practice shifts and the meaning of Real Presence evolves, the traditional theological concept of transubstantiation may lose its "natural" connection with the actual practice of the Eucharist and not function to express the meaning of *Real Presence.* It is not that these shifts are good or bad. It is not that one understanding of the Eucharist is or is not the only proper one. As with the evolution of eucharistic theology in the Middle Ages, it is simply the case that the tradition has evolved—a point that Church leaders, theologians, and liturgists should have realized would occur, especially had they recognized what Geertz, Boone, and Schreiter have noted in their research: shifts in one part of meaning systems or discourse practices, such as shifts in ritual behavior, inevitably evoke shifts in other parts of the system or practice.

The negative conclusion is that doctrinal formulas alone cannot carry the identity of a tradition; the positive conclusion is that living faith traditions may thrive and maintain an identity even as doctrinal formulas change, even radically.

Understanding Specific Beliefs

To understand a given belief, action, or attitude, one has to understand where and how it fits within the web. One must understand which other elements of the web are relevant to determining its meaning. Abstracting a belief from the web and formulating it as a theological proposition in order to analyze it philosophically may be legitimate. But asking whether a proposition (such as "The bread

---

[13] Ibid., 105.

and wine of the Eucharist are transubstantiated into the Body and Blood, Soul and Divinity of Christ, while the accidents remain the same") is an item of tradition or asserting that it must be accepted as the belief appropriate to eucharistic practice whether or not it is connected with the rest of the web in which it is imbedded may leave its practical meaning indeterminate at best and its relevance extrinsic to the practice in which participants come to believe in the Real Presence, as noted above. If the significance of a proposition is indeterminate in the context in which its significance is determined for believers, then how could it matter that that proposition expresses a traditional belief that is properly to be held? If it is indeterminate and dubiously relevant to the practice that forms the belief, how could it express a belief definite enough to define that practice? For the "traditional belief" abstracted as a verbal token from its appropriate context can easily lose—and some would argue already has lost—any practically determinable meaning. What could be at stake in defending a traditional explanation of Real Presence if participants in the eucharistic celebration can't see how it is connected to and alive in the practices of those who seek faithfully to live in the tradition that incarnates the Catholic vision? In short, the problem of carrying on and passing on a tradition literally cannot be solved by the prescription of a linguistic convention that is not organically connected with the practices that constitute the tradition.

This point is relevant to understanding traditions other than the Catholic tradition, too. In general, traditions prescribe and proscribe some actions. What must I do to be a good or true Buddhist or Baptist? How can I live as a left-handed Tantrist or a Sivite? What must we do to be good subjects of the British crown? What constitutes the good practice of law, medicine, or real-estate management? Sometimes the answers to these questions are identified as "moral rules," "good practice of the law," "professional standards," "appropriate beliefs," or "traditional customs." The opposites can often be seen defined as "sin," "medical malpractice," "unprofessional behavior," "falsehood," or "taboo acts." The most obvious and analyzable actions are ritual acts, which I have used above, but these are not the only sorts of acts a practice prescribes. And if a practice has evolved significantly, an attempt to impose rules, standards, beliefs, or customs from an earlier form of the practice will seem—and may be—anachronistic.

But here a problem arises. Often theologians and philosophers overlook the importance of attitudes and actions in a tradition. They collapse a traditional belief's significance into a mere proposition, a cognitive belief. This is the problem noted in chapter 2 of treating the items passed on, the *tradita*, as the sum of a tradition, and in the present chapter prescribing one term to formulate the doctrine of the Real Presence. But collapsing a conviction or living belief into a proposition, as if that is all there is to it, simply won't do. For instance, some Christians have said that one can't be a Christian until one realizes one is a sinner. One has to *take oneself to be* a sinner.[14] This is not merely a belief one holds true. It involves an important attitude to all of one's life. It is not a nominal belief, whose meaning might be captured in a bare proposition, but a conviction that shapes one's life; to realize the significance of this conviction requires learning how to *be* a sinner, how to recognize the graced nature of the world in which God never withholds divine aid, and thus how to realize redemption through repentance, forgiveness, and reconciliation. In doing so, this traditional belief not only necessarily shapes the participants' lives, but also must be reshaped by the participants' lives as new patterns of what it means to be a sinner, where grace can be found, and how reconciliation can be sacramentalized all emerge. Similarly, Catholics may no longer be clear on whether they are present at a divine sacrifice to which they are united with Christ the sacrificial victim as Christ's mystical body or whether they are present at a ceremonial meal in which they are united with each other in their gratefulness for the gift of the life-giving spiritual food that is the Body of Christ. Of course, the proper view is not to separate these, but to say that the eucharistic celebration is both. However, the Eucharist as ritual meal is a retrieval of an ancient tradition by the twentieth-century liturgical movement in Catholicism; more "traditional" Catholic liturgical theology, actually the theology of the Council of Trent (1545-63), which dominated Catholic eucharistic theology to the twentieth century, ignored or downplayed the significance of Eucharist as ritual meal in favor of it being a "sacrament and sacrifice."[15] New patterns of ritual behavior reshape the participants' attitudes, new significances of the doctrine of the Real Presence emerge, and the meaning of the linguistic token changes.[16]

---

[14] I owe this example to Stanley Hauerwas of Duke University.

[15] See, for example, Clifford Howell, *Of Sacraments and Sacrifice* (Collegeville, Minn.: Liturgical Press, 1952) for an example of a theologically sophisticated popular treatment of the liturgy in the pre-Conciliar era.

[16] Whether the doctrine of transubstantiation remains the best theological terminology to make sense of this belief in the present remains debatable. Clearly, in the past, one could hold the belief in the Real Presence without the doctrine of transubstantiation (see, for instance, Macy, "The Eucharist and Popular Religiosity," and the literature cited therein).

Once we are clear on the relationship of beliefs to the practices that constitute a tradition, one implication is obvious: A tradition cannot be learned by learning propositions, as if memorizing a catechism would teach one how to live a faith, or memorizing the rules of aviation would teach one how to fly. Even the practice of memorizing a catechism must be intimately linked with a number of devotional and moral practices in which the catechism's propositions can make sense. A catechism may convey a version of the vision that animates a tradition, but it is "empty" or "boring" or "dry" or "irrelevant" if it is not connected intimately with the attitudes and actions that people undertake.[17] The goal of participating in a practice may be known verbally or "notionally" (in John Henry Newman's terminology), but if it is not accepted as a life-shaping belief or "really" (as Newman put it), then it is empty, and likely either participation will wane or the proposition will "fade out" as it is insignificant for the life of participants. It is hard for Christians, for instance, to hope for heaven in a culture wherein immediate gratification is the norm, or to understand what holiness of life could be in a culture idolizing conspicuous consumption and material possessions. To believe in heaven and hope for eternal life require participating in a practice or practices that are *not* immediately gratifying, but which will shape one into a person worthy of heaven.[18] To seek holiness requires participating in practices that shape one's desires *not* to consume and to have "things," but to love God and one's neighbor as oneself. The means are *knowing how* to engage in those patterns of actions and attitudes that seek the goal and carry the vision; mere *knowing that* cannot suffice. Mere notional belief will not do.

This is not to say that at least a basic understanding of doctrine is not necessary, just that it is not sufficient. Above I discussed the

---

[17] Jay P. Dolan reports an extreme example of this in the Spanish missions of New Mexico in the eighteenth century. The friars who did not know indigenous languages taught the Native Americans the catechism, which they memorized in Spanish while not knowing Spanish. The Native Americans were, not surprisingly, tepid and indifferent in their Catholic religious practice. Many of them, however, did learn Spanish and became interpreters for the friars, and thus would have some understanding of the doctrines they had memorized. Nonetheless, they tended to lapse from Catholic practice into their own indigenous religious traditions which meant something to them, as the Catholic tradition did not and could not (see Dolan, *The American Catholic Experience*, 56, 61-68).

[18] Lest someone think otherwise, I do not mean by this that people "earn" heaven. However one interprets the parable of the Vineyard (Mt 20), I think it shows that worthiness is not necessarily connected with earning.

necessity of some basic skills and abilities as a constituent of good practice and praxis. Analogously, someone who has no clear idea of the content of a tradition is not in a position to participate well in the practice. One implication of the present approach is that catechesis is best understood in a practical way. One learns the meaning of the *tradita* as one is inaugurated into participating in the practices of the tradition. Once one is a solid practitioner—which includes a creative reception of the tradition, as the following chapter shows—one can be in a position to teach others the tradition by inaugurating them in the practices that constitute the tradition.

We can summarize this approach to understanding a tradition as a set of practices up to now in six points. First, one cannot know the meaning of a concept or a proposition unless one knows how it is used, how it fits within a practice. As concepts and propositions can fit in multiple ways in multiple practices, they may by polyvalent in their significance. Second, practices shape persons and reshape them, their beliefs and their attitudes. To become a Christian or an architect or a pilot requires learning the disciplines or practices that constitute Christianity or architecture or piloting. Of course, the practice of Christianity and the practice of architecture are radically different in the first and the twenty-first centuries, and the practice of piloting powered aircraft did not exist in any form until 1903. The practice of the reception of the Eucharist also changed radically with the reinauguration of the practice of daily or frequent communion for the laity in response to the 1905 decree of Pope Pius X, *Sacra Tridentina Synodus*.[19] The problem is not to notice the diversity in practices but to find their constancies.[20] Third, as contexts change, practices change. When people carry old practices into new places, they are changed in the process of transmission. As new skills are developed, the education of a practitioner may also properly change. These changes require changes in the practices, if the practices are to thrive. Fourth, as practices change, the significance of the concepts and beliefs they carry change. Fifth, since traditions cannot be reduced to bare *tradita*, that is, things passed on, traditions must be constituted, understood,

---

[19] C. Ledré, s.v. "Pius X, Pope," *New Catholic Encyclopedia* (New York: McGraw Hill, 1967).

[20] William A. Clebsch, in his discussion of the wild diversity of ways Christ appears to people and the lack of any single constant (save a bare and practically meaningless referent to Jesus of Nazareth) put it this way: "The point is not that there have been no Christophanic constancies, but that constancies have been unimportant in Christophanies" (*Christianity in European History* [New York: Oxford University Press, 1979], 19).

and communicated in and through practices. As suggested above, traditions are best understood as communicative practices, in which the communication of the "how to" is as important as, or more important than, much of the "what" communicated. How to love God with one's whole mind, whole heart, and whole self is primary; doctrines about God, mind, heart and self are derivative.[21] Sixth, one knows the meaning of things passed on, the *tradita,* by how they inhere in the practice or practices in which they are at home. Hence, it makes sense to identify tradition as a practice or complex set of practices in which initiates learn how to participate in local communities that teach them how to live in and live out that tradition.

Problems in a Practical Theory of Tradition

This approach to tradition seems itself rather untraditional. One objection is that this approach seems to make practices rigid, even unchangeable, save by accident or circumstance. Doesn't this analysis fall into the trap of making the whole practice "found, not made"? Are we not excluding the possibility of intentional reform? The development or evolution of a tradition described here seems unintentional. What of the possibility of intentional, planned reformation?

My response is that of course traditions and practices can be reformed. However, two points need to be noted. First, as suggested in chapter 2, an individual cannot reform a tradition any more than an individual can change other social patterns like racism or sexism (which themselves may be understood as traditions). Any proposal for reformation must be accepted by the practitioners who put it into practice. If the participants in the tradition, through whatever mechanism from horrible coercion to completely free choice, put into practice the proposal for reform, then and only then, is a tradition reformed. Second, I see no way to predict whether a successful proposal for reform will constitute the reformation of a practice or the instantiation of a substitute practice. Clearly the practice of surgery

---

[21] A similar point is made by Sharon Welch, *A Feminist Ethic of Risk* (Minneapolis: Fortress, 1989), 129ff. She claims that solidarity—a moral practice concerned with material and spiritual welfare—is a necessary condition for the possibility of transformative communication. Welch both relies upon the communication theory of Jürgen Habermas and departs from it in ways pioneered by Anthony Giddens. I find her work in this area important and persuasive.

was reformed when asepsis and anesthesia were introduced, but the practice remained surgery. Yet the reformation of the practice of auricular confession by many of the reformation churches and the institution of private forms of confession may be better understood as rejection of an old practice and the beginning of a new one in its place.

Now an obvious counter-response would be to invoke an account of development like John Henry Newman's in his *Essay on the Development of Christian Doctrine*. Practices and traditions are not rigid but nonetheless develop in a reasonable way. Yet Newman's account of development is a *retrospective*, not a *prospective* view. It describes past developments and derives notes or tests of development from historic developments. It does not, and cannot, prescribe or predict how development is to take place in the future or which line of possible development is the authentic development of the past. Moreover, Newman wrote the *Essay* in a very specific context: to respond to objections made to his commitment to Catholicism. It is not a fully developed theory but is "directed towards a solution of the difficulty" of variations in Church teaching. It is "an hypothesis to account for a difficulty."[22] Even if it has accurately identified the proper tests or notes for the authentic development of an idea, it cannot say (as we shall see in chapter 4) how such rules should be applied in the future. Hence, if the discussion in chapter 4 is accurate, then this counter-response fails to count against the main point that traditions are malleable, even unpredictable, in their development.

Moreover, a specific problem plagues some forms of theories of the development of doctrine. The problem is the conflation of development with progress. The presumption that "we" have made religious progress or become more religiously advanced (holier? wiser? more moral?) because "we" have a more "developed" notion of the papacy, the Eucharist, or religious liberty than our forbears cannot be sustained. By preferring a pattern of inculturation and contextual adaptation, the practical theory of tradition avoids even the appearance of the impertinence that we somehow have "improved" Christianity over the achievements of earlier ages to which theories of development can be prone.

If theories of development are not teleological, then *development* may just be another word for *change* in response to new circumstances,

---

[22] John Henry Newman, *An Essay on the Development of Christian Doctrine* (London: James Toovey, 1846 < 1845 >), 27.

a view Avery Dulles has identified as "historical situationism."[23] This is not to say that some changes are degenerative or mistaken. To identify a change as a development is simply to say that it is a "good change," one that does not destroy the identity of the tradition that develops. But how one recognizes the difference is not clear since even Newman's rules are retrospective rather than prospective, nor is it clear just how identity is to be recognized through change over time. How those rules for recognizing appropriate changes are to be applied in any future circumstances is not ascertainable in the present.

A progressive theory of development is caught on the horns of a dilemma: either the arrogance of teleology or the indeterminateness of rules for evaluating changes. The dilemma of development strongly suggests that any robust or progressive theory of development cannot be a solution for this problem of accounting for doctrinal change. This dilemma stands behind theologians' practical abandonment of development as a credible theory of doctrinal change, a point discussed at length in chapter 4. Yves Congar summarized this when he wrote that "history was understood less as a continual process of 'development,' that is, as a progress achieved through a gradual unfolding of what was already implicit, and more as a series of formulations of the one content of faith diversifying and finding expression in different cultural contexts."[24]

A second objection that can arise from some critics would be that I have ignored the (alleged) fact that an elite sets the rules of the practices. Someone might raise an objection like the following: When one looks at business practices, governmental practices in general and taxation practices in particular, one sees that power elites set the rules of the practice. If one looks hard enough, one can see that this applies to medicine, religion (especially the Catholic religion, where the "elite" can be identified as the pope and the Roman curia), and

---

[23] Avery Dulles, *The Resilient Church: The Necessity and Limits of Adaptation* (Garden City, N.Y.: Doubleday, 1977). Dulles adapts this terminology from George Lindbeck, "The Problem of Doctrinal Development and Contemporary Protestant Theology," *Man as Man and Believer*, Concilium 21, ed. Edward Schillebeeckx (New York: Paulist, 1967), 138-39. Neither Dulles nor Lindbeck espouses a progressive or teleological theory of development.

[24] Yves Congar, O.P., "Church History as a Branch of Theology," in *Church History in Future Perspective*, Concilium 57, ed. Roger Aubert (New York: Herder and Herder, 1970), 87. That no expression of the "one content of faith" is given outside a specific cultural context requires a nuanced understanding of what that "one content" is; chapter 6 addresses this issue in terms of revelation. It should also be noted that although Newman's account of development may be open to a "progressive" understanding, Newman did not presume that approach.

other practices as well. The practice of medicine is now so heavily institutionalized that elites like the World Health Organization define the practice of caring for certain illnesses, for example, prescribing ventriculostomy and monitoring of intracranial pressure for patients in a coma from acute head trauma.[25] The practice of taxing incomes in the United States is less than a century old and governed by strict, if nearly incomprehensible, rules enforced by what is clearly a power elite, the Internal Revenue Service. It was instituted by an act of legal authority.

My response to this objection is to recognize its truth for some "deliberately invented" practices, but not for all practices. Like Hobsbawm's deliberately invented traditions, "deliberately invented" practices are those that are constituted by an exercise of authority. However, many invented practices are not practices in the sense used in this essay. Certainly the activity of taxing incomes is not a practice, although the practice of tax law is. Taxing incomes is a means to the end of harvesting enough money to run a government; properly, it should be governed not by "rules" (which require some judgment for their application), but by "algorithms," which seek to avoid use of judgment as far as possible. The practice of tax law requires interpretation, argument, and so forth, and involves understanding and resolving disputes over how tax formulas should be applied—a practice that calls for judgment as part of the practice.

As noted above, *practice* has a specific meaning. Not all practices, as that term is used in ordinary parlance, in fact, are practices. Many are skills or abilities honed by repetition. These are not practices, at least not in the full sense of the term. The practice of medicine as undertaken today is a more complex issue.[26] If one can distinguish the practice of medicine from making money from practicing medicine, the former remains a practice in which skilled practitioners train

---

[25] See the transcript of Nova documentary #2411, "Coma," aired on PBS on 7 October 1997 as accessed at < http://www.pbs.org/wgbh/nova/transcripts/2411coma.html >. The practice guidelines for this sort of treatment were accepted as standard practice on 15 May 1997. Although the WHO wants these to be worldwide guidelines, neither skilled neurosurgeons nor the mildly sophisticated equipment required for this procedure are available outside hospitals that have developed significant trauma care facilities. Even such a "universal" prescription cannot be fulfilled if the context is not appropriate.

[26] For a history of the political and social machinations involved with establishing the practice of medicine in this country as limited to medical doctors and the limitation on the number of practitioners, see Paul Starr, *The Social Transformation of American Medicine* (New York: Basic Books, 1982).

new practitioners and recognized boards of peers establish standards of good practice based on clinical research. In general, even if "elites" declare the rules for practices *in the sense of practice used herein*, the application of these rules remains up to the practitioners. If the rules are not generally accepted by the practitioners, they fail to be the rules of the practice, as we shall see in chapter 4. This is especially visible in religious practices, as the extended discussion of Catholic Eucharist practices above indicates.[27]

What gives strength to this objection is the fact that people are frequently the victims, patients, or clients of practitioners. They seem to have no power or authority over against an elite group. This form of practice "for" clients of the practice raises profound social and personal ethical issues, especially when the practitioners' clients have not freely chosen to be subjects of the practice.[28] However, responding to this objection, finally, cannot be done wholesale but must be done in the context of examining specific practices: one must ask if the "good" the practice seeks is truly *good*, and one must ask if the practitioners seek the "good" of the practice or have some other goal (such as accumulating wealth) for which people use the practice and which in their doing deforms their practice to ends not intrinsic to the practice. In sum, elites may try to institute or regulate practices, but either the behavior of the practice must be coerced (in which case the "practice" is a simulacrum or counterfeit of a practice) or the rules of the practice must be accepted and implemented by the practitioners. So while this objection does properly point out the fact that elites do wield power, it fails to show that practices as herein understood, can be imposed on people as practices rather than rigid behavioral norms.

More important, elites are authoritative *within* a tradition, not *over* a tradition. The exercise of power occurs within a practice or set of practices. The exercise of power other than individual brute force over another individual is possible only because a practice, tradition, or system of practices makes it possible to exercise power. The power of politicians occurs within the political system. The power of entrepreneurs is exercised within economic systems. Similarly, the

---

[27] For a discussion of declarations that fail to work, see my work in speech act theory contained in *The Evils of Theodicy* (Washington, D.C.: Georgetown University Press, 1991), 13-15, 46-52, 70-76.

[28] For the history of an experiment in which those experimented upon were victims of American medical practice, see James H. Jones, *Bad Blood: The Tuskegee Syphilis Experiment* (New York: Free Press, 1981).

pope and the Roman curia are authoritative *within* the tradition, not *over* the tradition. The practice of referring disputed questions to Rome for resolution, adapted from the practices of the Roman Empire, is the practical root of papal primacy.[29] Over the centuries, the patterns of authority in the Catholic Church evolved in response to shifts internal to the practices distinctive to the Catholic community and in response to changes in practices "external" to the Catholic community, practices in which Catholics participated but did so not so much as Catholics but as citizens or subjects or buyers and sellers. The acceptance of papal infallibility at Vatican I marks a stage in the evolution of the practice of authority. Vatican I responded especially to shifts in European political practices, notably the canonization of political freedoms.[30] As practices generally shift in response to cultural and other forces, so do patterns and practices of authority within practices also shift.

A third objection might be that participants in a religious tradition do think that their beliefs have an ontological reference or are making truth claims. An objection could go like this: The analysis herein ignores claims like the Catholic claim that there is a deposit of faith transmitted through the apostolic witness and that this constitutes the tradition. The present analysis caricatures this sort of theological view by taking its proponents as reducing the deposit of faith to *tradita*.

My response is to note that it is not uncommon for "traditionalists" and—in very different ways, for "positivists"—to reduce the tradition to repetition of behaviors or formulas, to equate the deposit of faith with the *tradita* transmitted. At its extreme, this approach to religious traditions can be pathological. The petrification of a tradition by its participants renders such traditions both brittle and hegemonic.[31] Positivists' reduction of (typically, opponents') traditions to "mere mechanical repetitions" of behavior is blind to the connections among behaviors, attitudes, beliefs, and intentions. The "rule theory" to be

---

[29] See Klaus Schatz, *Papal Primacy: From Its Origins to the Present*, trans. John A. Otto and Linda M. Maloney (Collegeville, Minn.: Liturgical Press, 1996).

[30] Ibid., 156. That the shape of the practice of authority remains in flux and in dispute within the Catholic Church is clear. See, for instance, John R. Quinn, "The Exercise of the Primacy and the Costly Call to Unity," in *The Exercise of the Primacy: Continuing the Dialogue*, ed. Phyllis Zagano and Terrence W. Tilley (New York: Crossroad/Herder, 1998), 1-28, and the following essays commenting on Quinn's paper.

[31] For an argument on the criteria for recognizing religious pathology (and "fundamentalism" as a pathological tradition), see Charlesworth, *Religious Inventions: Four Essays* (Cambridge: Cambridge University Press, 1997), 147-51.

proposed in chapter 4 avoids both the reduction of the deposit of faith to formulas and also the tendency to invent novel traditions deliberately. I also claim that this approach is consonant with a Catholic view of tradition, although I do not address those normative theological issues until chapter 6.[32] Here we can note that a simple theory of propositional truth won't do.

Moreover, to know—however imperfectly—the tradition, one has to know not merely formulas of faith, but to know *how* the deposit of faith constitutes the ongoing life of the church. One cannot take the tradition as the formulas alone: That is a form of reductionism. To know how to live the tradition is required. The practice of receiving, living in, and passing on a tradition will certainly yield formulas that practitioners believe are true, but the formulas are neither the foundation nor the invariant constituents of a developing tradition. Those devoted to the tradition who want to avoid reducing *traditio* to *tradita* are, in my view, engaging in the rule-governed practice of living within a tradition; I am attempting herein to analyze what they are doing without slighting their truth claims.[33]

Conclusion

So far I have argued that a tradition is best understood as a nexus of vision (belief), attitude (dispositions, affections), and style (pattern of action) constituting complex practices. My argument consists not in deduction but in using some specific cases, especially the case

---

[32] One of the main points of Congar's *Tradition and Traditions* is to avoid the equation of the tradition with documents or texts or monuments. In chapter 3, "The Subject of Tradition," he presents the two fundamental propositions that constitute, in his view, the Catholic position: "(1) Documents are not the sole constitutive element of Tradition, which cannot be either conceived or defined without the inclusion of its *living subject*, which is (primarily) the Holy Spirit, and (visibly) the Church with its assisted magisterium. (2) The Church and the magisterium have *no* autonomy whatever in regard to the *depositum fidei*. But this deposit must not be identified with documents or monuments" (454).

[33] My own view, in brief, is that successful reference to what-there-is is not a *condition for* a proposition to be appraised as true, but a *consequence* of a proposition's being true. Whether what some would call ontological truth claims are in fact true cannot be shown by a further claim that they refer; the attempt to refer properly is up to us; whether we succeed is up to the way the world is; and there may be multiple ways to succeed, many propositions that successfully refer to the way things are. These *obiter dicta* will, I hope, be clearer when we come to more strictly theological issues in chapter 6.

of the Catholic doctrine of the Real Presence. This doctrine is embedded primarily in a ritual practice of worship to make the point. Of course, this is simply one practice among the many that are central to the Roman Catholic tradition; there are many others. That such worship is a practice with a goal we can identify (all too simply) as praising God, a means of participating in the meal/sacrifice, carried on by expressed or unexpressed ritual rules (rubrics) by a community of worshipers who live under the governance of the Christian vision should be clear. If the analysis is illuminating, then that is good reason for accepting, I would say, this "practical" definition of a tradition.

Obviously, this is not a complete understanding of the tradition. That is far beyond the scope of this text. But if the Eucharist is the central liturgical action of the Catholic community, then it can serve as the prime example for this analysis. The web of Catholic creedal beliefs, attitudes, and other practices can be tied into the practice of the Eucharist, although I have not done so here. That is work for another time and place.[34]

I have also tried to show along the way that a tradition shapes participants and that the participants, especially when they form a community, reshape traditions in the way they receive and enact them. This is especially true with regard to the shifts in Catholic eucharistic practices, although we can see it in other practices as well.

If a tradition is constituted as a set of practices, then how can we identify a practice? Without an identifiable practice, we can't know what we are talking about! Chapters 2 and 3 have undercut "beliefs" as determiners of practices. Moreover, if practices are to have the characteristics of a tradition—making communication possible and shaping identity—what shapes the practices? My answer to that question is "rules" akin to grammatical rules. Chapter 4 explores the "grammar" of tradition as the rules of a practice.

---

[34] Methodist Geoffrey Wainwright has written an influential Eucharist-centered theology (see *Doxology: The Praise of God in Worship, Doctrine, and Life: A Systematic Theology* [New York: Oxford University Press, 1980]).

FOUR

The Grammar of a Tradition

The previous chapters attended to a multifaceted central practice of the Christian tradition, the Eucharist, and explored a practical theory of tradition. The present chapter completes that exploration by attending to the trickiest aspect, the rules of a practice. For, in addition to the end or goal or purpose of a practice, and the means needed to reach that goal, a practice proceeds according to rules. *Rules* can be understood as guidelines for participating in a practice, as a *grammar* can be understood as the guidelines for understanding a language. Rules show how the elements of a practice are connected.

The role of rules in and for practices is often misunderstood. This chapter seeks to spell out a "rule theory" of practice—and a fortiori of tradition. In doing so, the chapter highlights the ways in which rules are followed. In the practical theory of tradition, engaging in rule-governed practices is the way in which the tradition is received. The tradition is enacted in and handed on in particular practices. A tradition does not exist in some ethereal abstract realm outside all practices. Like authority, the tradition is *in* the practices, not *above* or *beyond* them. The present theory claims that traditions indeed *are* the practices.

The chapter begins by exploring what it means to follow a rule. This turns out to be more complex than implementing an algorithm, for there may be many ways of acting that constitute "following a rule." The second section shows what is needed to evaluate practices and the acts undertaken in them. After a short discussion of the status of rules, the penultimate section shows that the practical account of tradition is a development of other recent accounts of tradition. But this leads to the problem of discerning what is an authentic development of a tradition and what is a corruption of a tradition. As a way of approaching this question, the final section provides an analysis of a difficult case in the development of Catholic doctrine.

Rules and Practices

When we consider ritual practices as the bearers of tradition, the rules are easy to find: Rules are the written and unwritten rubrics that guide the practice, govern behaviors, shape attitudes, and prescribe the beliefs involved in the practice. As contexts change, the tradition changes, and so the rules may change, as chapter 3 showed. It is the place of rules in nonritual practices, the changeableness of rules, and the concept of following that need to be worked through.

It is more difficult, perhaps, to see practices as "rule governed" in areas other than rituals. In rituals, at least some are obvious. Rules are visible as the rubrics, the choreography, the prescribed positions and behaviors of ritual. Whether the inauguration of a president, the celebration of a marriage, or the singing of the national anthem ("you must stand for the singing of the anthem if you are physically able to do so"), the rubrics are often clearly laid out. Yet rubrics are not the only rules.

Once a practice is recognized as a web of actions, beliefs, and attitudes, the rules that tie these together with the purposes of the practices can be made clear. What is interesting about rules, however, is their status in a practice. Rules are the "grammar" of a practice. As a grammar is a set of rules for speaking or writing a language, derived from our performance practices of speaking and writing, so the rules relevant to practices are those that are the grammar of engaging in those practices. Rules are crucial guides to practice. But if rules are crucial, what is it to follow rules?

In a deceptively simple way, one can say that to follow a rule is to engage in the behavior it codifies. Linguistic theory suggests we can analyze rules into three types. First are *pragmatic rules*. These codify the ways in which (the where, when, and how) one does something, including speaking; rubrics are the obvious example. Second are *semantic rules*. These codify what actions and words mean; definitions are one example. Third, there are *syntactic rules*, which codify how various actions and words can be related to one another.

The rough distinctions between types of rules can be conveyed by examples of rule violations. Failure to enact pragmatic rules may be inappropriate or inept performances ("How could you tell such a filthy joke here in the convent?" "That was a beautiful cartwheel; but 'not in class,' Jennifer." "That was a 'love tap'? You nearly broke my arm!"). Violations of semantic rules exhibit confusions about the meaning of actions and words in performance ("No, Tim, sticking your tongue out does not show respect to Aunt Gertrude." "He doesn't know the difference between starboard and port."). Violations of syntactic rules put various words and/or actions together in a "wrong" way in performance ("That good Baptist preacher was convicted of bootlegging!" "His talking about overcoming prejudice is like Hitler supporting Jewish rights." "That wasn't a sentence; I have no idea what she meant."). However, violations of syntactic rules, like Jesus' rearranging the kingdom of God, or Buddha declaring that members of all castes (not just Brahmins) might reach Enlightenment, or foregoing pleasures in a hedonistic culture may be prophetic, boundary-shifting actions.[1]

Obviously, the distinctions among the three types of rules are not entirely sharp. To claim clear distinctions would be deceptive.

Rules do not generate successful performances. One cannot develop a set of rules sufficient to regulate or generate a performance or an action (a point which will be developed below). This sort of rule theory might make it seem possible that one might be able to develop such a code and that such a code of rules would in some way be an "agent," bringing about actions.[2] That, too, would be confused. Nonetheless, if we are aware of these pitfalls, we can take rules as codes of practices.

The ability to understand and to follow a rule is not demonstrated by being able to state the rule but by knowing how to put it into practice; someone who can't put a rule into practice doesn't really understand the rule. A teacher doesn't test accounting students' understanding of the rules of accounting by giving them a test on the content of a rule they have memorized. One tests them by giving them a new problem or situation to see if they have the know-how to apply the rule. A state does not license physicians only on the basis of their being able to pass written tests about the rules for good diagnosis and treatment. The state requires the completion of internships and/or residencies in which the newly minted doctor with "book knowledge" is supervised as an apprentice in learning how to apply that knowledge in order to become a physician, a participant in the

---

[1] See Robert J. Schreiter, *Constructing Local Theologies* (Maryknoll, N.Y.: Orbis Books, 1985), 66. Schreiter does not construe these acts as syntactic violations.

[2] Some writers could be read as if rules were agents. For instance, discussing early Christianity, George Lindbeck writes: "Three regulative principles, at least, were *obviously at work*" (*The Nature of Doctrine* [Philadelphia: Fortress Press, 1984], 94, emphasis added). Also see Schreiter, *Constructing Local Theologies*, 114-15, for comments on the limited success of Chomsky's transformational-generative grammar project.

practice of medicine. The practice of teaching is not one in which knowledge about a subject is sufficient to make a good teacher. Good teachers not only know their subjects and convey information, but they also know how to empower students to become adept at understanding the subjects themselves. It is a practice, like medicine and accounting, learned by doing. In general, one has a concept or knows a rule if and only if one can apply it well, can put it into practice.

Two clarifications will help us understand the status of rules more precisely. First, it might seem that this approach conflates rules and concepts. This would be a confusion *if* concepts were equated with data or information. It may seem a technical point, but one can have all the data one needs without having concepts that make sense of the data. One of the debates concerning artificial intelligence is whether computers can "think." Computers can certainly store and manipulate data. If they can form concepts from the data and apply those concepts to further data, then, at least in some sense, computers can think. If given the data philosophers use to construct concepts of justice, a computer could come up with a recognizable and defensible concept of justice, for instance, that would be strong evidence in favor of its being able to think. Concepts go beyond data or information. They are (often) generalizations derived from data and applied to further data. One has a concept when one has the imagination to form it from data and to apply it to data. Hence, concepts look very similar to rules in that understanding both rules and concepts is knowing when they apply and how to apply them. Concepts look very different from the data or information from which they are constructed, and to which they cannot be logically reduced (a point often overlooked by those who tend to think of education as the process of transmitting data to the students). They differ in that rules can usually be (even though they are not always) stated in imperative form (for example, "Always act justly"), whereas concepts may be single nouns (for example, the concept of justice).

Second, rules are not algorithms. Of course, some algorithms are written as rules, "Whenever *A* and *B* occur, you must *C*." One example of an algorithm is found in computerized stock trading. A simple form of such a rule would be, "Whenever stocks *a* and *b* lose 10 percent of their value, sell those stocks and stocks *c*, *d*, and *e* as well." However, humans have to decide whether to use such programs. And occasionally they backfire—as in the October 1987 stock crash on the New York Stock Exchange. Since that time, further algorithms were put in place to stop a repeat of such an event. But these algorithms do not guide further computer-based program trading; they halt it. Although human judgment is not always fully in control, the trading halt creates the possibility that humans can exercise human judgment about the situation—judgment that goes beyond algorithms.[3]

Rules are guides to engaging in a practice. It would seem, then, that following rules (at least roughly) would be necessary for participating in practices just as following grammatical rules (at least roughly) is necessary for communicating in a language. If one wants to participate in the practices of communication, one has to follow the syntax, semantics, and pragmatics of the language—maybe not very well, but well enough to be understood. But since rules are not algorithms, the question arises: Can there be more than one way of following a rule?

Following a Rule

As in all practices, there are rather different levels of competence in knowing how to follow rules. McClendon, whose concept of a practice was discussed in chapter 2, follows MacIntyre in making the point about the role of rules in practices. In his very influential rule theory of doctrine, Lutheran theologian George Lindbeck has made a similar point for Christian doctrines construed as *regula fidei*, the rule of, the formula of, the grammar of faith.[4] But what is often forgotten in the discussion of rules is an insight put in various ways, but put most pithily by James C. Edwards: "A formula doesn't apply itself."[5] A rule does not apply itself.

The curious thing about rules is this: Ultimately there is no rule for applying a rule. Sometimes the most difficult thing about understanding a rule is discerning when it applies. Consider a moral rule: It is always immoral directly and intentionally to kill an innocent human being. As formulated, it is universal. So it should be always applicable. However, is every incident of bombing economically valuable targets in war a violation of it? Bombs kill the innocent civilians along with combatants. Bombing is an intentional act and the result of that act

---

[3] See *Barron's Magazine* (12 July 1999): MW67. I owe clarification on this point to Bill Riker.

[4] See Lindbeck, *The Nature of Doctrine*, 18, 94. While Lindbeck's theory is in some ways very insightful, it has some significant flaws; see the chapter on Lindbeck (co-written with Stuart Kendall) in Terrence W. Tilley, et al., *Postmodern Theologies* (Maryknoll, N.Y.: Orbis Books, 1995), 91-113.

[5] James C. Edwards, *The Authority of Language: Heidegger, Wittgenstein and the Threat of Philosophical Nihilism* (Tampa, Fla.: University of South Florida Press, 1990), 162.

seems directly to kill innocent noncombatants; such loss of life is "collateral damage," anticipated but not desirable results (not consequences) of bombing. Just-war theorists, proponents and opponents of therapeutic abortion, and debaters about capital punishment have constructed arguments about the circumstances in which this fundamental moral rule is and is not applicable, and about how it is to be applied.[6]

Of course, one can formulate a rule for applying a rule, a "second-order rule." But how does one know when that second-order rule applies? Well, then one can formulate a "third-order rule." But the same problem arises. This cannot go on to infinity. Rules must come to a halt. We run out of time and patience. We do not have the ability to formulate and apply an endless list of rules. Eventually one stops the regress (preferably before it reaches infinity). We acknowledge that we can go no farther. We come to a "bedrock" when rules run out. Then one has to say, "This is the way we do it." At the end of rules for acts we simply encounter the practice: This is the way we do it.

This "ending," however remains unsatisfying. Too often we disagree in practice. Simply pointing to a practice as if it were the final word cannot solve conflicts within a practice about how a rule is to be followed. Nor can it solve a conflict arising between practices, such as the practices within Christianity of the just warrior and the pacifist. A homely example will help sort out these problems with regard to following a rule.

Consider an ordinary pedestrian traffic signal (I have in mind a specific signal, but one which is replicated widely in the United States). This signal, in its component for pedestrians, can be in three states when it is functioning. It may have a white sign lit steadily against a dark background. This sign says "Walk."[7] It may have a red sign flashing against a dark background. This sign reads "Don't walk." It may have a red sign lit steadily against a dark background, also saying "Don't walk."

We know the rule: "Walk" means it is safe to cross the street (but watch out for drivers turning into the street you are crossing anyway). "Don't walk," whether flashing or not, means it is not safe to cross the street and you should wait until the "Walk" sign appears. This is what most of us have been taught since infancy, if we live in

---

[6] For further discussion of this issue, see Terrence W. Tilley, "The Principle of Innocents' Immunity," *Horizons* 15/1 (Spring 1988): 43-63.

[7] Of course, the notion of a sign *saying* is already heavily encoded, not only with the particularity of this type of sign saying something, but with the concept of a sign *saying*.

cities or towns with traffic signals. Since people who follow this rule wait when the sign says "Don't walk," we can call them waiters.

But what would we say if someone told us that they were part of a group who followed the rule differently if the sign were *flashing* "Don't walk." They had been taught, they tell us, something different. A flashing "Don't walk" sign signifies, they say, that one has to hurry, to move quickly or to run. It does not mean that one has to wait, but that if one doesn't wait, "Don't walk." We can call them quicksteppers— or, perhaps, New Yorkers. One may wait if one wants, but it is better for one, if one can, to step quickly to cross the street in the face of a flashing "Don't walk" sign.

What would we say of such people?[8] We may refer to the fact that some people are brought by their training to differentiate the two sorts of appearances of "Don't walk" (as we may not have been trained). We might notice that they follow the "Don't walk" rule differently if the sign is flashing rather than lit steadily. We might also say that they understand or follow the "Don't walk" rule. Hence, waiters and quicksteppers seem both somehow to follow the "Don't walk" rule, but they do so in different ways.

Do we want to say that quicksteppers don't understand the rule? That they don't understand what the sign is "ordering" them to do? No. We should say, perhaps, that they understand it differently, at least differently from us, if we are waiters. Tourists from Midwestern towns who become pedestrians or drivers for a brief period in downtown New York or Washington or Boston make various remarks about "the traffic" and "the drivers" and "the pedestrians" in those cities. The way they follow (or fail to follow) traffic rules is different from "the way we do it in Kansas." We might want to say that the way the rule is meant or what the sign means determines which steps are to be taken. But what is the criterion for the way the rule is meant? What is the correct criterion for knowing what "Don't walk" means? Is there a second-order rule to say what the rule "Don't walk" means that the waiters understand and the quicksteppers do not? Or is it that the quicksteppers understand and the waiters do not? Well, we

---

[8] The basic point is found in Ludwig Wittgenstein, *Philosophical Investigations*, 3d ed., trans. G. E. M. Anscombe (New York: Macmillan, 1958 <1953>), §§189-90. I am paraphrasing Wittgenstein here; Wittgenstein uses a more sophisticated example to make the point. I explore this rather simple practice because once we see the problems with typical analyses of this elementary practice, we can see that analogous problems of an extremely larger magnitude would emerge if we were to try to analyze complex practices, such as eucharistic practices.

could just simply stipulate that one group is right on the basis that its way is the *right way*. But not only is that circular, it begs the question we are asking: Which is the "right" way to follow a rule when the "right" way is disputed? We also don't want to go into an infinite regress. Well, then is the right way the way *we* always follow the rule? But who is "we"? If we are the group of waiters, why should our practice be a criterion when "they," the quicksteppers, have been taught differently? Why prefer the way we are taught to follow the rule or the way they do? Does anything really make quicksteppers' practice inferior to waiters' practice, or their way of following a rule wrong in comparison with the waiters' way?[9]

Confronted by such conundra, people sometimes want to answer these questions by saying that the difference is merely a matter of interpretation. Each group "interprets" the rule differently. They have different "ideas" of what the rule means, and each group "chooses" its interpretation. We have a plurality not only of interpretations, but even of strategies for interpretation.[10] However, this strategy doesn't solve the problem but merely removes it one step. Now we have to account for the difference not only in terms of what people do, but also in terms of a mental event that generates ideas or interpretations that then bring them to act as they do. But this confronts us with the same problem, only at a different level. Are there rules for forming good ideas or good interpretations? If so, how are they applied? If not, how can we interpret whether an interpretation is good?

---

[9] Of course, a power elite may, utilizing whatever means it has, command a specific interpretation. However, as noted in chapter 1 regarding the dispute over the lectionary, if such interventions are arbitrary, the interpretations given can only be maintained by the exercise of power extrinsic to the interpretive process. Similarly, a police officer may properly enforce the law the "waiter" way, but that will lead to serious resistance in New York; the law will only be obeyed under the threat of the use of excessive force in its application.

[10] David Tracy, among others, makes interpretation key to all understanding. While his important and insightful work cannot be ignored, the present work explores a different approach for reasons that will become obvious in the discussion below. The basic difference is fundamental: Tracy takes the root model of interpretation to be understanding a historical, classic text or a quasi-text (see Tracy, *Plurality and Ambiguity: Hermeneutics, Religion, Hope* [San Francisco: Harper & Row, 1987],10-11). The present work takes the root model of interpretation to be performing a ritual or a song or a symphony. Obviously, textual interpretation is necessary for performing a piece and the interpretation of a classic is a performance; the two approaches have much in common. However, making performance practice primary avoids some problems in interpretation theory and surfaces insights that the hermeneutical approach valorized from Schleiermacher to Tracy obscures, especially the concrete contexts in which interpretation occurs.

The pattern is clear: We can easily get into an infinite regress of interpretations, just as we got into an infinite regress of rules.

To explore this issue, I want to use an "ordinary language argument." This sort of argument notes the importance of what people ordinarily say when they are using their native language well. It is especially appropriate for understanding practices—for the use of language is one form of practice. These arguments are not necessarily decisive, a point recognized by one of its strongest proponents, John L. Austin: "Certainly, then, ordinary language is *not* the last word: in principle it can everywhere be supplemented and improved upon and superseded. Only remember, it *is* the *first* word."[11] Failure to note that oftentimes our technical vocabulary obscures important distinctions that can be teased out from ordinary language can result in philosophical (or other) obfuscations. Those philosophers who claim "everything is interpretation" run the risk of obscuring important distinctions ordinary language preserves.

Thus, an ordinary language argument can ask whether all responses to sensory stimuli are interpretations. Does a person throwing up her arm in response to a man lunging at her with a knife "interpret" the action? If she does, she stands no chance of warding off the attack. Does the defensive tackle in football perform a mental act of interpretation to respond to the block of the offensive guard? If he does, he is knocked out of the play because his reaction needs to be practically instantaneous to be effective. *Interpretation takes time;* we interpret what is not clear to us. Hence, to say "I interpreted his movement instantaneously and responded to it" sounds odd. It would be better to say, "I responded to his movement," or "I reacted to her action." Does the defensive player in basketball "interpret" the fakes of the offensive player? Or does the player *recognize* them for what they are—or fail to do so and get "faked out"?

My point is that some acts are clear enough not to require interpretation. Some acts require immediate responses. Some people we recognize, even across a room. We can learn, as football linemen do, to respond to some acts immediately, as though they are unambiguous. We do learn to respond to some speech acts immediately, especially when the context removes any possible ambiguity, for example, an order from a sergeant to a private, a call of "Fire!" in a theater, and so on. That our responses, linguistic or otherwise, are learned does not make them interpretations. That we learn to recognize people

---

[11] John L. Austin, "A Plea for Excuses," in *Philosophical Papers*, ed. J. O. Urmson and G. J. Warnock (Oxford: Clarendon Press, 1961), 133.

"from their walk," for example, does not mean that when we "recognize" them we engage in an act of interpretation. Obviously, many acts do require interpretation because they are ambiguous. Clearly, we sometimes are hesitant and have to take time and "decide" whether we recognize a person. Certainly, some texts require interpretation because they are multivalent. Moreover, some acts may be intentionally deceptive, such as the fakes of the basketball player or some pronouncements of government officials; we may respond to them immediately, but "after training" or "upon reflection" we can learn how to recognize them for the deceptions they are and how to respond properly. Interpretation takes time; so does learning other practices. However, hermeneutical practices are not universal, but limited to those who have the time to clarify the multivalent or to confuse the clear. In many cases interpretation is like the training wheels we discard when we have learned how to ride a two-wheel bike. We engage in practices skillfully, gracefully, intentionally, and creatively without intervening acts of interpretation.

Hence, resorting to mental acts of interpretation as an explanation for different ways the rules are followed makes the problem worse. By postulating a mental event of interpretation, we introduce yet something else to explain, lose the possibility of immediate responses and learned reactions as ways of following rules, and run into the danger of yet another infinite regress. As it is clear that interpretation is not something we always do in responding to another, this is not a path to follow, if an alternative is available.

What if we say that the basis for the differences in the ways waiters and quicksteppers have been taught and learned the rule about "Don't walk" is not a difference in a hidden "mental act" of interpretation? What if we say that we and they are *trained to follow* (not interpret) the rule "Don't walk" in wildly different ways? And is this not the case with us? Do we not ordinarily just follow the rule blindly without thinking about it? Is this not why "New Yorkers" are at home with the way the rules are followed in downtown Manhattan, and Kansans with the way the rules are followed in Wichita—but not New York? If this is accurate, then we can avoid introducing explanations that are harder to explain than the behavior they were designed to explain.

However, we run into other problems if we take the explanation not to be a "mental event," but a difference in practices in which we and they are trained to follow rules in certain ways unquestioningly, thoughtlessly, or blindly. In this case, if we wanted to ask, Which one is correct?, what could we say? "I never thought about it"? "I don't know how to think about it"? Are we forced into relativism (which may not matter much in this example but is a problem in other areas, for example, religious traditions)? Must we decide simply by retreating to our own practice and asserting it as our norm? It is circular, as noted above, to appeal to our own practice when the normativity of two different practices that follow the "same" rule differently is in dispute. That doesn't solve the problem either. How do we get beyond the Scylla of relativism and the Charybdis of arrogance?

On the one hand, the appeal to an interpretation is finally an appeal to another rule: Interpret this sign this way. We are caught in an infinite regress of rules. There is not, ultimately, a rule for applying a rule. On the other hand, we are left with the differences and no way to say which is the right way to follow the rule. There is just "what we do" and "what they do," our way of engaging in the practice and theirs. The alternative to infinite regress seems a vicious form of relativism wherein no judgments can be made about which way of following the rule is preferable.[12]

Moreover, the problem is even worse. Consider now the wide variety of circumstances in which you might be standing in front of a pedestrian traffic signal. You are standing with a bursting bladder on one side and a bathroom across the street; or with a bus across the street closing its doors; or with no motor vehicle traffic in sight in the middle of the night; or carrying a baby; or with a toddler at your side. Do you apply the "Don't walk" rule in each of these circumstances? Or do you just ignore it? If you follow it, which practice do you instantiate, that of the waiters or of the quicksteppers? In which do you participate? Which practice would you "pass on" if you were to teach the rule? The waiters' (ours) or the quicksteppers' (theirs)? Do you merely say that the rule of waiting does not apply in these circumstances? The waiter with the bursting bladder might say just that. But by what rule do you know when *not* to apply the rule that normally applies? Answering that question would start us on another infinite regress. But that leaves us with no answer to the question, Given the circumstances, which rule do you follow or ignore, and how do you decide? Once we actually examine the many contexts in which this rule might be applied, the issues multiply and a general rule-theory or interpretation-theory solution to the problem seems impossible.

---

[12] An analogous point could be made if we construed the quicksteppers and waiters as participants in different practices. The issue then becomes not one about how one follows a rule in one practice, but about the practice in which one ought participate.

In light of all these difficulties, what we need to do to solve this worsening problem is to recognize that the issue can be solved neither by recourse to hidden mental acts of interpretation nor by recourse to the conception of a practice as a blind and repetitive following of rules. The solution, finally, is where we began: in the act. We quicksteppers and waiters both know what the rule means. We realize we can follow it in various ways. We can even agree on what would clearly constitute a violation of the rule: walking slowly across an intersection in the midst of heavy traffic in the face of a flashing "Don't walk" sign. The question we are asking is how "Don't walk" applies to us here and now, in specific situations. *In short, understanding how to follow or apply a rule is not essentially an exercise in either rule-governed interpretation or repetition, but in understanding how to act.* This is not to say that we do not ever engage in merely repetitive rule-following behavior. Nor does it deny the claim that facility at using interpretive rules to interpret complex phenomena and texts is sometimes necessary. To follow a rule may require neither interpretation nor repetition. To follow a rule is to act, and sometimes to act in unexpected or creative ways that seem to "break" the rules of a practice. But even then we determine that it is wiser to place ourselves under the regime or in the practice in which the rule we follow has its home than not to enter that practice or decide the rule does not apply.[13] We "decide" to play basketball or learn (at least rudimentary) life-saving skills.

Differences between our imaginary disputants, the waiters and quicksteppers, are like differences among Christians struggling to

---

[13] In *The Wisdom of Religious Commitment* (Washington, D.C.: Georgetown University Press, 1995), I argued that the issue of the rationality of religious belief is not finally an epistemic issue in the technical sense (for example, whether person p at time t is warranted in believing proposition n, "God exists," given circumstances q,r,s) but an issue of prudential judgment.

I also do not intend to exclude cases of the rebel, one who breaks a rule out of principle or desire for personal gain but acknowledges that the rule *should* apply to his or her behavior. These cases can be understood in various ways, but I would tend to think of the former as an attempt to get a rule changed and the latter as the case of a supervening rule (for example, Always look out for number one first, last and foremost) being applied. It also seems the case that in at least some cases of principled rule-breaking the point might well be to show a way to reform a practice. It also seems that many of the latter cases would be deceptions at a fundamental level: like the deep penetration spy who works for years in a government in order to get into a position from which to better serve his or her masters, so the person who participates in a practice while breaking its rules may be duplicitous, playing, as the spy is, by a different and hidden set of rules.

understand how to live out their tradition. In the sixteenth century, for instance, the disputes between those Protestants and Catholics who practiced infant baptism (*pedobaptists,* as their opponents called them) and those who practice believers' baptism (*anabaptists* is the name that stuck to them) were not differences about interpreting rules but over the proper grammar of Christian life. Anabaptists appealed to the New Testament practice as their model and repudiated the "mainstream" practice as a tool of the state. Pedobaptists appealed to the tradition and the necessity for baptism to wash away original sin. Was the dispute about baptism a mortal conflict over interpretation or over burning issues in theological syntax (necessarily connecting baptism and sin, a connection not much made before Augustine or in the Orthodox Churches), religious semantics (the meaning of baptism), and pragmatics (who is to be baptized and when)? Construing that dispute as one of interpretation is certainly possible, but construing it as one about what is the rule of the tradition and how is it to be followed with regard to this crucial ritual action may well be more illuminating. Intractable disputes about the ordination of women, the legitimacy of contraception, the legitimacy of some divorces, the necessity of celibacy for clerics, the roles of teaching authority, and so on can all be illuminated if one takes them *not* as merely matters of interpretation, but as disputes about how to live in and live out a tradition in the practices that constitute it.[14]

Given that such disputes are, at any given time, intractable, this approach suggests that the question to be raised is not one of interpretation, but one of the wisdom of entering a practice. It may seem trivial to ask whether it is wiser to be a waiter or a quickstepper. But that question is not always trivial: Is it wiser for a Christian community and its members to engage in believers' baptism or infant baptism? To allow and encourage women to preside at Eucharist? To find various forms of contraception not unnatural? What we have been saying is this: Just as there are not grammatical rules sufficient for an agent to produce excellent speaking or writing, so having or describing good judgment in other practices is not exhaustible by interpreting rules. Finally, we are thrown back on our acts and practices:

---

[14] Lindbeck, *The Nature of Doctrine*, 91-111, "tests" a rule theory of doctrine by arguing that it clarifies the issues regarding Christology, Mariology, and infallibility among those who dispute those doctrines. While the theory does not solve these disputes, it suggests patterns for understanding the disputes that may make possible progress beyond earlier logjams. One could argue that the recent Lutheran-Catholic agreement on justification is an example of the power of such an approach.

This is what we do and that is what they do. If we are thrown back on acts and practices, then how can we come to judgment *about* acts and practices?

Coming to Judgment

Performing a *good* act or performing an act *well* cannot be reduced to algorithmic repetition or to giving a correct interpretation. We may evaluate some skills, especially complex motor skills, on the precision of repetition. We may evaluate some interpretations on the basis of their lucidity or insight. However, neither of these is sufficient for recognizing a good act. We recognize a good act or a well-done act in an act of judgment, that this act is one of following a rule well, even though it may be an odd way to do so.[15]

As with other acts, sometimes coming to judgment involves acts of interpretation; sometimes *interpretation* is not the right word to use, but rather *recognition* or *response.* We do not interpret some actions, such as a well-thrown block in football or a well-executed fake in basketball. We recognize them. If we see a child flailing about in a swimming pool and a fully clothed adult jumping in the pool, we don't interpret the adult's act as a rescue but rather recognize it. If nurses or physicians see a specific wave pattern on a cardiac monitor, they do not interpret it as ventricular tachycardia; rather, they arc trained to recognize it and to begin emergency procedures to save the patient's life. In so doing, they act well. Such rescuers and medical professionals may be congratulated not for a correct interpretation but for a quick and correct response, for acts that display good judgment, for good acts that are well done.

Even in those cases in which interpretations are necessary, interpretations come to an end; that end is determined by an act of judgment. One can interpret a polyvalent text almost endlessly, but eventually in the performance of a play, the writing of a commentary or review, or the singing of an art song in recital, one puts one's interpretation "on the line"; one's interpretation is put into practice. Generally, interpretations are put into practice for an audience. Although its significance is often overlooked, hermeneutical theory presupposes

---

[15] A similar argument might be made by those influenced by Hans-Georg Gadamer, who would claim that interpretation is not reducible to the rules of any method or theory (see H.-G. Gadamer, *Truth and Method,* 2d ed., trans. Joel Weinsheimer and Donald G. Marshall [New York: Continuum, 1989]).

that the interpreter interprets a text (or other artifact) *for an audience*. In so doing, the interpreter may engage in the play of interpretations without reaching any judgment. But this may not be of use to an audience (unless the point is not to *give* an interpretation for an audience, but to teach it about interpreting). But properly an interpreter comes to judgment in the sense of *judgment* used here: an act in the practice of interpretation. In some instances, one may snap to judgment without engaging in any extended process of interpretation. The point is that not all interpretations come to judgment. Some do; some do not. Nor do all judgments involve interpretation. Some do, but some involve reactions, responses, or readings that may require great expertise, but that are not really interpretations.[16]

Each of these acts is performed and evaluated in the context of a practice: football, basketball, life-saving, medicine. Well-performed acts in one practice may be bad acts in another practice. A football block is a foul in basketball. A ball-fake would be ludicrous in a patient's room. This is not to suggest that there are not acts and patterns of acts that can be found in many practices—an act can be a good one to perform in many practices, for example, greeting someone; or bad in almost all practices, for example, a hard right cross to someone's jaw (usually a good act only in boxing). But most (and perhaps all) acts are performed as exercises in a practice.

Since rules are not sufficient to determine any act, including an act of judgment, one way to approach the problem is to ask, How do we learn good judgment? How do we learn when we come to the end of rules or reasons, to the "bedrock" of our practices, to the point at which the only response is, That's just what we do! That's the way we act! The problem is that a general answer to this question cannot be given. Hence, the quest for a foundation for our rules and practices reaches a dead end. The reason for asserting the lack of a general answer comes from the work of Ludwig Wittgenstein.

An important implication of Wittgenstein's *Philosophical Investigations* is that there are no general rules for coming to the end of explanations of rules (or practices). As Peter Winch put it:

---

[16] This ordinary-language argument could be expanded. For instance, a physician may interpret the wave form for someone (say a patient's relative) who cannot recognize it or a cardiologist may interpret a set of recorded wave forms (an electrocardiogram) for other physicians who cannot read (not interpret) cardiograms as effectively as the cardiologist. I see no reason to collapse these acts of reading and recognizing into acts of interpretation. Most precisely, interpretation is what experts do for a non-expert or for another expert when interpretations are up for grabs. Scripture scholars, docents in art museums, lawyers and judges, and other experts usually interpret for non-experts.

Wittgenstein does *not* characteristically follow a reminder that explanations come to an end with any such general question as "*Where* do they end?" And I believe to ask the question is to betray a misunderstanding. Spinoza thought that because explanations have come to an end there must be something which has no further explanation, a *causa sui*. But Wittgenstein's point is not at all like that—it is a *criticism* of such an outlook. He does not think that explanations come to an end with something that is intrinsically beyond further explanation. They come to an end for a variety of quite contingent and pragmatic reasons, perhaps because of a practical need for action, perhaps because the puzzlement which originally prompted the search for an explanation has evaporated (for one reason or another).[17]

What we do is *not* a foundation for our practice; it *is* our practice. Our explanations come to an end not because we reach a foundation, but because we have no need or no way to go further in the practice of explaining our practice!

In one sense, we can go on and on looking for explanations. But eventually we give up and come to judgment, judgment in act. But there is no rule telling us when we should come to judgment. We do so for various reasons. In any case, we come to judgment that *this* is where the explanations end.

Displaying what constitutes good judgment would require writing a book like Aristotle's *Nicomachean Ethics*. I cannot write that book— and, given the variety of practices, a modern Aristotelian ethics would either be very abstract (and thus self-defeating) or be nearly interminable because good judgment seems to be specific to actual practices, contexts and traditions—and to cover good judgment in even a few paradigm practices would require both remarkable expertise in many practices and remarkable ability to step back from first-order practices and engage in the second-order practice of theorizing about them. But the reasoning I find cogent can be summarized in this short, abstract way: We learn good judgment just as we *learn how* to practice medicine, architecture, historical research, teaching, basketball, or liturgies, by a certain kind of imagination that enables us to imitate creatively the practices of people who engage in these practices well.

---

[17] Peter Winch, "Discussion of Malcolm's Essay," in Norman Malcolm, *Wittgenstein: A Religious Point of View*, ed. with a response by Peter Winch (London: Routledge, 1993), 104.

By learning how they do it, we learn good judgment; we learn good judgment by imitating their exemplary instantiation of a practice. To discern good judgment in practices, we imitate those who engage in good judgment in crossing streets, in good writing or speaking, in knowing when to stop burrowing in archives and come to judgment, in discerning when surgery is indicated, or in good performance in any other practice.[18] That there may be many good ways of engaging in some practices is simply a fact about the world; there are also many more bad ways. The difference is often all too obvious. Moreover, imitation is necessarily not slavish imitation or mere repetition, but creative imitation, what philosopher Paul Ricoeur calls *mimesis*$_3$.[19] In short, the criteria for good practice are given by what good practitioners do.

But perhaps the most fundamental disputes are over recognizing exemplars in a practice. Which of the various practitioners is a "good"

---

[18] This seems to be what Wittgenstein is getting at in *Philosophical Investigations* in the following sections: "240. Disputes do not break out (among mathematicians, say) over the question whether a rule has been obeyed or not. People don't come to blows over it, for example. That is part of the framework on which the working of our language is based (for example, in giving descriptions). 241. 'So you are saying that human agreement decides what is true and what is false?' It is what human beings *say* that is true or false; and they agree in the language they use. That is not agreement in opinions, but in form of life." What Wittgenstein seems to mean here is that mathematicians don't have disputes because they participate in a practice in which they all have the requisite training to know what a valid proof is and can make that judgment when they analyze a proposed proof. This does not obtain in religion or politics, where we do sometimes come to blows. "242. If language is to be a means of communication there must be agreement not only in definitions but also (queer as this may sound) in judgments. This seems to abolish logic, but does not do so.—It is one thing to describe the methods of measurement, and another to obtain and state the results of measurement. But what we call 'measuring' is partly determined by a certain constancy in results of measurement." What Wittgenstein seems to be saying here is that, using our present example, if we differ from others in what counts as obeying the sign "Don't walk," we may not even be able to communicate clearly about what each of us is doing, much less figure out ways of deciding who's "right."

[19] See Paul Ricoeur's discussion of *mimesis*$_3$ in his *Time and Narrative* I, trans. Kathleen McLaughlin and David Pellauer (Chicago: University of Chicago Press, 1984), 70-82. For one example of the use of exemplars for religious understanding, see David Burrell, *Exercises in Religious Understanding* (Notre Dame, Ind.: University of Notre Dame Press, 1974); for a different approach that uses life stories to explore the doctrine of atonement, see James Wm. McClendon Jr., *Biography as Theology: How Life Stories Can Remake Today's Theology*, 2d ed. (Philadelphia: Trinity Press, 1990 < 1974 >). Each of the exemplars Burrell and McClendon studies exemplifies different patterns that can all be subsumed under Ricoeur's *mimesis*$_3$.

practitioner? Is Quincy Quickstepper or Wanda Waiter a good practitioner? Are they both? Is Angie Anabaptist or Peter Pedobaptist a good practitioner? Are they both? Here I think we hit rock bottom, at least for our purposes. Like "getting" a joke, recognizing exemplars is not something any explanation can make occur. Recognizing good waiters or quicksteppers is not a matter of interpretation (or we get into the mental rules infinite regress) but a cultured or learned response, an act of judgment or appraisal.[20] For while an explanation may help you understand why a joke was funny, it cannot enable you to "get" the joke in the same way that someone who "gets" it spontaneously does. So too with the recognition of exemplars. *Rules don't apply themselves, but exemplars show how rules are to be applied in a practice.* Exemplars show how to act, how to practice. And exemplars are finally recognized, not cognized. In the end, we point at certain people and say, "If you want to understand how we do things, *this* is the way we do things!"

Finally, the turn to the practice of exemplary practitioners is the resolution or dissolution of the problem of interpreting rules and of coming to judgment—not a very satisfactory or systematic one, but a recognition that explanations come to an end at various places in various contexts for various reasons and that realizing that we have come to an end of explanations and of rules is simply an act of judgment undertaken in a specific context—an act that may simply go wrong.[21]

Practices, especially religious practices, are fragile; communities of practitioners are also fragile. We want to understand the "right" way to engage in practices and the "right" way to believe, not only because we want to be authentic and faithful participants in the tradition, but also because we want to be able to pass on a vibrant tradition to those who succeed us in the tradition. We would like to find a rule that could guarantee that the tradition we have been blessed to inherit can bless those to whom we bequeath it. But no rule can guarantee that our performances will be "right." No interpretation will validate itself. No authority can assure a tradition will thrive. No exemplar can prescribe a guaranteed pattern of success. Learning all we can, we simply must act as well as we can.

---

[20] This is at least analogous to what Lonergan calls an insight. See B. J. F. Lonergan, S.J., *Insight: A Study of Human Understanding* (New York: Philosophical Library, 1957). See below, pages 163-70, for a discussion of appraisals.

[21] Ideally, governing boards for invented or institutionally linked practices would be constructed not to perpetuate a power elite but to recognize the ability of a group of exemplary practitioners.

The Status of Rules in Practices

If rules can be interpreted in such varied ways, and if rules for good interpretation and judgment cannot finally be specified, what status do rules have? What good are they?

First and foremost, rules are not metaphysical entities of some sort, independent of our practices.[22] They are not Platonic ideals that exist independent of what we do and that somehow inform what we do. Nor can they be imposed a priori on our practices by an independent or arbitrary authority—except in instances like the imposition of rules of translation for the lectionary discussed in chapter 1 or the promulgation of rules for treating head trauma discussed in chapter 3. Such forms of imposition are possible because in each of these sets of practices these authorities have the responsibility for discerning and promulgating rules that can guide good practice. Rules are not sufficient and not often necessary to give rise to practices; our practices give rise to rules. Grammar doesn't give rise to language; language gives rise to grammar. Rules are shorthand guides for learning how to engage in practices.

Nonetheless, practical rules shape the ways in which practitioners engage in practices. Their purpose is to remind us and others how we can carry on the practices and reach the goals our practices envision—good worship and good medical treatment are, respectively, the goals of the practices noted above. But fundamentally, as we have noted, rules are always open to novel applications, and the practice can change as a result of such applications. What counts as good English grammar has changed as English has evolved. What constitutes *good* practice changes in all living practices extended over time and place. As language teachers have discovered, teaching rules is not sufficient for teaching a language; but to attempt to ignore rules completely would make teaching languages practically impossible. Except possibly for some artificially constructed practices or exercises (for example, chess, board games, bridge) where the basic rules, axioms, or

---

[22] This is *not* to say that rules may not, in some sense, refer and need to refer to actual entities or states of affairs. This position differs from Lindbeck, *The Nature of Doctrine,* 19, who says that the "only job that doctrines do in their role as church teachings is regulative." However, doctrines are the written and/or remembered content of *acts* of a community or the authorities within that community. To do their job properly, such acts must also have specific referential force (see Terrence W. Tilley, *The Evils of Theodicy* [Washington, D.C.: Georgetown University Press, 1991], 35-38).

postulates are algorithms laid out (algorithmically, logically) before the practice is instituted, our common practices and traditions come first, and the rules that govern them follow.[23] Yet even in these cases of "artificial" practices, we can differentiate players who have truly grasped the game and those who are novices: the former know how to follow the rules much more exquisitely than the latter—and how to deal with "rules" that are in conflict with one another.

The formation of a constitution for a nation is an example of the priority of practice over rules. Given a set of actual or desired practices that have structured or should structure a form of life, constitutions attempt to formulate the rules implicit in such practices. For instance, the right to vote given to property-owning males in the U.S. Constitution at its origins reflects the practice of power at the time. The movements toward universal adult suffrage over the past two centuries are successful attempts to change that practice by those who were eligible to participate in it. The only ones who could effectively change the rules in response to the calls for justice for the disenfranchised were the land-owning males. The practice of suffrage is instituted in a certain context and as either the context changes or a widespread desire to amend the practice occurs, the shape of the practice is altered by a change in the rule. But the basic point remains: Practices come first; rules second.[24]

Second, as noted above, George Lindbeck has developed a very influential rule theory of doctrine. In effect, Lindbeck has argued that doctrines are not statements of belief but the rules of the grammar of faith.[25] If doctrines employ or state concepts as understood above, there is very good reason to believe that doctrines may well

---

[23] Even in the cases of complex artificial games like bridge or chess, judgment and inspired guesswork—or a computer simulation of judgment and statistical probabilities of opponents' future moves—seem necessary for playing the games.

[24] This position seems to create severe problems as it is formulated for natural-law theory, at least in some of its strong constitutive forms. It can be overcome by a Sellarsian move in which our rules are recognized as made by us and warranted in use, but which reflect, more or less well, the natural law. Of course, the Sellarsian move reduces correspondence with the natural law to no use in the process of *justifying* moral or other claims. But doesn't that actually reflect the shape of the arguments anyway? I will take up this point again in chapter 6.

[25] The phrase "the grammar of faith" is taken from a book by Lindbeck's one-time colleague, philosopher Paul Holmer, *The Grammar of Faith* (New York: Harper & Row, 1978). See especially Terrence W. Tilley, "Incommensurability, Intratextuality, and Fideism," *Modern Theology* 5/2 (January 1989): 87-111. This paragraph draws on material published in Tilley, *Postmodern Theologies*, 95.

have at least a rule-like status in the Christian religious traditions. Moreover, one crucial insight of this theory helps the present investigation: Lindbeck has argued persuasively that there are rules implicit in the tradition that can be used to guide the *development* of the doctrines in the tradition. Consider the following, in which Lindbeck calls these rules "principles":

> First, there is the monotheistic principle: there is only one God, the God of Abraham, Isaac, Jacob, and Jesus. Second, there is the principle of historical specificity: the stories of Jesus refer to a genuine human being who was born, lived, and died in a particular time and place. Third, there is the principle of what may be infelicitously called Christological maximalism: every possible importance is to be ascribed to Jesus that is not inconsistent with the first rules. This last rule, it may be noted, follows from the central Christian conviction that Jesus Christ is the highest possible clue (though an often dim and ambiguous one to creaturely and sinful eyes) within the space-time world of human experience to God, i.e., to what is of maximal importance.[26]

Lindbeck is *not* claiming that these rules are sufficient to generate or guide the tradition. Not only are other rules needed, but how these and others are to be applied may be matters of dispute—Christians have many more divisions in practice than do waiters and quicksteppers. He does, however, sustain the claim that some form of rules articulated more or less like this can be derived from a set of practices, a form of life or tradition, that can be identified or distinguished as Christian. Unless it implied these rules (or ones formulated similarly), a practice extended over time and space as a tradition probably could not be recognized as Christian.[27]

---

[26] Lindbeck, *The Nature of Doctrine*, 94.

[27] Ibid., 96. Some might see these principles as *constitutive rules*, that is, those rules that must be followed to make Christianity possible, analogous to the rules of the Constitution of the United States that make the government possible. The rules with which we are occupied here then would be construed as *regulative rules*, that is, those rules that Christians must follow to be Christians, analogous to the laws and regulations of the United States Law Code and various administrative codes that show citizens how they must behave to live lawfully in this country. However, Lindbeck's principles are not *positive* rules, but *negative* ones; we cannot imagine how to recognize any community without some form of them as a Christian community. More important, these rules are not sufficient

Yet these principles are not in fact doctrines. Although Lindbeck proposes a "rule theory of doctrine," his primary rules are not official doctrines but rules for the expression of doctrines. Lindbeck calls these "operational doctrines."[28] Given what we have said about rules and applying a rule above, these rules might be applied in wildly different and creative ways depending upon the context. But it would again take us far beyond the limits of this book to explore the particular rules that constitute the body of Christian doctrine. What we can see is how a rule theory of doctrine links practices and traditions more generally.

In sum, rules are not metaphysical entities, or rigid algorithms, or contentless directives. They are shorthand guides derived from good practice with the purpose of guiding those who wish to learn or understand a practice, just as grammar is a shorthand guide derived from good speaking and writing with the purposes of guiding those who wish to learn how to communicate or to understand how speakers and writers of a language communicate. In the process of learning, we may learn rules before we become good at a practice. But it is otherwise when considering the constitution of a practice: *Practice first; rules second.*

A tradition endures through time not by following rules, but by the fact a community of practitioners continues to act in ways that carry on and carry out such a practice, perhaps even when not all of the circumstances in which it originated still obtain. The community follows the rules of the practice in new contexts, perhaps being faithful by radically changing the rules. The discussion of the Eucharist in chapter 2 provides an extended example of this point. The debate about the status of baptism mentioned above provides an example of an unresolved dispute. But we have seen that following a rule is not a simple exercise that can be carried out mindlessly; nor can the results of following a rule well be predicted in advance. This raises the question, How do we discern whether a shift in the practice, whether deliberate or not, is an authentic development of the

---

to constitute any specific Christian community. Finally, it is not clear that the distinction between constitutive and regulative rules can be drawn in a way that would apply to religious communities as it seems to apply to governments. The former may or may not be conceived as founded in a "constitutive" social contract with definite rules, and the distinction seems based on a contractarian understanding of societies and communities. Religious communities certainly (and perhaps political ones as well) arise from shared practices, not from explicit social contracts.

[28] Ibid., 75.

practice, a degradation of the practice and the tradition, or the creation or invention of a novel tradition? This question is much more difficult to answer than the question of how traditions are carried on.

Constancy and Change in Traditions

Among those who have invested energy in answering the question of constancy and change, the issue is usually discussed in terms of development. The most distinguished approach is John Henry Newman's *Essay on the Development of Christian Doctrine*. This essay is typically taken to be both a philosophical and theological treatise.[29] As an exercise in philosophy, it provides both a theory of the relationship between the variable and the invariant elements in a tradition and a phenomenology of authentic development. As an exercise in theological apologetics, it takes the theory and argues that Roman Catholicism embodies the most authentic development of Christian doctrine. Whether the theological exposition determines the shape of the philosophical work is moot; elements of both are inextricably intertwined throughout the essay.

Yet the essay is not really a philosophical or theological treatise. As noted in chapter 3, it is a response to a difficulty. Moreover, both the phenomenology and the apologetics definitely rely on historical investigation, an approach that was both Newman's intent—and the grounds for strong criticism by one of his opponents, as Jaroslav Pelikan has shown:

> Newman began to work on the *Essay on Development* in March 1844. In the front of the notebook in which he was to set down his ideas and fragments for the *Essay*, he instructed himself: "Write it historically, not argumentatively. Begin . . . historically." One of the Anglican replies to the *Essay on Development*, that of William Archer Butler, caught the importance of this factor in Newman's argument. "It is essential to this theory," wrote Butler, "to abide *all* true historical conclusions"; for Newman, he argued, history could not be "merely the narrative of facts, but the law of

---

[29] I am indebted to Edward Jeremy Miller for discussions that helped clarify for me the force of the *Essay*.

doctrine." Therefore, "the fundamental error of the whole system indeed may probably be stated to consist in this very thing, that it conceives Christianity is to be investigated *as a mere succession of historical events* in order to determine Faith."[30]

Newman uses historical investigation, then, to tease out the notes or tests (Pelikan calls them "criteria")[31] for authentic development. These notes or tests apply not only to the Christian tradition (although the illustrations of them are primarily drawn from Christianity). The use of contingent historical events to provide criteria for what is the true faith gives rise to Butler's criticism.[32]

However, Butler's criticism misses the mark. For Newman, the Idea of Christianity *appears in* a succession of historical events but is not *reducible to* them. The faith *is* what it is. The events *show* what it is. Butler, like many philosophers, collapsed two issues. His claim confused what *constitutes* faith (an ontological claim) with how we *recognize* which claims express the faith (an epistemological claim). Newman is clear that the idea of Christianity, the faith, never changes essentially. What clearly develops is the expression of that idea. "These expressions [creeds and dogmas] are never equivalent to" the idea. Nonetheless, those expressions "live in the one idea which they are designed to express, and which alone is substantive. . . . Catholic dogmas are, after all, but symbols of a divine fact, which, far from being compassed by those very propositions, would not be exhausted, nor

---

[30] Jaroslav Pelikan, *Development of Christian Doctrine: Some Historical Prolegomena* (New Haven, Conn.: Yale University Press, 1969), 37, citing (for Newman) papers on *Development*: copy book and fragments on *Development*; Newman MSS, in the Oratory of St. Philip Neri, Birmingham (microfilm in the Yale University Library), B2I and B2II, Batch 135; and (for Butler) William Archer Butler, *Letters on Romanism in Reply to Mr. Newman's Essay on Development*, 2d ed. (Cambridge, 1858), 144.

[31] In the 1845 edition of the *Essay* Newman called these principles "tests"; in the 1878 edition, this had become "notes" of authentic development. The shift is important, at least theoretically, as we shall see below.

[32] This is, of course, another version of what Van A. Harvey called "the familiar dictum 'Christian faith cannot be dependent on the probabilities of historical research,' a dictum that was accepted in essence if not in wording by Lessing, Kierkegaard, Herrmann, Kähler, and the dialectical theologians" (*The Historian and the Believer* [New York: Macmillan, 1966], 249). Harvey found this dictum "muddled." I agree, but the "unmuddling" proposed here differs from Harvey's approach.

fathomed, by a thousand."[33] The historical events that constitute development, thus, do not determine what the faith is, but rather express and show the faith.

It is difficult to overstate the importance of the distinction of what a thing is and what expresses and shows it. This is not at all the same distinction as the classic philosophical distinction between appearances and reality. Faith is a divine gift that is lived in and lived out. The life of faith is a life lived under the guidance of a Christian vision. The articulation of that vision and the practice of the faith may vary from time to time and place to place. Christians use *these* expressions and engage in *these* practices and avoid *those* expressions and practices. Yet none of these expressions and other practices are sufficient to express fully and completely the gift of God itself. They are expressions of that gift. That gift can be known through them if it can be known at all. The faith, then, is not reducible to any one articulation of the vision or any one way of practicing the faith. The faith is the faith, and the expressions are that by which we come to recognize and eventually to understand what it means to live in and live out that faith. What we can say is that there are expressions, that is, articulations and practices, that are or are not, to use Newman's term, "authentic developments."

Newman discerns seven tests or notes of authentic development. The first is *preservation of the idea*. If a judge abandons justice as a basis for rendering judgments and turns to bribery, the judge fails to preserve the idea of justice. If a community claiming to carry on the Christian tradition abandons its center in Jesus, it would not be an authentic development but a degradation of the tradition or the initiation of a separate tradition. Newman finds this hard to apply to Christianity, but spends 116 pages (in the 1878 edition) applying it to the Church of the first six centuries and referring in a footnote to his

---

[33] John Henry Newman, *An Essay on the Development of Christian Doctrine*, 2d ed. (London: James Toovey, 1846), 56-57; Newman is here quoting from his *University Sermons*. The version cited is a reprint of the 1845 edition with a few trivial corrigenda noted on p. xv. The 1878 edition of the *Essay* (reprint edition, Westminster, Md.: Christian Classics, 1968), 53, omits the sentence about dogmas being symbolic and the two sentences before it, which construe creeds and dogmas as "the creations of our minds," either because Newman's meaning of over forty years earlier would be misunderstood in a Roman Catholic context or because he had more substantive concerns about such constructivism and the use of "symbol" in that later context. As chapter 6 will show, the present approach would find support in the omitted lines.

argument that it applies to the Roman Catholic Church now. The second is *continuity of principles*. If a development implies different principles for acting, different *rules* in the sense used in this book, it is inauthentic. When the Greek soldier began returning to his city-state defeated in battle with his shield rather than on his shield, this is a corruption of principles. If a community abandoned principles like the three principles that Lindbeck identified (see pages 107-8 above), it would abandon the Christian tradition. *Power of assimilation* is the third. Newman says that this is an "eclectic, conservative, assimilating, healing, moulding process, *a unitive power* is of the essence."[34] Aquinas's ability to "baptize" Aristotelian categories and utilize them in the expression of Christian faith would be an authentic development (as judged by a Roman Catholic, at least). The fourth is *logical sequence*. This is not "deductive validity" but something like "fittingness." The dogma of the Immaculate Conception, unknown in scripture and controverted for much of the history of Christianity, could be seen as fitting into a logical sequence in the development of devotion to Mary.[35] The fifth is *early anticipation of later developments*. Newman's use of this is polemical. Because it is so easy to point to early "anticipations" of almost any theological doctrine (indeed, of any tradition, as Hobsbawm has pointed out), this test or note simply does not work to distinguish authentic development from "corruptions." Sixth is *an addition that is conservative* of what has gone before. It is difficult to find an example that clearly illustrates this test or note. Catholics might argue for purgatory and indulgences and evangelicals for literal inerrancy. Both sorts of doctrines are additions intended to conserve the meaning of the tradition present in the earliest community and the scriptures it generated; both also seem (to their opponents) not to conserve what has been taught. Seventh, a true development displays *chronic vigor*. A "flash in the pan" fails this test. What counts as chronic, however, is unclear.

Perhaps the main problem with these notes or tests is that they don't function very well—*pace*, Pelikan—as criteria. First, it is not clear what status they have, even for Newman. In the 1845 edition of the *Essay*, he called these "tests," and in the 1878 edition he called

---

[34] Newman, *Essay on the Development of Christian Doctrine* (1845), 186; (1878), 74, emphasis added in the 1878 edition.

[35] In *The Nature of Doctrine* Lindbeck develops a "taxonomy of doctrines" (84-88) that enables him to articulate a nuanced understanding of the "late developing" Catholic Marian dogmas and infallibility (94-106).

them "notes." The crucial point is that one can *apply* tests, but one cannot apply notes. One can only discern whether some specific development had or didn't have those notes. Tests can be applied imaginatively and prospectively to evaluate a contemplated or hypothetical development. Notes can only be discerned retrospectively in an extant practice. Whether this difference was in Newman's mind as he revised the *Essay* is a moot point.

Second, the actual tests or notes themselves don't function very well in circumstances in which authenticity of development is in dispute. The first test/note (preservation of the idea) seems clear, but it doesn't apply to the development of doctrine but to the way individuals put an idea into practice or fail to do so. The example is rather obvious, but the problem is not with such coarse substitutions. Substituting "memorial meal" for "Real Presence" is clearly a failure in continuity; but it is not clear that Jean de Brébeuf, S.J., substituting "atonesta" in the seventeenth century (as discussed in chapter 3), fails to be in continuity, or that substituting "transignification" for "transubstantiation" today fails the continuity test. The third, fourth, fifth, and sixth are not individually or jointly sufficient to resolve the problem of discerning authentic developments from corruptions. The seventh is useful, but only after enough time has passed to test an alleged development. We are left with the second test, continuity of principles. But this test, in practice, is identical to the rule theory of doctrine: What remains constant are the principles for faith in action, and even these principles shift their meaning as the language in which they are articulated evolves or changes (third-century Greek is not twelfth-century Latin is not twenty-first-century English; as noted in the introduction, terminological identity may mask substantive change and terminological diversity may mask substantive identity). Hence, Newman's work may provide a way to understand development in general and the relation of the historical and cultural expressions of the Idea of Christianity. It may also provide a theological legitimation for significant shifts in a tradition over time. However, it does not help us in discerning which developments in particular cases are authentic and which are corruptions. Indeed, given the argument about the priority of practice here, Newman's work cannot provide such a guide because it attends not to what is primary in the expression, the practice, but to what is secondary, the doctrines or doctrinal rules that are derived from and guide practice.

Another theory for constancy in tradition is mentioned by Alasdair MacIntyre. MacIntyre tightly connects practices and traditions with the narratives (the vision, in the account here) that they carry and that carry them. He finds that traditions ebb and flow depending on whether they enable the participants to exercise the relevant virtues. As he writes, "Lack of justice, lack of truthfulness, lack of courage, lack of the relevant intellectual virtues—these corrupt traditions just as they do those institutions and practices which derive their life from the traditions of which they are contemporary embodiments."[36] MacIntyre's point is accurate—no shared practice can be undertaken, much less endure through time and become a tradition, unless its practitioners learn the virtues that make a shared human life possible. Moreover, MacIntyre's account is not developed in support of a reactionary account of immobile traditions. As he put it, "Thus the narratives which we live out have both an unpredictable and a partially teleological character. If the narrative of our . . . lives is to continue intelligibly . . . it is always both the case that there are constraints on how the story can continue *and* that within those constraints there are indefinitely many ways that it can continue."[37] Yet when it comes to distinguishing authentic developments from corruptions, as with applying Newman's notes or tests, there are problems in applying MacIntyre's insights. He tells us what *constitutes* a healthy tradition but does not tell us how to *recognize* a healthy tradition. He does not give us tests to distinguish healthy from failing traditions.

In later work MacIntyre argues that the "rival claims to truth of contending traditions of enquiry depend for their vindication upon the adequacy and the explanatory power of the histories which the resources of each of those traditions in conflict enable their adherents to write."[38] However, people will come to differing judgments over whether one tradition of inquiry or another has greater "explanatory power," a point we noted about Newman's notes/tests. In a practical context, the issues are whether participants in one practice can both learn from other practices how to engage in their own practice better, and whether they can correct deficiencies in others' practices. It is difficult to see how MacIntyre's approach could be applied. MacIntyre's insights, while useful, especially for displaying the nature of traditions of inquiry constituted by extended arguments, are

---

[36] Alasdair MacIntyre, *After Virtue: A Study in Moral Theory* (Notre Dame, Ind.: University of Notre Dame Press, 1981), 207.

[37] Ibid., 201.

[38] Alasdair MacIntyre, *Whose Justice? Which Rationality?* (Notre Dame, Ind.: University of Notre Dame Press, 1988), 403.

not helpful when there is a dispute over what constitutes good practice or a tradition worth living in and living out.[39]

In short, neither Newman nor MacIntyre provides criteria for distinguishing which contemporary versions are authentic developments faithful to the past instantiations of the practices that constitute traditions and which changes are in fact deliberate inventions, innovations, or degradations that violate the received and ongoing traditions. If turning to theory has not been of use, another approach is to consider a specific case of change.

A Case of a Change in Tradition

In 1864 Pope Pius IX issued the encyclical *Quanta Cura*. Accompanying this encyclical at the order of the pope was the famous *Syllabus of Errors*. Citing two previous messages of Pius IX, one of the errors condemned is "Every man is free to embrace and profess that religion which, guided by the light of reason, he shall consider true."[40] In 1965 the Second Vatican Council, in its *Declaration on Religious Freedom (Dignitatis Humanae)*, proclaimed that "the human person has a right to religious freedom. . . . In matters religious no one is to be forced to act in a manner contrary to his own beliefs. Nor is anyone to be restrained from acting in accordance with his own beliefs, whether privately or publicly."[41] Faced with this patent contradiction, John Courtney Murray, S.J., in his introduction to the document, wrote: "The notion of development, not the notion of religious freedom, was the real sticking-point for those who opposed the Declaration even to the end. The course of development between the *Syllabus of Errors* (1864) and *Dignitatis Humanae* (1965) still remains to be explained by theologians."[42]

---

[39] This point that the discrimination is not fully settled between rivals is acknowledged again by MacIntyre in his Gifford Lectures, *Three Rival Versions of Moral Enquiry: Encyclopedia, Genealogy, and Tradition* (Notre Dame, Ind.: University of Notre Dame Press, 1990), 214-15. Nonetheless, MacIntyre places his bets on "tradition," and specifically the Aristotelian-Thomistic tradition of philosophical inquiry.

[40] *The Syllabus of Errors* (1864), in *Religion from Tolstoy to Camus*, ed. Walter Kaufmann (New York: Harper & Row, 1961), 183; this is proposition 15 of the eighty condemned propositions.

[41] Walter M. Abbott, S.J., ed., *The Documents of Vatican II* (New York: Guild Press, America Press, Association Press, 1966), 678-79, no. 2.

[42] Ibid., 673.

Opposition to religious freedom did not end in the nineteenth century. In 1955 Murray was silenced by Roman authorities because he advocated freedom of religion as a positive political good rather than a (barely) tolerable political evil.[43] Less than a decade later, Murray's position would be in large part vindicated by the promulgation of *Dignitatis Humanae* at the Second Vatican Council. This is not only a radical reversal, but given that "the Church thinks in centuries," a practically instantaneous turnaround.

Nearly thirty-five years later, no convincing theory of development has accounted for the "course of development" that allows a clear contradiction in 1965 of what the highest magisterial authority in the Church taught in 1864. Some tortuous accounts have attempted to show an alleged continuity between these two statements. However, as J. Robert Dionne put it, "there can be no doubt whatever that the Council reversed the position of Pius IX and his successors," that the teaching of *Dignitatis Humanae* is "not continuous" with the earlier doctrine, and that arguments in favor of continuity are, at best, "tendentious."[44]

Clearly, the change in teaching on religious freedom would fail to have what Newman identifies as the notes or tests of an authentic development. There is no continuity of principles; indeed, as the conservative minority objected at the Second Vatican Council, this is a *reversal* of principles. There is hardly an "early anticipation of later

---

[43] See Donald E. Pelotte, S.S.S., *John Courtney Murray: Theologian in Conflict* (New York: Paulist Press, 1976), 51-59.

[44] See the meticulous analysis of J. Robert Dionne, S.M., *The Papacy and the Church: A Study of Praxis and Reception in Ecumenical Perspective* (New York: Philosophical Library, 1987), 147-94; quotations at 192, 193. Dionne analyzes only an argument of Roger Aubert's as "tendentious," but this judgment applies mutatis mutandis to other arguments that focus on doctrinal development. Dionne proffers a very complex account of a multiplicity of ways in which changes in authoritative Church teaching on various subjects have occurred. Crucial to his account is the reception of Church teaching. Dionne, however, argues that "*reception was a reciprocal movement*" (293). "Reception" does not merely apply to the acceptance of papal teaching by the rest of the Church, but also to the pope listening to what bishops, theologians, and local Churches were saying in making and modifying magisterial teachings. Dionne shows that there were various forms of interaction between the papal teaching office and the rest of the Catholic Church that led to change in teaching. Dionne implicitly recognizes that authority is not concentrated in the papacy or the curia or the bishops, even in the Catholic tradition, but is distributed in different ways through the community of practicing Catholics. See the discussion of authority in chapter 6 for a "practical" understanding of this point.

developments." To claim that the later teaching is conservative of what has gone before would be very difficult to argue.[45]

The papal magisterium in the nineteenth century was adamant in its condemnation of what we today would take to be some basic human rights. For instance, in 1832 Gregory XVI condemned freedom of conscience as an "absurd and erroneous opinion," a "derangement," and a "pestilence" because of which "kingdoms which flourished by reason of wealth, of rule, and of glory perished."[46] Pius IX built on Gregory's teaching by continuing to condemn freedom of conscience and religion, the separation of Church and State, and public education independent of ecclesiastical control.[47] Both also condemned what we would call civil disobedience and conscientious objection to government orders. They decried revolution as an action directed against God, the author of all authority. Even their more diplomatic successor, Leo XIII, warned in 1885 against revolution as a "rebellion against the divine will. . . . To cast aside obedience and by popular violence to incite to revolt, is therefore treason, not against man only, but against God."[48] In 1895 Leo advised American Catholics that it would be "very erroneous" to draw from the evidence of the Church's flourishing in the United States that the independence of the Church from the State is to be considered "universally lawful and expedient."[49]

To understand this opposition to human rights in Roman Catholic teaching, one must look at the context. In 1789 the Catholic Church was the established religion of France, her "eldest daughter" and main

---

[45] The document itself links its new support of political freedom of religion with teaching about the religious response to God: "It is one of the major tenets of Catholic doctrine that man's response to God in faith must be free. Therefore no one is to be forced to embrace the Christian faith against his own will. This doctrine is contained in the Word of God and it was constantly proclaimed by the Fathers of the Church" (*Dignitatis Humanae,* no. 10; numerous references to historic sources are made). Beyond noting the fact that the citations of St. Augustine advocating freedom could be countered with at least as many from Augustine's writings opposing this notion of freedom, the fact that this document draws such a *political* implication from the tradition that supports (however intermittently) a free *religious* response to God is clearly a novelty.

[46] Pope Gregory XVI, *Mirari Vos* (15 August 1832) in *Readings in Church History,* ed. Colman J. Berry (New York: Newman Press, 1965), 3:41.

[47] *The Syllabus of Errors* 15, 47, 55, 77, 78, in Kaufmann, *Religion from Tolstoy to Camus,* 163-70.

[48] Pope Leo XIII, *Immortale Dei* (1 November 1885) in Berry, *Readings,* 3:94-95.

[49] Pope Leo XIII, *Longinqua Oceani* (6 January 1895) in *Documents of American Catholic History,* 2d ed., ed. John Tracy Ellis (Milwaukee, Wis.: Bruce Publishing, 1962), 498.

support outside of Italy. In France, throne and altar were interlocked in a political-ecclesial structure. Thus, when the French Revolution reined in and later overthrew a despotic monarchy, it also destroyed the Church's established position in the name of "the rights of man and citizen." The details need not concern us here, but the papal magisterium "learned" that advocacy of human rights was inseparably connected with disastrous revolution against traditional authority, especially when the ideals of the revolution degenerated into a reign of terror in the 1790s. This "learning" was reinforced by the revolutions of 1830 and 1848 (in which Pius IX had to flee Rome in disguise), and the Italian *Risorgimento,* which reduced the temporal possessions of the pope, the Papal States, to the 109 acres of Vatican City. The modern tradition in the nineteenth century of the papal magisterium opposing political human rights, then, is rooted in its reaction to the horror of revolution for human rights and against God-given authority. In the twentieth century, as the papacy came to terms with its loss of the Papal States, it emerged as a leader in the campaign for human rights. The papacy, however, has always understood human rights within a specifically Catholic tradition, which links rights with duties and which orders rights hierarchically. The recent teaching about rights is based in a theological anthropology that finds that the human person is intrinsically social and dignified because each and all are created in the image and likeness of God.

It is not my point to argue here that such opposition was wise or unwise or that the more "positive" views of recent decades are an improvement over earlier rejections of human rights. Nor is it my point to note that the teaching office of the Church is "reactive" rather than "proactive" in many of its pronouncements. Nor is it my point to note the fact that the official teaching authority of the Church has indeed practically reversed itself on a whole range of social and political issues, not only on religious freedom. The documents of the Second Vatican Council, as well as the encyclicals of John XXIII, *Mater et Magistra* (1961) and *Pacem in Terris* (1963); Paul VI, *Populorum Progressio* (1967); and John Paul II, *Laborem Exercens* (1981), *Sollicitudo Rei Socialis* (1988), and *Centesimus Annus* (1991)—all of which later encyclicals build on *Rerum Novarum* (1891) of Leo XIII and *Quadragesimo Anno* (1931) of Pius XI—recognize substantial, positive human economic and social as well as political rights.

My point is simply to notice, with Dionne, that focusing on doctrinal statements, statements that are *tradita,* cannot explain the changes. In fact, considered as statements they are simply reversals, fractures in the tradition. In Newman's terms, they would be "innovations" not "developments."[50]

Finally, it is not my point to offer a theory of development. As noted in chapter 3, theories of development can easily run into the dilemma of development. Even Dionne does not have a theory of development but rather an analysis of how the praxis of the Church, especially the practices of fraternal correction and mutual support between the central teaching authority and other groups and individuals in the community of the Church, gives rise to changes in official teaching.[51] Lindbeck does not have a theory of the development of doctrine. However, his "taxonomy of doctrines" suggests that one can make more sense of changes in doctrine if one takes a basically *contextual* rather than a *developmental* approach. Lindbeck, like Congar (as cited in chapter 3), finds that some rules (although not their formulations) are essential and permanent, some conditional; some of the conditional rules are reversible, some irreversible.[52] A conditional, irreversible doctrine (for Catholicism) might well be the doctrine of the Immaculate Conception. A necessary condition for the doctrine to be able to make its point is the presumption of the theory of the seminal transmission of original sin; if that theory of sin is not presumed, then the doctrine is pointless, but if the theory is presumed the doctrine is necessary. A conditional, reversible doctrine might be the doctrine of the human right to have freedom of

---

[50] Some Roman Catholics on the "far right" consider the Second Vatican Council and especially the celebration of the Mass in the vernacular to be a fracture in tradition so deep that they find the official Church to be heretical and/or schismatic from the "true" Church. They are sympathetically portrayed by Michael Cuneo, *The Smoke of Satan: Conservative and Traditionalist Dissent in Contemporary American Catholicism* (New York: Oxford University Press, 1997); also see Mary Jo Weaver and R. Scott Appleby, eds., *Being Right: Conservative Catholics in America* (Bloomington, Ind.: Indiana University Press, 1995). If one were to consider magisterial doctrinal statements and ritual prescriptions as texts without contexts, and take verbal identity among them as the key for continuity in a tradition, then the position of these "far right" Catholics would not only be a tolerable option, but clearly the most appropriate one. Obviously, this book argues that verbal inerrancy cannot be a criterion of continuity, so the traditionalists' premise is not tenable.

[51] Dionne, *The Papacy and the Church*, esp. 366.

[52] See note 35 above. I have adapted Lindbeck's approach for use here. It is not clear in Lindbeck's account either how one could discern whether a given novel formulation of a rule presumed permanent and irreversible is a legitimate formula or how one could establish which rules were permanent, essential, and irreversible, and which conditioned. Such practical issues are obviously important, but cannot be resolved by a taxonomy.

conscience. If the doctrine is or is seen as *necessarily* constituted in a regime that is anti-ecclesiastical, such as that of the French Revolution in its later phases, it could and should be repudiated by the Church as part of an attack on the Church. However, if the doctrine of the human right to freedom of conscience is *not* conditioned by such an alliance with an anti-ecclesiastical government, then it can and perhaps should be supported by the Church. Neither Dionne nor Lindbeck offer *normative theories of the development of doctrine*, but *descriptive accounts of doctrinal change* that note that doctrinal formulas shift as contexts—the contexts of practices and environments—change. And if conditions change unpredictably, then changes in doctrines may be unpredictable as well. Theories of development attempt to find continuity where it cannot be found.

If the argument here is accurate, then it is not possible to devise a theory to predict future changes in *tradita* or to legitimate past changes. As MacIntyre notes, the past constrains the future changes in a tradition, but within those constraints, a tradition may develop in unpredictable ways. Continuity in tradition cannot be guaranteed by rules, by rules for following rules, or by anything other than carrying on and carrying out the tradition itself by participating in the practice or practices that constitute the tradition. Such traditions may change radically. In fact, in order to live in a tradition as contexts change, we must constantly invent the tradition. If conditions and contexts change and practices are not adapted and changes in them "invented," the tradition withers away.

What makes two different patterns of practice, then, the same tradition is nothing less than the recognition that they are "the same," that "we" share the same practice with "them." Shared practices must be shaped and reshaped as they are undertaken and inculturated in different contexts. We recognize that continuity not *in theory* but in the practice of engaging in an act of judgment or appraisal that recognizes continuity. These judgments vary, but they are always in the present. That they must be responsible to the past is a truism. How they are responsible and whether they are responsible are present judgments. When communities fissure, parts of the community have "come to judgment" that, however similar, the practices that constitute their traditions are not the same, that one way is faithful to the past and the other not, and that the communities cannot live in and live out the same practice together.

In *Faust*, Goethe wrote, "In the beginning was the deed." I would add, "And also in the end."

Conclusion

We now have seen that a tradition can be understood as a practice or set of practices; that as a practice, a tradition shapes persons and that persons reshape traditions in the way they individually and together receive and enact them; and that traditions can be recognized and understood by learning their "grammatical rules" and how to apply them. We have explored both the constancy and the variety of traditions. We have found that there is not (and I would argue there cannot be) a theoretical criterion of constancy in a tradition.

Yet even if we can't, at this point, discern rules for evaluating traditions, we have argued that the rules of a tradition are like its grammar. However malleable and however variously applied, a set of rules can provide at least "negative" principles for recognizing a tradition. If a set of practices does not include rules formulated in a manner we can recognize as expressions of rules that Lindbeck's three basic principles also express, we cannot recognize it as a Christian practice. The question is whether this understanding of rules and practices has enabled us to have an understanding of tradition that avoids the problems which have plagued other accounts, especially the problems captured in the "made" *vs.* "found" accounts of tradition.

I believe that it has. To show this, in chapter 5 I will argue that we can write a grammar for the Catholic Intellectual Tradition. What we should discover are not doctrines but general principles that give some shape to this tradition; that is, principles without which the tradition would not be recognizable, but also which can include a variety of different kinds of intellectual activity as fitting in this tradition. At the end of that chapter, I will show how this approach overcomes the problems other approaches have in understanding traditions.

FIVE

Toward a Grammar of the Catholic Intellectual Tradition

As noted in the introduction, it is far beyond the limits of the present text to develop a "grammar" of Catholicism. The Catholic tradition is so complex, so well studied, and so dynamic that even a tentative attempt to describe that grammar would be a major book in itself, a systematic theology. In order to bring out an instance of this sort of approach, this chapter attempts to sketch the grammar of an aspect of the Catholic tradition, the Catholic Intellectual Tradition (CIT).

With the advent of Catholic studies programs at Catholic universities in the United States,[1] many institutions have begun exploring the CIT. Yet, when asked what this tradition is, people have difficulty articulating its content or even its significant practitioners. When considering specific authors, there are some who are clearly in the tradition: Teresa of Avila, J. F. Powers, Pierre Teilhard de Chardin, Willa Cather, G. K. Chesterton, John Ford. There are some who are clearly *not* in the tradition, but whose works influence many thoughtful Catholics: Fyodor Dostoevsky, Chaim Potok, Elie Wiesel, Robert Bellah. There are some who are in the tradition or out, depending how you define it: Graham Greene, Ignazio Silone, Martin Luther, James Joyce, Martin Scorsese, Mary Daly, Andres Serrano, Seamus Heaney. Yet what this CIT is—what they are a part of or on the edge of—remains a problem. This chapter sketches a way to begin solving that problem.

The purpose of this chapter, then, is threefold. First, I want to illustrate the understanding of tradition given in chapters 2 through 4.

---

[1] See, for instance, Thomas Landy, "Catholic Studies at Catholic Colleges and Universities," *America* 178 (3 January 1998): 12ff.

Second, I intend to show that there is reason to believe that there is a polyvalent, polysemous nexus of vision, attitude, and style variously enacted by exemplars and more pedestrian folk that we can legitimately call the Catholic Intellectual Tradition. And third, I want to begin writing a grammar of that tradition.[2]

This tradition is also not dependent on or a creation of the institutional structures of the Catholic Church. Obviously, institutional authorities in the Church attempt to set the rules for Catholic religious practices, including the practice of believing; an account of the issue of authority in the Catholic tradition will be sketched in chapter 6. However, just as the Catholic Intellectual Tradition is broader than theology, it is also broader than the religious practices of Catholics. While Catholic intellectuals often do attend to and participate in Catholic religious practices, the institutional authorities do not and cannot "set" the rules for the CIT, a tradition that is not institutionally bound.[3] Catholic intellectuals may be affected by the institutional authorities, but the CIT is not constituted by those authorities.

This chapter discusses five rules of grammar of the CIT. These are *not* principles that I am prescribing for Catholic intellectuals to follow. These are not principles I *want* to be the grammar of the CIT. Rather, the claim made here is descriptive. These are the rules that emerge from the practices undertaken which constitute the tradition. These rules are the "grammar" of this tradition. I do not claim that these rules are exhaustive or sufficient. Nor is their formulation unchangeable. Like Lindbeck's three basic principles, they are "negative rules": If an intellectual's work could not be construed as fitting

---

[2] This chapter does not equate the Catholic Intellectual Tradition with Catholic theology or philosophy. Obviously, Catholic theology and philosophy are parts of this tradition but not the whole. Of course, sometimes Catholic theologians or philosophers may dominate this tradition, but that is not, so far as I can see, a necessary fact about the tradition. Moreover, I would argue both that Catholic theology requires many other rules for its explication and that insofar as a theology fails to follow these rules, it will not be Catholic, even if its formulas seem orthodox. The Catholic Intellectual Tradition is, then, much broader than theology, especially theological orthodoxy.

[3] An institutionally bound practice is a practice that one can undertake only if one has a requisite status or role in an institution. An institutionally free practice is a practice that one can undertake without regard to one's institutional status or role. Only a judge, for instance, can give a ruling during a trial, although anyone might give an opinion. The significance of institutionally bound and institutionally free practices is explored in the context of speech act theory in Terrence W. Tilley, *The Evils of Theodicy* (Washington, D.C.: Georgetown University Press, 1991), 33-34.

with (at least) most of them, it would be hard to understand that work as an exercise in this tradition. It might be possible to add other rules and to come up with a set of "constitutive rules" for the tradition. It is likely that these rules are not unconditional, but they may be permanent. It seems certain to me that the formulations of the principles offered here are neither unconditional nor permanent nor unsurpassable. But the claim here is that these are a set of central and distinctive rules that can be used to define—to allow us to see the extent and limits of, at least roughly—this tradition.

Moreover, I do *not* think that any of these principles is exclusive to the CIT. I am certainly aware of other traditions that exhibit one or more of them or formulations much like them. There are works and authors that are clearly items of the CIT, but which may exhibit only one or two of these principles; and there are works that may exhibit one or two of these principles but obviously are not a part of the Catholic universe. All this means is that there are marginal and borderline cases, as there are in any attempt to characterize something as big as this tradition. What would cause this thesis to need revision would be to find a body of work—or perhaps even one or two very significant works—that are clearly not part of the universe of the CIT, but clearly fit all, or even most, of these rules; or to find a body of work that clearly is part of the universe of the CIT, but that fails to be an expression of the rules I formulate. If these states of affairs should obtain, then, at minimum, a rethinking of these principles would be needed.

An Analogical Imagination

The first rule is that the CIT is characterized by a predominance of an analogical imagination over a digital or dialectical imagination.[4] The analogical imagination can be seen as active in a specific

---

[4] The concept of the analogical imagination was worked out by Catholic theologian David Tracy, *The Analogical Imagination: Christian Theology and the Culture of Pluralism* (New York: Crossroad, 1981), esp. 405-45. Tracy is, of course, concerned primarily with modern and contemporary theology, but his concept is certainly extendable to premodern eras.

Although characterizing a Protestant imagination as *dialectical* and a Catholic imagination as *analogical* cannot be hard and fast, and is certainly unfair to some Protestants and some Catholics and some who have feet in each camp, that the "both/and" response to polarities is generally Catholic and the "either/or" response generally Protestant seems a fair, if rough, characterization of the basic imagination of two different sets of practices shaping differing intellectual traditions.

intellectual practice; it seeks to discern the similarities or the unities that exist among events, entities, or states of affairs that seem different.[5] Since the publication of Catholic theologian David Tracy's book *The Analogical Imagination*, much methodological reflection in theology has illustrated the distinction of the Catholic analogical imagination from the Protestant dialectical—or to use an electronic metaphor, digital—imagination.[6] Tracy's work has been influential not only in theology but also in cultural studies.[7]

The most general characteristic of the analogical imagination is to treat dilemmas or paired types as "both/and" in contrast to the "either/or" of the digital imagination. The story told by historian Alec Vidler about the great Catholic philosopher Baron Friedrich von Hügel, related in chapter 2, can be seen as illustrating the analogical imagination in practice. As noted there, von Hügel worked with two very different "explanations" of religion, one "naturalistic" (based in historical criticism) and the other "supernaturalistic." To hold these two explanations together requires precisely an analogical imagination. The analogical imagination can see them both as true, each within its

---

[5] See Tracy, *The Analogical Imagination*, 408, where he discusses the search for an adequate conceptual language for contemporary theology and characterizes the language of analogy in the following: "Two major conceptual languages have served as the principal candidates for this task in theology: analogical and dialectical languages. Both language traditions, I believe, continue to function as the classic *theological* languages par excellence. The first of these languages, analogy, is a language of ordered relationships articulating similarity-in-difference." Sociologist Andrew M. Greeley has argued that his research not only supports David Tracy's understanding of the analogical imagination as distinctively Catholic theology, but also finds it a constituent of the popular Catholic imagination (see "Theology and Sociology: On Validating David Tracy [The Analogical Imagination]," *Journal of the American Academy of Religion* 59 [Winter 1991]: 643-52; and *The Catholic Myth: The Behavior and Beliefs of American Catholics* [New York: Scribner's, 1990], chap. 3.

[6] Prime among these areas has been the methodological disputes over the use of and interpretation of narrative in theology. Tracy is the prime representative of a "Chicago" school, while George Lindbeck exemplifies the opposing "Yale" school. Although it unfortunately neglects those of us who take a different approach (Catholics like John Shea in *Stories of God: An Unauthorized Biography* [Chicago: Thomas More, 1978] and other writings, and "Berkleyans" like James Wm. McClendon Jr. [a Southern Baptist], Michael Goldberg [a conservative Jew], and the present writer [a Roman Catholic]), a clear analysis of these differences is in Gary Comstock, "Two Types of Narrative Theology," *Journal of the American Academy of Religion* 55/4 (Winter 1987): 687-717.

[7] Lee Lourdeaux, *Italian and Irish Filmmakers in America: Ford, Capra, Coppola, and Scorsese* (Philadelphia: Temple University Press, 1990) suggests the presence of an analogical imagination in these otherwise diverse producer-directors.

own realm, and can see the connections between them; despite the crucial differences von Hügel could easily argue that one is concerned with the realm of "primary causality" (that God brings beings into being and sustains them) and the other with the realm of "secondary causality" (that these beings are independent and creative actors whose being is sustained by God, but whose actions are authentically their own). Naturalistic explanations hold within the realm of secondary causality, but not primary causality, a point that Vidler misses by presuming the explanatory value of a "public/private" split in religiosity (I will later discuss the problems with this split). The ability to hold the "both/and" view is characteristic of the analogical imagination.

Literary critic John B. Breslin, S.J., describes the analogical imagination in his introduction to a startling anthology of contemporary "Catholic" short fiction:

> The Romantic belief in salvation through art has long since proved bankrupt. . . . The burden of having to reinvent Sacred Writ in each generation has done writers no favor; it has only created a proliferating tribe of ever more ingenious scribes to interpret, or deconstruct, their texts. But a literal-minded Christian attitude that denies any connection between literature and the Bible, between metaphor and revelation has been no more helpful. It distorts the very message it claims to serve by severing the divine and the human, pretending that God's Word could come to us in any other way than human words.
>
> Insofar as it is possible to speak of a "Catholic sensibility," it means an attitude that avoids both of these extremes, instinctively preferring the conjunctive "and" to the disjunctive "or."[8]

Many evangelical Protestants, for instance, are quite sure they know that there is a radical difference between the saved and the lost: Either one accepts Jesus Christ as one's personal Lord and Savior or one does not. A typical Catholic, when confronted by an earnest evangelical asking her whether she accepts Jesus as her personal Lord and

---

[8] John B. Breslin, S.J., "Introduction," *The Substance of Things Hoped For: Fiction and Faith: Outstanding Modern Short Stories*, ed. John B. Breslin (New York: Doubleday, 1987), xiii.

Savior may well react with puzzlement. She may not be so sure the issue is quite so clear cut.

Catholicism has typically attempted "both/and" solutions to problems. The Catholic imagination "baptizes" pagan practices, like the Christmas tree; uses pagan feasts, like "stealing" the date of the birth of Jesus from Mithraism; seeks not so much to confront people being evangelized with the gospel as to inculturate the gospel, as shown by missionaries and Church leaders from Jean de Brébeuf in the sixteenth century, to Matteo Ricci in China in the seventeenth century, to contemporary debates over integrating various African motifs into Christianity. The "Catholic error" is to form a syncretic religion in which "too much" of the non-Christian is incorporated and tends to dominate; the dialectical error is to sunder what might be joined analogically.

A second feature of the analogical imagination is that Catholics live in a sacramental universe. Gerard Manley Hopkins's brilliant poem "God's Grandeur" expresses this as well as anything: "The earth is charged with the grandeur of God; it will flame out." The sacramental universe is not necessarily a magical one or an enchanted one—although those are certainly at least analogues of the sacramental universe. It is expressed in the awe and wonder in the first paragraphs of Stuart Dybek's haunting story, "Hot Ice":

> The saint, a virgin, was incorrupted. She had been frozen in a block of ice many years ago.
>
> Her father had found her half-naked body floating face down among water lilies, her blond hair fanning at the marshy edge of the overgrown duck pond people still referred to as the Douglas Park Lagoon.
>
> That's how Eddie Kapusta heard it.[9]

Dybek's story details an earthy religion, with beliefs in miracles and in a saint who had drowned defending her honor "helping" people who prayed to her after her death. Her body came to rest in a freezer chest in a dying ice house on the south side of Chicago. Knowing it sacrilegious to allow a "saint" to be lost when the ice house was to be demolished the next day, two young street-wise punks, Eddie and his friend Manny, "rescue" her:

> "It feels like we're kidnaping somebody," Eddie whispered.
> "Just think of it as ice."

---

[9] Stuart Dybek, "Hot Ice," in Breslin, *The Substance of Things Hoped For*, 85.

"I can't."

"We can't just leave her here, Edwardo."

"We'll think of something."[10]

Eddie *can't* just think of "it" as ice or as a dead body. She is both of those—and a saint, too. To his thoroughly analogical imagination, her body is the ultimate sacramental, a complete "first-class relic."

Catholic interest in items of material religion, holy water, holy oil, relics, holy cards, rosaries, and indulgences, and even a frozen dead saint (to name but a few), may be seen as magical, but are also sacramental, occasions on which divine grace and presence can be effectively present in humanly crafted things. These items are not just water, but water that cures; not just olive oil, but oil that heals; not just body parts of a dead person, but relics of a saint who was close to God and is close to the devout. Material religion even in its roughest forms can be an expression of this sacramental imagination.[11]

This sacramental imagination can be distorted and debased. Eddie and Manny's religion is not only sacramental but superstitious magic. Relics can become charms, holy water a panacea, and indulgences commodities to be sold. Not only does the Church need always to be reformed, but so does the imagination. The analogical imagination must pray, "Lead us not into temptation, to superstition and syncretism."

But there is an even worse debasement, exemplified in Don De-Lillo's surreal National Book Award winning novel *White Noise*.[12] The protagonists of DeLillo's novel are a blended family. The narrator, Jack Gladney, is an academic; he invented "Hitler studies." "When I

---

[10] Ibid., 111.

[11] Colleen McDannell, *Material Christianity: Religion and Popular Culture in America* (New Haven, Conn.: Yale University Press, 1995) offers a powerful understanding of the importance of religious artifacts for popular religious devotion. McDannell does not, however, clearly distinguish in chapter 5 ("Lourdes Water and American Catholicism") a significant difference in Catholics' use of material items from most of those used by Protestants. Both traditions had substantial visual and architectural representations of the holy, but Protestants did not eat the Body of Christ, drink Lourdes water, or rub holy oils on their bodies as Catholics did. Catholics' nostrums tended to be "sacred," while those of the rest of the culture did not. McDannell does suggest that the "consumption of Lourdes water also resonated with another nineteenth-century health practice: homeopathy" (147) but doesn't utilize Tracy's understanding of the analogical imagination as a way of understanding how Catholics tended to handle their material religious culture items differently from Protestants.

[12] Don DeLillo, *White Noise* (New York: Viking Penguin, 1985). I owe this reference to Julie Byrne of Duke University. My interpretation of the significance of the story is at odds with her more benign interpretation.

suggested to the chancellor that we might build a whole department around Hitler's life and work, he was quick to see the possibilities. It was an immediate and electrifying success. The chancellor went on to serve as adviser to Nixon, Ford and Carter before his death on a ski lift in Austria."[13] He and his wife Babette have children from previous marriages. Babette reads aloud from tabloids to the blind in a shelter in which they have fled from a toxic cloud. No one reacts to the incredible absurdities ("diet sunglasses") they hear. Jack retreats:

> I went back to our area. I wanted to be near the children, watch them sleep. Watching children sleep makes me feel devout, part of a spiritual system. It is the closest I can come to God. If there is a secular equivalent of standing in a great spired cathedral with marble pillars and streams of mystical light slanting through two-tier Gothic windows, it would be watching children in their little bedrooms fast asleep. Girls especially.[14]

Bedrooms are cathedrals. Fast food provides eucharistic solace. The shopping mall is the church they flock to in times of anxiety. Shopping is worship. You can buy whatever you need at the mall and market. Yet the end of the novel shows that this is not a sacramental world but a flat one. Jack is in a supermarket check-out line:

> The terminals are equipped with holographic scanners, which decode the binary secret of every item, infallibly. This is the language of waves and radiation, or how the dead speak to the living. And this is where we wait together, regardless of age, our carts stocked with brightly colored goods. A slow-moving line, satisfying, giving us time to glance at the tabloids in the racks. Everything we need that is not food or love is here in the tabloid racks. The tales of the supernatural and extraterrestrial. The miracle vitamins, the cures for cancer, the remedies for obesity. The cults of the famous and the dead.[15]

The slow-moving line is not the line for communion—or is it? The tabloids are not stained-glass windows telling stories—or are they? The cults are not of the saints—or does the Gladneys' world have

---

[13] Ibid., 4.
[14] Ibid., 147.
[15] Ibid., 326.

tabloid saints? DeLillo portrays a world in which the "spiritual system" is the flattest, most disconnected parody of a sacramental universe. When the analogical imagination is lost, the absurd becomes the Mysterious and commodities are transubstantiated into sacraments by the spiritually starved in a world empty of the presence of God.

The world is, in the Catholic sacramental imagination, not necessarily a beautiful place. Nonetheless, Catholic romantics imagine that the beauty of creation remains despite the defilement of sin. It is at root a graced universe, though it may be a harsh and dreadful grace (to paraphrase Dorothy Day), a grace seen in and through the Crucifixion. One example of this acceptance of creation as still good, even while groaning in travail, is the Catholic theological conviction that accepts that the strength of the mind remains despite the incompetence of the will naturally to will the good; we may know what is good, but cannot do it without grace. Catholics can imagine that the goodness of creation displays God's glory even though we know that the universe is fifteen or more billion years old and recognize that Genesis 1 is a post-Exilic Jewish myth countering the Babylonian Enuma Elish and does not record the creation of the world in 4004 B.C.E. The analogical imagination finds no war between religion and science, just some difficulties to be overcome to accept both religion and science.[16] Even Marian apparitions, which occur in specific times and places, not in some generally diffuse way, are expressions of the sacramental universe. Mary does not appear either here or there, but both here and there and seemingly everywhere, but not to everyone! For the analogical imagination, sacramental grace—like Mary—can pop up almost anywhere.

Nor is the world of the sacramental imagination always brightly illumined by a divine radiance. As Stephen Schloesser put it, in the "century of the Great War, the Great Leap Forward, the Stalinist famines, the Holocaust and Hiroshima . . . a sacramentalism which does not somehow take the 'really, really dark' as its fundamental starting point will not be genuinely Catholic."[17] Even a sacramental universe

---

[16] Admittedly, some U.S. Catholics have been influenced by Protestant fundamentalists' views of scriptural inerrancy over the last few decades. This would not apply to them. But the traditional Catholic understandings of scripture do not accept the sort of literal interpretation that would exclude the necessity of recognizing the multiple senses of scripture, from the literal to the mystagogical.

[17] Stephen Schloesser, "When You Read Catholic Writers Everything Is Really, Really Dark': Twentieth Century Sacramental Modernism," unpublished paper prepared for the Roman Catholic Studies Group of the American Academy of Religion (22 November 1999), 6. The title is taken from a comment of Annie Dillard.

is not transparently bright. The analogical imagination is always in danger of construing the world optimistically, of papering over the tragic dimensions. In the era of "man-made mass death," to ignore the culture of evil is naive, at best. Yet evil is not all there is. "If the death-world were the only world, the resulting monolith would spell the end of all life."[18] The sacramental imagination cannot deny the power of evil, but it also must recognize that the world in which evil exists is nonetheless God's creation.

A third aspect of the analogical imagination is the incarnation. Protestant thinkers like Kierkegaard have highlighted the radical paradox of the incarnation: the Infinite become finite. Protestant logicians like Thomas V. Morris have written densely packed philosophical arguments to show that the incarnation is not a logical impossibility—it took Morris over two hundred pages to make his admittedly defensive argument. In the end he sought only to show that some arguments allegedly proving that the classic doctrine of the two natures is incoherent are refutable, and so "there seems to be no obstacle in principle to the acceptability of the widespread Christian assumption that it is possible that it is rational to believe Jesus to be God Incarnate."[19] That Kierkegaard and Morris are concerned about the incarnation should not be surprising. But the shape of their concern is profoundly un-Catholic (that is *not* a criticism, but simply a description). For better or worse (and it may well be worse—all Christians owe debts of thanks to digital thinkers like Kierkegaard and Morris) Catholics take the incarnation for granted. They don't tend to respond with Kierkegaardian angst or a Morrisian exposition of logical possibilities. It infects their image of the Church—the Mystical Body of Christ is a Catholic metaphor. It shapes their fictions—François Mauriac's presumption of the humility of God in the birth of Jesus in his short story "A Christmas Tale" exemplifies this.[20] It forms their theologies, both academic and popular: the (limited) Puritan tendency to minimize Christmas and the focus of much Protestant theology on the doctrine of the atonement and on the importance of the cross over the incarnation and the harsh smell of the stable where Jesus was born exemplify this.

---

[18] Edith Wyschogrod, *Spirit in Ashes: Hegel, Heidegger and Man-Made Mass Death* (New Haven, Conn.: Yale University Press, 1985), 25.

[19] T. V. Morris, *The Logic of God Incarnate* (Ithaca, N.Y.: Cornell University Press, 1986), 204.

[20] F. Mauriac, "A Christmas Tale," in Breslin, *Substance of Things Hoped For,* esp. 20-21, 27.

This is not to deny the importance of the cross or of the doctrine of the atonement or the need for redemption. The sacramental universe can be "really, really dark." Soteriology is at least necessarily a part, and arguably even the basis, of Christology for the analogical imagination. But redemption of humanity is not the *sole* reason Christ came into the world. And theories of the atonement are not a staple of contemporary Catholic theology, however important the cross is for Catholic theologians. Contemporary U.S. Catholic theologian John Shea put it this way: Christ "came primarily because he wanted to, not because we needed him. This is the reason of a friend whose presence brings dignity and worth. An old catechism holds that our reason for existing is to enjoy God forever. The incarnation is the declaration that God has the same idea."[21] The analogical imagination understands that the incarnation occurs because God wanted to be part of our shared narrative, but also because we humans needed divine presence to heal our fracturedness. As any theologian would, Shea also finds that the "cross is the grounding of the Christian community, its symbol of realism, and its ongoing principle of critique."[22] Yet Shea also says:

> The Cross is God loving us from the inside. God has accepted those aspects of our lives we ourselves have disowned and denied. We fight the awareness of our guilt, proving ourselves innocent at all costs. We fear suffering and death so fiercely that it dominates our imaginations and dictates to us the shape of our days. If Creation is God's presence to our beauty, the Cross is God's presence to our pain and twistedness.[23]

---

[21] Shea, *Stories of God*, 128. North American Hispanic/Latino theologians' concept of *mestizaje* is a very rich practical theological appropriation of an incarnational imagination. Their distinguishing foci are practical religion and negotiation of difference in realms in which divergent cultures and religious expressions meet (see especially Roberto Goizueta, *Caminemos con Jesús: Toward a Hispanic/Latino Theology of Accompaniment* [Maryknoll, N.Y.: Orbis Books, 1995] on *mestizaje* as "empathetic fusion" [119-22]; María Pilar Aquino, "Theological Method in U.S. Latino/a Theology: Toward an Intercultural Theology for the Third Millennium," *From the Heart of Our People: Latino/a Explorations in Catholic Systematic Theology*, ed. Orlando O. Espín and Miguel H. Díaz [Maryknoll, N.Y.: Orbis Books, 1999] on *mestizaje* as "intercultural discourse" [35-37]; and the literature they cite.

[22] Shea, *Stories of God*, 158.

[23] Ibid., 152.

In this Shea links both incarnation and "at-one-ment" in a way in which the sacramental presence of the divine in the human is redemptive. Our pain and twistedness may be dark, but that darkness does not swallow up the divine light.

As an imperative to express this rule, we can formulate it this way: In a universe sacramentally graced by the incarnation, seek "both/and" before "either/or."

A Universal Hope

The second principle of the Catholic Intellectual Tradition is that there is hope for everyone and everything. There is nothing that cannot be or could not have been redeemed. Whatever else one wants to say about much of Flannery O'Connor's fiction, short stories like "Revelation" and "The Lame Shall Enter First" presume that everything is redeemable. In the former, that is just what Mrs. Turpin is forced to learn. In the latter, as in Tobias Wolff's poignant short story "The Liar," and many devotional family romances of the earlier part of this century, what could have been redeemed is lost not by tragic flaw or inevitability but by self-deception, a wicked choice, or a foolish rebellion. It is not that people are predestined for eternal damnation or even that they are eternally damned. What is "lost" is always tinged with the lost hope for what might have been, had things gone otherwise.

For hope to be possible, the conditions for despair must exist. For hope to be possible, certainty must be impossible; these are incompatible epistemic attitudes. One cannot hope to be true what one is certain is true; one cannot be certain to be true what one hopes to be true. An important factor that differentiates this form of hope for redemption from an optimistic attitude is that the latter need not recognize the "darkness" in and of the world. If everything is redeemable, everything is in a condition to need redemption—and redemption cannot be certain. I have argued elsewhere that one doesn't even have to believe in God to pray to God. Hope that God exists is enough.[24] And in a world wherein darkness threatens to overcome the light, hope for the redemption of all is sufficient.

To clarify this principle of redeemability, it can be contrasted first with the Calvinian doctrine of double divine predestination. Few contemporary Protestants, of course, accept predestination by God

---

[24] Terrence W. Tilley, "'Lord I Believe: Help My Unbelief': Prayer without Belief," *Modern Theology* 7/3 (April 1991): 239-47.

of some people to hell and some to heaven; nonetheless, it is a doctrine that cannot be found in the Catholic tradition. Where it is even approached, as in the development of Jansenism in Port Royal in the seventeenth century, it is condemned. Indeed, few Catholics, and even some professional theologians, truly understand how the doctrine of predestination is, in a Calvinist universe, an awe-inspiring necessary implication of the doctrine of the sovereignty of God, a doctrine Catholics also accept but do not see as entailing predestination.

The hopeful principle of the redeemability of everything can also be contrasted with the optimistic doctrine of universal salvation, adopted by people as diverse as liberal Protestant theologian John Hick and, apparently, neo-orthodox theologian Karl Barth.[25] Catholics do not tend to believe that all things must turn out for the good. Voltaire parodied a version of this view in *Candide*, a piece intended at least in part to show the problems with Leibniz's claim that this is the best of all possible worlds. The Catholic Intellectual Tradition has a tendency to hope, but not to optimism. Karl Rahner expressed it well in an interview late in his life:

> "An orthodox theologian," Rahner says dryly, "is forbidden to teach that everybody will be saved. But we are allowed to *hope* that all will be saved. If I hope to be saved, it is necessary to hope that for all men as well. If you have reason to love another, you can hope that all will be saved."[26]

Whatever optimism the Catholic tradition has is a hope, not a fact, not a certainty. In my judgment, however, this is about as far as the Catholic tradition can go and remain Catholic. Certainty is excluded. Commonly, this hope is tempered by a sadness over what has been lost or may have been lost. One resigns oneself and the "lost" to a God whose will and mercy is beyond comprehension and thus beyond certainty.[27]

---

[25] See John Hick, *Death and Eternal Life* (New York: Harper & Row, 1980 <1976>), 242-61, esp. 259; and the enigmatic comments of Karl Barth, *The Humanity of God* (Richmond, Va.: John Knox Press, 1960), 61-62.

[26] Eugene Kennedy, "Quiet Mover of the Catholic Church," *New York Times Magazine* (23 September 1979): 66-67. Also see Hans Urs von Balthasar, *Dare We Hope "That All Men Be Saved"? with a Short Discourse on Hell,* trans. David Kipp and Lothar Krauth (San Francisco: Ignatius Press, 1988), which makes a similar point.

[27] Inevitably, this raises the issue of salvation in other faith traditions. For a review of recent Catholic theological approaches to this issue, see Terrence W. Tilley, "A Recent Vatican Document on 'Christianity and the World Religions,'" *Theological Studies* 60/3 (June 1999): 318-37.

To give an imperative for this principle, we can say, "Hope that all can be redeemed and treat everything as intrinsically redeemable, but only saints are surely redeemed."

An Inclusive Community: "Here Comes Everybody"

The third grammatical rule of the Catholic Intellectual Tradition is that it is for everybody. The Catholic imagination cannot see the Church as a sect for the saved but must envision it (however paradoxically) as a holy body of sinners.[28] The introduction of multiple possibilities for confession in the Middle Ages, rather than confession as a once-in-a-lifetime sacrament, indicates that everyone, even the greatest sinner, can find a home here.

The confessional has occupied a central place in Catholic fiction and autobiography. Heinrich Böll's "Candles for the Madonna," for instance, is narrated from a participant's perspective. The narrator, a failing manufacturer of candles, is jealous that two young lovers, after a night together, could *realize* their sinfulness, *confess* their sins, *repent,* and *be absolved*, while he could not. The narrator, oppressed by sin more vague, can confess his sins, but only when he leaves his candles for the Madonna can he be free of sin.[29] The story makes no sense save for the practice of confession. And the confessional, finally, is for everybody. Both the flagrantly sinful lovers and the bland old businessman who never does much of anything sinful can find grace there.

Richard Gilman was a convert to Catholicism from Judaism—for six years, anyway. His poignant, if narcissistic, autobiography is devoted almost exclusively to the period of his conversion and struggle to stay in the Church he finally left. The Yale professor and self-confessed promiscuous lover records his last confession and his aridity of soul at length. We pick up the story as this final confession, in a little church in Paris, comes to an end:

---

[28] That this creates theological problems is obvious. For an exploration of the problems of sinning members and the holiness of the Church in two twentieth-century theologians, see Dennis Doyle, "Journet, Congar and the Roots of Communion Ecclesiology," *Theological Studies* 58/3 (September 1997): 461-79. What neither denies is the holiness of the Church or the sinfulness of its members; but how this paradox is understood created and creates great rifts in Catholic ecclesiology.

[29] Heinrich Böll, "Candles for the Madonna," in Breslin, *Substance of Things Hoped For*, 197-207.

> At the end, I asked him how I could go on practicing the
> Faith in my present state of only partial and increasingly
> reluctant belief, adding that I foresaw a time when a sense
> of insincerity would keep me from doing it altogether. "And
> what if you do not *practice* it?" he asked me. "What if you do
> not go to Confession and Communion and all the rest? Do
> you think you will not still be a Catholic, do you think God
> will throw you away?"[30]

God does not throw Gilman away, however much he wants to be left
alone. He relates a later incident:

> A woman dear to me told me recently that she thought that
> divinity pulled the soul, the immortal part, out of the self,
> the way sexual joy did. I knew what she meant, but then I
> threw against her—a born Catholic, a woman with "sins" of
> lust in her dossier—the fact of the Church, its formal pro-
> scriptions; how, I asked her, could she go on feeling herself
> Catholic while *disobeying*. I live, she said, I'm a sinner, the
> Church is for sinners, I won't give it up, it doesn't know
> everything and it's not synonymous with God. I belong to
> it, and so do you, if your hurt and pride could let you see.[31]

But his pride gets in the way of seeing that he fits in the Church. In
railing against the God who brought him into the Church and then
left him feeling high and dry, he writes, "No, you offered me Grace,
how can I get round it? And I spurned it, how can I get round that?"[32]
Of course, he can't get round either of these. But God has not, as his
final confessor told him, thrown him away. The Church is for everybody—that's why there is a sacrament of reconciliation. However
oppressive the confessional has been felt by some—and there is no
denying that it has often been a disciplinary regime that enforced
humiliation or what French theorist Julia Kristeva calls abjection—
the wisdom of Gilman's confessor and his woman friend remains in-
tact: You can always return, if you will, as you are, for this is a Church
for all sinners, and a Church in which all really are sinners, none
(yet) saints.

---

[30] Richard Gilman, *Faith Sex Mystery: A Memoir* (New York: Simon and
Schuster, 1986), 219.

[31] Ibid., 250.

[32] Ibid., 251.

And in confession, a flawed or imperfect act of contrition is good enough for absolution, for reconciliation with God, and for finding the joy in releasing one's burdens. Some have found this sort of religion superstitious—and to fall into superstition is a very dangerous temptation for sacramental believers. But the tradition is inclusive, not exclusive. And this inclusivity is reflected in the sacramental practice, which includes the imperfect. It is not superstitious, a point I have made elsewhere.[33]

The Roman Catholic Baltimore Catechism #3 teaches, for instance, that there are two kinds of contrition that one could have for one's sins, although the words of the prayer known as the Act of Contrition are the same.[34] One, an imperfect act of contrition, "is that by which we hate what offends God, because by [sin] we lose heaven and deserve hell; or because sin is so hateful in itself." Generally, Catholics understood imperfect contrition as motivated by a fear of hell as punishment for one's sins. To say the prayer with imperfect contrition "is sufficient for a worthy confession, but we should endeavor to have perfect contrition." The other, a perfect act of contrition, "is that which fills us with sorrow and hatred for sin, because it offends God, who is infinitely good in Himself and worthy of all love." To say the Act of Contrition with perfect contrition "will obtain pardon for mortal sin without the Sacrament of Penance when we cannot go to confession, but with the perfect contrition we must have the intention of going to confession as soon as possible, if we again have the opportunity." Generally, Catholics understood perfect contrition as motivated by love of God. Imperfect contrition is just that: imperfect. It is not superstitious, or "too little" to earn forgiveness. It signifies that this is a

---

[33] See Terrence W. Tilley, "The Philosophy of Religion and the Concept of Religion: D. Z. Phillips on Religion and Superstition," *Journal of the American Academy of Religion* 68/2 (June 2000): 345-56.

[34] The catechisms were accessed at < http://www.catholic.net/RCC/Cat-echism >. The relevant lesson from which quotations in the text are taken is Lesson 18 of Baltimore Catechism #3; Baltimore Catechism #2 does not have the teaching about perfect contrition being sufficient for forgiveness of sins without confession and does not call imperfect contrition *attrition*. The contemporary *Catechism of the Catholic Church* is essentially similar, but it makes explicit that fear can be the motive of imperfect contrition: "The contrition called 'imperfect' (or 'attrition') is also a gift of God, a prompting of the Holy Spirit. It is born of the consideration of sin's ugliness or the fear of eternal damnation and the other penalties threatening the sinner (contrition of fear). Such a stirring of conscience can initiate an interior process which, under the prompting of grace, will be brought to completion by sacramental absolution. By itself however, imperfect contrition cannot obtain the forgiveness of grave sins, but it disposes one to obtain forgiveness in the sacrament of Penance" (1453).

sacrament for everybody, even those who cannot work up a "proper" motive for repentance. In its literature, in its theology, in its concern for missions to those who have not heard of Christ, a mark of the Catholic Intellectual Tradition is that it is not elitist or exclusivist.[35] The mark of the Church relevant here was articulated best by James Joyce and was, I believe, one of the reasons he lapsed: "Here Comes Everybody."

"Everybody" includes the saints. The CIT is shaped by the notion of the church as the communion of the saints—and saints and sinners past and present are often vitally near. But some of the oddest people are saints. For instance, it may be a happy accident, but in fact the Buddha was named a Catholic saint. He is inscribed in the Roman martyrology. He was canonized as St. Josaphat because the Enlightened One's asceticism and devotion were so impressive. "Josaphat" is a rendering of *boddhisatva,* a Buddha in practice in the Mahayana traditions. What is more remarkable is that the story of his life and canonization were told without shame in the classic book *Butler's Lives of the Saints*, where his feast day is given as November 27.[36] That a short version of the history rather than an unexamined tradition was canonized in the devotional literature suggests that "everybody" in "here comes everybody" is really rather inclusive.

For an imperative for our third principle, may I suggest, "Here comes Everybody! Don't keep them out if they want in—or even if they don't."

A Public Church

The fourth principle of the Catholic Intellectual Tradition is an acceptance of the worldliness of the Church in particular and of religion more generally. What this means is that the CIT doesn't take the Church or religion to be constituted only in the private sphere and to

---

[35] For an important work contrasting U.S. Catholic Intellectual Traditions and their practical inclusivity in contrast with the Euro-American image of the intellectual as the brave and creative (male) academic, see Sandra Yocum Mize, "On the Back Roads: Searching for American Catholic Intellectual Traditions," in *American Catholic Traditions: Resources for Renewal*, ed. Sandra Yocum Mize and William Portier, The Forty-second Annual Volume of the College Theology Society (Maryknoll, N.Y.: Orbis Books, 1997), esp. 5-10. The inclusivity is not Mize's point, but the research in her essay and the works she cites can support that claim.

[36] However, recent "updated" versions of Butler's *Lives* note that this saint is "legendary" and acknowledge that he is the Buddha.

be strangers in the public square. The Church is an agent in the secular culture. Religion is a public practice. It cannot finally be privatized, even if it can be separated from the State.

I find this point very hard to document but ubiquitously exemplified. Chapter 1 noted that the author of *Byzantium* presumed a private/public split in the description of the provenance of the diptych ivory icon. She presumed that the split characteristic of the modern world applied as well in the ancient world. That presumption affects her very perception of the provenance of the piece. I do not, and so I question her judgment and her analysis. In chapter 2 I also reinterpreted Alec Vidler's analysis of Baron Friedrich von Hügel's holding of two different explanations simultaneously. Vidler also presumes the characteristic split of the modern world and not only ignores evidence of public modernism, which he knows well, but also fails to interpret the Baron's practice in a manner consistent with his own philosophy. The differences in interpretation seem trivial, perhaps, but indicate a major difference in vision.

Many people have criticized "the Church"—meaning by this, usually, the hierarchy of the Church or the teaching authority of the Church—for meddling in areas it should keep out of. How dare the Church censor books by placing them on the Index? How dare the Church work for decency in the movies and promulgate not only an evaluation of films from a moral and religious point of view—as well as from an aesthetic one—but even have people pledge to follow the Church's ratings of the movies, a practice followed in some places in U.S. Catholicism in the twentieth century? How can the Church seek public money for private education? What do the bishops know about war and peace? What do the bishops know about economics or the death penalty? How could Pope Alexander VI divide the Western Hemisphere between the Spanish and the Portuguese? Why didn't Mother Teresa of Calcutta tend to her poor and shut up about abortion as a social plague? All of these questions, and a host of others, presume that the Church is not a public and worldly institution but should confine itself, if it is to be a *church*, to the private and the spiritual.

If the Church is a sacrament, it cannot but be worldly. Voluntary associations can be private, but a sacrament cannot. It is this radically different presumption about the nature of the Church that underlies this difference, especially in the United States and in the nations that have religious diversity within their borders. Maureen A. Tilley tells the story of how shocked her mostly Protestant students at the Florida State University were when they discover that the Orthodox Church can be a department of the State in some southern and eastern European countries. They have great difficulty understanding how a church (like almost everything) cannot be strictly private in a communal society. Although there are significant differences between Orthodox and Catholic ecclesiologies, both practical and theoretical, neither tradition presumes that the Church is private or voluntary.

Jonathan Z. Smith, in *Drudgery Divine*, shows how the questions Protestants and Catholics ask structure both their research strategies and their results when they study the world of Christian antiquity.[37] Smith writes:

> One cannot adopt as a historical model, that which was initially developed as a historical myth: the notion of a pristine church during the first five centuries; followed by a period of ten centuries consisting of an initial stage of "mixture," then total (Roman) "idolatry"; and, finally, a new age *in qua Deus Ecclesiam iterum ad fontes revocavit*—and argue simply that the later Roman church syncretized as a result of its expansion or its entanglement with the ("pagan") empire, while the early church remained, miraculously, both more insulated and free—or some other version of the regnant Protestant mythos, even if it be expressed in the more "scientific" dualisms of "charisma and routinization" or "sect and church."[38]

The "Protestant" presumption of a Church unsullied by its contact with the politics, economics, and religions of Late Antiquity must be contrasted with a Catholic presumption of the publicness of the

---

[37] Jonathan Z. Smith, *Drudgery Divine: On the Comparison of Early Christianities and the Religions of Late Antiquity* (Chicago: University of Chicago Press, 1990), 34: "If there is one story-line that runs through the various figures and stratagems briefly passed in review, it is that this has been by no means an innocent endeavour. The pursuit of the origins of the question of Christian origins takes us back, persistently, to the same point: *Protestant anti-Catholic apologetics*. It will be my contention, in the subsequent chapters, that this is by no means a merely antiquarian concern. The same presuppositions, the same rhetorical tactics, indeed, in the main, the very same data exhibited in these early efforts underlie much of our present-day research, with one important alteration, that the characteristics attributed to 'Popery' by the Reformation and post-Reformation controversialists, have been transferred, wholesale, to the religions of Late Antiquity. How else can one explain, for example, the fact that the most frequent distinction drawn in modern scholarship between the early Christian 'sacraments' (especially the Pauline) and those of the 'mystery cults' is that the latter exhibit a notion of ritual as *ex opere operato*?"

[38] Ibid., 114-15.

Church. The CIT should not—even though some Catholic scholars may[39]—separate the Church from the cultural influences on it or the culture from the churchly influences on it.

There is a corollary principle that follows from this principle of publicness and the principle of sacramentality. In their academic work Catholic intellectuals *tend* to be not only non-reductionist, but anti-reductionist.[40] This corollary helps us to understand, in part, why the Catholic Intellectual Tradition, and Catholic theology in particular, has clashed with certain aspects of the Enlightenment tradition. Of course, part of the story is the unhappy political reversals the Church felt in the nineteenth century. But even before these events, Catholic thinkers saw much Enlightenment thought as reductionist, as not merely explaining but rather explaining away religious faith and practice. When some Catholic theologians, especially those labeled modernists a century ago, made substantial use of critical history and philosophy, their theology was condemned, even though most of their claims regarding scripture, history, and human experience could be acceptable today.

Reductionism seems to have an elective affinity with the digital imagination: *either* religious beliefs are Freudian illusions or Marxian opiates and the proper way to understand them is to reduce them to their real material causes and to recognize the material interests that provoke them; *or* they are immune from analysis, because they are uniquely religious. This is especially clear in the work of J. Samuel Preus.

In *Explaining Religion* Preus has invented a tradition of scholarship that legitimates contemporary reductionistic approaches to religion. The basic tenet of this research paradigm "treats religion as an element of culture. . . . I shall refer to [this paradigm] as 'naturalistic' rather than using the more common but misleading label, 'reductionistic.'"[41] The central claim of the reductionistic or naturalistic approach is that once we find the natural (social, psychological, economic, political, and so forth) origins of religion, we have explained religion. Nothing more need be said. The anti-reductionist thesis is this: Religion is,

---

[39] Ibid., 114 n.52, cites Hugo Rahner, *Greek Myths and Christian Mystery* (London: 1963; reprinted, New York: 1971), 24-27, as an example of this.

[40] Margaret Steinfels helped me to see the importance of this principle; it may be independent, but I think it is an implied, rather than an independent, principle. Of course, all these principles may be co-implicated.

[41] I have argued this in "Polemics and Politics in Explaining Religion," *The Journal of Religion* 71/2 (April 1991): 242-54, a review essay centered on J. Samuel Preus, *Explaining Religion: Criticism and Theory from Bodin to Freud* (New Haven, Conn.: Yale University Press, 1987), quotation on ix.

like literature, poetry, philosophy, sport, or war, a web of complex practices that cannot be explained without remainder by being reduced to simpler terms (like social psychological or economic ones) or private concerns. Anti-reductionism implies that one ought to be skeptical about the possibility that an explanatory reduction can completely account for these complex human practices. Surely physiological, psychological, social, economic, and political factors contribute to each of these practices. But to say, for instance, that the power or meaning or even success of Verdi's opera *Nabucco* is due *without remainder* to non-musical factors, such as political and economic factors of the Italian *Risorgimento*, combined with the maturing of *bel canto* singing techniques, is to reduce the marvelous to the obscure.[42] Surely it is logically possible that a complete knowledge of all the relevant "natural" factors would provide an exhaustive explanation of the power of an opera, or even of the rises and declines of opera as an art form. But it is also possible that such an explanation of an indefinite number of factors would take more time and space than are available for us to give it. Moreover, religious factors may be no less "natural" than musical ones, a possibility methodologically excluded by the reductionists, but one available if one's research methodology includes the possibility or the presumption that the universe is sacramental, as Friedrich von Hügel's methodology evidently did. Reductionists and anti-reductionists can agree that religions are sets of complex practices. They methodologically disagree about the possibility of our needing reference to anything beyond the "natural" (using "natural" in a scientific and social-scientific sense exclusively) to explain or understand religious phenomena.

A reductionist like Preus can note that religion is no more autonomous when it comes to analysis than literature or political theory. But the anti-reductionist notes also that it is not less autonomous than the other realms. We are skeptical about reducing music or literature to physiological and political causes. Analogously, we should be skeptical about reducing religion to psychological and sociological causes. Nonetheless, as all these practices involve human beings, we cannot but expect to find social and psychological dimensions of them that are surely amenable to explanation.

---

[42] The spontaneous singing by crowds of mourners of the chorus "*Va pensiero,*" Verdi's setting of Ps. 137 in this opera, during his public funeral may be relevant here; even if Catholics (as most Italians were in 1901) realized that Verdi was not given a Church funeral, the use of his music, composed for an operatic spectacle, as at least a quasi-religious commemoration suggests that the co-implication of secular and sacred was and is alive and well at least in some parts of the world.

The anti-reductionist would also argue that it is the reductionist who bears the burden of proof in these matters. Certainly it is plausible to explain some religious believing as a result of nonreligious factors. For instance, William James's description and evaluation of the religious life of Louis Gonzaga might easily be taken as an account that could bear that burden of proof by explaining St. Louis's strange behavior as a sad but understandable response to the psychological and social pressures of his Church and home.[43] But if one attempts to reduce Søren Kierkegaard's or Dag Hammarskjöld's faith to social and psychological causes, the anti-reductionist may suggest that the reductionist has missed the point and may well be methodologically self-blinded to the possibility that we live in a sacramental universe. In my judgment, reductionism is plausible on a retail basis in certain cases, but not as a wholesale explanation of religion. This rejection is, I believe, a principle, albeit a derivative one of the Catholic Intellectual Tradition that does not presume religion is unworldly or private.

Certainly Dorothy Day would agree with our principle of religious worldliness. And surely she is a part of the CIT. Her autobiography, *The Long Loneliness*, is de facto an argument for belief in God "after Marx."[44] It made a very public argument for a religious faith. It took on the main opponent in the war for the souls of the working class— Marxism and its reductionist account of religion. Another part of her very practical argument was her witness—her public works in publishing the *Catholic Worker* and her practice of founding houses of hospitality. Day's concept of religion is clearly a public one.

Religion is not a private affair but a vastly public one for the CIT; the Church is not merely spiritual but also worldly; and attempts to reduce religion to nonreligious factors lead to misunderstanding religion. For the CIT, our imperative could be, Don't presume religion is a private, nonsocial, nonpolitical practice, and yet don't presume that religion can be reduced to social, political, economic, or psychological causes.

A Gracious God

The fifth principle of the CIT is that a gracious God is the source and creator of all good things. This principle may simply be a corollary of the first and second principles. Nonetheless, it can be spelled out independently. The Council of Florence (1483-45) put it this way:

---

[43] William James, *The Varieties of Religious Experience* (New York: Collier-Macmillan, 1961), 278-81.

[44] This point is made in Sandra Yocum Mize, "Dorothy Day's *Apologia* for Faith after Marx, *Horizons* 22/2 (Fall 1995): 198-213.

> The holy Roman Church firmly believes, professes and preaches that the one true God, Father, Son, and Holy Spirit, is the creator of all things visible and invisible. When God willed, in his goodness he created all creatures both spiritual and corporeal. These creatures are good because they were made by the Supreme Good, but they are changeable because they were made from nothing. The Church asserts that there is no such thing as a nature of evil, because every nature insofar as it is a nature is good.[45]

The CIT finds that whatever in the world is evil is not evil as a result of God's determination but as a result of the mutability of finite things. Nothing is evil by nature; neither does sin occur by God's determination.

In a less theological vein, sociologist Andrew Greeley affirms not only the goodness of what comes from God, but that the Catholic imagination has God as closer to God's people than does the Protestant imagination. He has concluded from his survey data that "Catholics are more likely than Protestants to see God as an intimate other—lover, friend, spouse, and mother—and the world and human nature as basically good. . . . Catholics are more likely [than Protestants] to emphasize the presence of God."[46] These differences lead Greeley to a rather strong conclusion:

> Moreover—and this is the critical point—when one takes into account images of God, . . . the differences either disappear or are substantially reduced. The difference in religious behavior that exists between Catholics and Protestants can be accounted for by their different images of God, who is perceived as distant (father, judge, king, master) in the Protestant imagination and present in the Catholic imagination (mother, lover, friend, and spouse).[47]

---

[45] *The Church Teaches: Documents of the Church in English Translation*, ed. John F. Clarkson, S.J., et al. (St. Louis: B. Herder Book Company, 1955), 44.

[46] Greeley, *The Catholic Myth*, 55.

[47] Ibid. Greeley also correlates this view of God with sexual satisfaction within marriage (190ff.). He finds that 98 percent of Catholics believe in God (146). One wonders what happened to the other 2 percent or why they would identify themselves as Catholic. Obviously, feminine images for God are *not* exclusively Catholic. Both Protestant and Catholic feminist theologians have utilized this broader range of images and models for God (see, for example, Sallie McFague, *Models of God: Theology for an Ecological, Nuclear Age* [Philadelphia: Fortress Press, 1987]; and Elizabeth A. Johnson, *She Who Is: The Mystery of God in Feminist Theological Discourse* [New York: Crossroad, 1992]).

While the difference in images can hardly be absolute, the Catholic imagination does not see God as "wholly other" or disengaged from the world. Yet Catholics highlight the gift of the graciously present God creating what is good.

Perhaps the significance of this can be drawn out by a contrast with a Calvinist Intellectual Tradition.[48] The Calvinian Synod of Dort (1618) generally affirmed that humans could not resist divine grace; that Christ died only for the elect; that once a person received saving grace, it could not be lost; and that God had eternally issued a decree of divine predestination.[49] "On every level, the Synod of Dort defined the will of God in such a way that what God wills and what happens were virtually identified. Only the Fall was excluded from the divine decree; all else, including the results of the Fall for human life and destiny, was the outworking of God's immutable will."[50] Each person's bondage to sin, as a result of Adam's fall, is God's immutable will. The Synod of Dort did not solve the vexing problem of God's mercy— evidently some received it and others did not. But later Calvinists explained the mercy and justice of God by the doctrine of double divine predestination, as Dillenberger and Welch note:

> The later Calvinists' way of meeting the problem was through the concept of double divine predestination, under- stood as a declaration that God sends some to eternal life and some to eternal damnation. God is a God of glory, maj- esty, and power. Heideggerus [1696], for example, declared

---

[48] I do not mean to reduce a rich tradition of Calvinian intellectualism to a theological doctrine or set of doctrines. Clearly there is a Calvinist tradition that in this country is instantiated in the Puritans, especially America's greatest theo- logian, Jonathan Edwards; continued after a period in eclipse with the domi- nance of Scottish common sense philosophy in the nineteenth century; and continues today in the work of philosophers of religion working in the Calvinist tradition. Walter Ong, S.J., attributes much of early modern and modern thought (of which the rigorous Calvinist tradition portrayed here would be, perhaps, an extreme example) to the rise of Ramist logic (see *The Encyclopedia of Philosophy*, ed. Paul Edwards [New York: Macmillan, 1967], s.v. "Ramus, Peter"). If that the- sis is correct, it could go far to make much of "modern thought" potentially part of an intellectual tradition significantly different from the Catholic Intellectual Tradition. It is, however, beyond the scope of our work here to explore that thesis.

[49] See John Dillenberger and Claude Welch, *Protestant Christianity: Interpreted through Its Development*, 2d ed. (New York: Macmillan, 1988), 83-86. Dillenberger and Welch note that the Synod accepted single divine predestination, but that the tradition quickly accepted double divine predestination as normative.

[50] Ibid., 86.

that God's glory is expressed more clearly through the concept of damnation than through the idea of a just death for
human sins. "The supreme end is the glory of God repro-
bating;—the subordinate end is the righteous condemnation of the reprobated to death for their sins."[51]

This Calvinist view of the God of distant majesty is one in which
everything that happens comes from God; everything is God's will,
including that which damns a person to hell. In the contrasting Catholic view, God is not so distant and there is much greater hesitation
about affirming that ultimate evils come from God. The notion that
God could condemn people to hell who chose to sin by God's own will
for them—a strong view of predestination—is absent from Catholic
doctrine and foreign to the Catholic Intellectual Tradition.

Similarly, Calvinists affirmed the Spirit as God inspiring the scripture, but "inspiration no longer included participation in the reception and experience of revelation. The *book as such was revelation*
because it was written under the Spirit. . . . So the Bible was the Word
of God from cover to cover."[52] For the Calvinists, God's work in writing the Bible was direct; for the Catholics, not only did God use human authors, but the Bible as a book was only part of the story. As the
Council of Trent (1545-63) put it:

> The council is aware that this [all saving] truth and [moral]
> teaching that the apostles received from Christ himself or
> that were handed on, as it were from hand to hand, from
> the apostles under the inspiration of the Holy Spirit, and so
> have come down to us. . . . The Council . . . also accepts
> and venerates traditions concerned with faith and morals
> as having been received orally from Christ or inspired by
> the Holy Spirit and continuously preserved in the Catholic
> Church.[53]

The notion of transmission and of the existence of nontextual records
of revelation is noted by the Council of Trent. In 1943 Pope Pius XII
in his encyclical letter *Divino Afflante Spiritu* even acknowledged that
the Bible could contain "certain hyperbolic ways of speaking," "ap-

---

[51] Ibid., citing Heinrich Heppe, *Reformed Dogmatics: Set Out and Illustrated from the Sources* (London: Allen and Unwin, 1950 < 1861 >), 187.
[52] Ibid., 87, emphasis added.
[53] Clarkson, *The Church Teaches*, 45.

proximations," "paradoxes," and other modes of human expression. Interpretation requires recognition of the "form of expression or the literary type used by the sacred writer," a point which concedes that the book *qua* book is not inspired in a literalist sense.[54] Although some Catholics were and are literalist in their interpretation and the teaching authority in the Church has a tendency to affirm a literal scriptural inerrancy upon occasion, the Catholic Intellectual Tradition has traditionally been more nuanced in its reading of scripture than the Calvinian traditions.

Perhaps the difference can be caught in two different mottos: For the Catholic Intellectual Tradition we are to deal with whatever God has given us *Ad majorem dei gloriam*. This motto of the Jesuits suggests that we create and re-create out of the good God has given us for the greater glory of God. If some Protestants like Bach take this as a motto and some nonaffiliated folk like Wittgenstein would have liked to have taken it for a motto, then perhaps they fit to a certain extent in the Catholic Intellectual Tradition. Perhaps this is a sign that non-verbal arts—painting, non-sacred music, architecture—are more at home in the Catholic Intellectual Tradition than in a non-sacramental tradition. While not at all excluding the attitude expressed in a similar Calvinian motto, *Soli deo gratia, soli deo gloria*, the Catholic tradition finally recognizes that even if all good comes from God, for some goods it is not God *alone* who has produced them, but humans cooperating with God. And if there is evil in the world, including the ultimate evil of the loss of eternal life, it is not attributable to God.

An important corollary of this principle, especially in connection with the principle of the analogical imagination, is what Catholics often call the compatibility of faith and reason. As Pope John Paul II put it at the beginning of his encyclical *Fides et Ratio* (1998), "Faith and reason are like two wings on which the human spirit rises to the contemplation of truth; and God has placed in the human heart a desire to know the truth—in a word, to know himself—so that by knowing and loving God, men and women may also come to the fullness of truth about themselves."[55] In present terms, what people come to understand by the practices of knowing and living in and out of faith cannot ultimately be incompatible. In a sacramental universe "truth is one," and God has given humanity the ability to come to

---

[54] Ibid., 64-65.

[55] John Paul II, *Fides et Ratio*, no. 1, accessed at < http://www.vatican.va/ holy_father/john_paul_ii/encyclicals/index.htm >.

understand that truth. The pursuit of truth for the sake of truth, for instance, is thus one characteristic of universities and specifically of Catholic universities. The Catholic Intellectual Tradition has confidence in faith and reason.

The analogical imagination would have us understand that humans come to what is true by both faith and reason. Perhaps the deepest heritage in Catholic theology, the ongoing practice of reason informing faith informing reason, can be seen as begun by the apologists, carried on by Augustine and Boethius at the end of antiquity, renewed by Anselm, Abelard, Albert, and Aquinas (among many others) in the Middle Ages, and continued today. Indeed, "the compatibility of faith and reason" might well be a central rule for the practice of specifically Catholic theology.

So, an imperative for this section is easy: Treat all good things as a gift from a gracious God, with a corollary that all good things can be enhanced or defiled by human action.

Why Not Other Principles?

Why stop at five principles; aren't there others? There may be. However, introducing more principles than these would, I believe, exclude parts of the tradition that belong as recognizable components of the CIT. Some would bring forward a concern with philosophy, especially Thomistic philosophy. While many Catholic writers, especially those of the Catholic Renaissance in this country, are familiar with and utilize Thomistic principles, Thomism as a Catholic philosophical system is a tradition invented in the nineteenth century.[56] Catholic writers, artists, and theologians working before the Thomistic revival or after its current waning are not necessarily influenced deeply by Thomism. Some would bring forward a concern with the pope. While the papacy is a major component of the Catholic imagination today, it has not always been so. Greeley captures this in his typical puckish manner:

> "I can do without the pope," a middle-aged layman told me.
> "I'm a historian and I know that at most times in history
> Catholics had only the vaguest notion of who was bishop of

---

[56] For a history of this invention, see John Inglis, *Spheres of Philosophical Inquiry and the Historiography of Medieval Philosophy* (Leiden, Boston, Köln: Brill, 1998).

Rome. But I can't do without God or the Church or the
Blessed Mother."

Thus speaks the self-conscious Catholic imagination.[57]

The inclusion of a rule about the papacy would also serve to exclude
so much literature that strikes me as obviously Catholic—for example,
most of the stories in the Breslin collection and the work of Graham
Greene—that it is inappropriate. Some would bring forward a respect
for clergy and religious. But this would evidently exclude not only
the parodies that help define some aspects of the tradition, but also
the definite anticlerical strand within Catholicism. Some would suggest that the Catholic intellectual is an organic intellectual, emerging
from and working for (if not always in) the community that produced
him or her. But some Catholic intellectuals have been an elite and
not much connected with the community. Again, this is too restric-
tive a principle. Some might claim that concern with or devotion to
the Blessed Virgin Mary is essential. While such devotion may be, as
Greeley suggests in many of his writings, characteristic of recent and
contemporary Catholic devotional sensibilities, and thus a practice at
least currently central for the Catholic tradition, Marian images are
not de rigueur in Catholics' intellectual practices.

So far, then, these five principles form the grammar of the CIT in
the sense that a person, practice, or artifact that does not fit with
them or most of them is not part of the CIT or questionably part of
the CIT. While there may well be other principles, these rules—which
can and will be applied in unexpected and controversial ways as the
practice is inculturated in new cultural contexts—seem sufficient to
delineate the CIT.

Conclusion

The argument of this chapter makes it clear that traditions are
constructed. In the final part of chapter 4 and this chapter, one could
say that living traditions are invented and reinvented. Human beings
engage in practices that constitute traditions; as contexts vary, those
practices change, sometimes radically and sometimes deliberately.
The grammar of the tradition, we could say, is both made (by the
participants' practices) and found (as intellectuals reflectively analyze those practices and write rules for the practice like the present

---

[57] Greeley, *The Catholic Myth*, 147.

one). The grammar of the practices shapes us in the ways in which we live and move and have our being; but we also reshape and reinvent the grammar of the practices, and perhaps even change the rules as practices are translated into new places. In this sense traditions are necessarily both made and found. Hence we have resolved the issue that began this study. The historians' points made most clearly in chapter 1 seem vindicated: Traditions are made and invented. Yet they are also found, as they are practices handed on and their grammar is *there* to be uncovered, even though that uncovering itself is a construction. The rules are *there* to be followed, although the practice of following the rule may come to modifying the rule, even to inventing new rules (whether the community that constitutes and is constituted by that tradition will accept the new rule in a reconstituted or invented practice is a contingent matter; sometimes it will, sometimes it will not). We promised to avoid the dichotomy with which we began. By considering traditions to be enduring practices that carry *tradita* rather than focusing on the *tradita* as the bearers of the traditions, we have shown how to do so.

Let's recap the argument. Traditions are neither made nor found in any simple sense but rather are ongoing practices constantly being invented. Practices generate rules for continuing the practice. To recognize a tradition we can uncover its "rules," noting that rules and their application are both relatively constant in their continuity and often rather fluid in the inventive application of them. Whether inventive applications or changes in rules are to be constituted continuations or degradations of a tradition are contingent matters. I have proposed these five rules as those which structure a multivalent tradition that we call the Catholic Intellectual Tradition. This leaves us with one major unredeemed promise: How can the practical theory of tradition be connected with the traditional concerns found in a theology of tradition? Having shown that the division between those who claim traditions are made, made up, deliberately invented, and those who claim the traditions are simply found or given is not a tenable dichotomy, but that all traditions are invented and reinvented in various ways in response to contextual internal and external challenges, chapter 6 can move toward a theology of tradition.

Toward a Practical Theology of Tradition

Even if the practical account of tradition explored in chapters 2 through 4 and exemplified in chapter 5 satisfactorily describes how traditions are both made and found, substantial questions remain about the adequacy of this account for Catholic theology.

What have we claimed? We have claimed that traditions are invented and reinvented. They cannot be reduced to *tradita* (what is transmitted). They are enacted and transmitted in particular practices. We have claimed that neither the rules nor the beliefs essential to tradition are independent of the varying practices. We cannot say that practices are not local expressions of some ideal *Tradition* that exists in some Platonic realm beyond the horizons of our practices, which we can try to mimic; but from what practice-independent viewpoint could we make any substantial claim about such a *Tradition-in-itself?* We cannot say that our traditions get "closer to" *Tradition* as our traditions develop, a claim so haughty that it must be inconsistent with the humility of Christianity.

We have argued that practices are self-involving and self-creating. We become what we practice—whether physicians, bootleggers, Confucians, or Catholics. Practices shape communal and individual identity. We have suggested that some practices, especially those that constitute religious traditions in a religiously plural society, are fragile; they can be lost in the twinkling of an eye. A tradition can be lost should a generation fail to pass on the practices to its successors. We have shown that practices are malleable; a practice that remains so rigid as to be uninfluenced by the other practices that constitute a culture becomes a museum piece. To parody Newman: In heaven it may be otherwise, but for practices here below, to live is to change.

If these positions are correct, if traditions just are invented, constructed practices, then how can this approach to tradition connect to the theological issues to which tradition is traditionally related?

Many of the main conversation partners of *Inventing Catholic Tradition*, such as George Lindbeck, Robert Schreiter, and Alasdair MacIntyre, do not connect their theories to the loci of the theology of tradition. They finally have little to say about truth, revelation, and authority.

First, some accounts of religious traditions seem to have no significant place for truth. Lindbeck's construal of doctrines as rules, for example, is developed in opposition to the traditional claim that doctrines are simply propositions people believe. He calls this a "cognitive-propositional" approach, characteristic of premodern religion. Modernity has rendered such an approach problematic, at best. Lindbeck also seeks to avoid what he calls "experiential-expressivism." This he finds to be the dominant, modern, "liberal" position, which construes religious doctrines as linguistic expressions of a prelinguistic religious experience (often an experience of the Sacred or Holy alleged to be the same experience underlying many religious traditions). Such expressions may be true to experience, but they cannot be true or false as propositions can be.[1] They cannot "say of what is, that it is so, or of what is not, that it is not."[2]

Lindbeck distinguishes sharply between ordinary statements that believers make (first-order utterances) and rules that doctrines express. Doctrinal (second-order) rules regulate believers' (first-order) statements. While Lindbeck's theory makes room for a certain form of truth claims in first-order utterances of religious belief, he finds that second-order doctrines cannot be true or false. Their function is not to represent what is true, but to regulate the practice of believing. Believers can make statements that can be "true" or "false." Rules may be wise or unwise, appropriate or inappropriate, insightfully expressed or obtuse, but because they are not propositional statements, they cannot be true and they cannot be false. Ordinary believers' statements of their beliefs are not doctrines, although they may be in line with or fail to be in line with doctrines; that is, ordinary,

---

[1] See George A. Lindbeck, *The Nature of Doctrine: Religion and Theology in a Postliberal Age* (Philadelphia: Westminster Press, 1984), esp. 16-17, 47.

[2] While many formulations of epistemological realism are possible, this elegant version is from Susan Haack, "Confessions of an Old-Fashioned Prig," *Manifesto of a Passionate Moderate: Unfashionable Essays* (Chicago: University of Chicago Press, 1998), 21.

first-order utterances may follow the doctrinal rules or fail to follow the doctrinal rules.[3]

Moreover, if a tradition is *invented*, as the present approach argues, how can an invention be *true*? Inventions are useful or frivolous, damaging or helpful, socially responsible or ecologically destructive, and so forth. They are not true or false. So, if a tradition is a practice or set of practices that, in some sense, is invented and must be reinvented to thrive, as chapter 4 argued, then the present contextual, practical theory of tradition seems to have even less a place for truth than a pure cultural-linguistic theory of doctrine like Lindbeck's. Where is a place for "truth" in this "practical" account of tradition?

Second, none of the conversation partners for this work have much to say about revelation. This is a huge problem considering the connection of scripture and tradition with revelation in Catholic theology, especially from the Council of Trent (1545-63) to the Second Vatican Council (1962-65) and beyond. Lindbeck's cultural-linguistic approach to understanding the status of doctrine and Schreiter's semiotic account of the development and structure of local theologies do not deal with the concept of revelation. Are doctrines, then, unconnected to revelation? How are practices connected with revelation? Where is revelation in a practical account of tradition?

Finally, the practices of institutional authority are absent from most theories that have influenced the present text. In fact, an understanding of the authority of office is so absent that I have claimed elsewhere that such theories simply are not adequate to account for the multifaceted reality that is an enduring faith tradition, an apostolic tradition.[4] It is a fact that the Congregation for the Doctrine of the

---

[3] Throughout *The Nature of Doctrine*, Lindbeck converses with the "revisionist" or "hybrid" positions of Catholic theologians Karl Rahner, Bernard Lonergan, and David Tracy. Each of them, Lindbeck claims, combines "cognitive-propositional" and "experiential-expressivist" components. Their evident advantage over Lindbeck's account, at least at first glance, is that they have a place for recognizing the truth (or falsity) of doctrine, whereas Lindbeck does not. The present constructivist account is yet another alternative to the "cultural-linguistic" and "hybrid" accounts.

[4] See Terrence W. Tilley, *The Wisdom of Religious Commitment* (Washington, D.C.: Georgetown University Press, 1995), chap. 2. This is *not* to say that a scholar like George Lindbeck is insensitive to such issues; institutional authority concerns are very important for generating the theory detailed in *The Nature of Doctrine*. However, the theory offered therein is so formal that the actual exercise of institutional authority fades from sight almost completely. John Thiel has argued persuasively that were Roman Catholics to adopt George Lindbeck's form of postliberal theology, this would make a postliberal Catholicism "quite akin to the theological positivism expected by Pius XII in his encyclical *Humani*

Faith (CDF) can strongly shape liturgical and doctrinal practice, as demonstrated in chapter 1. It is a fact that national and transnational bodies like the American Medical Association and the World Health Organization regulate medical practices, as shown in chapter 3. One may regret or rejoice that the CDF has so much power in the diverse, multicultural community composed of practicing Catholics; one may find the AMA standards or the WHO regulations helpful or impossible, given the diversity of medical practices. However, unless a theory can *recognize* this fact of institutional, official authority as significant for understanding a tradition, the theory is inadequate. Not all practices have strong visible authorities. Some do not have officially appointed or elected authorities. Yet religious traditions have some form of authority, however constituted. How can we account for this in a practical theory of religion?

The present chapter explores three concerns that are fundamental for a practical theology of tradition: truth, revelation, and authority. If there is no connection between the present account of tradition and these loci of theology, then this account, however useful it may be as a sociological or linguistic or philosophical theory of tradition, has little or nothing to contribute to a theology of tradition. It is beyond the scope of the present chapter to offer anything more than a sketch of responses to these concerns. The point is not to resolve these three issues but to indicate ways in which they can be resolved as issues in fundamental theology. If positions like those sketched here can be developed, then the constructivist account of traditions as practices developed here is a live option for Catholic theology.

As the question of truth is the broadest, the first section argues for an "appraisal" account of truth appropriate for a practical theory of tradition. In light of this account, the second section places revelation in the practice of discipleship. In doing so I agree with Avery Dulles's claim that the "special identification of revelation with Christ is almost a commonplace among modern theologians."[5] The third section addresses the issue of authority. In a formal sense, authority

---

Generis" (John Thiel, *Imagination and Authority: Theological Authorship in the Modern Tradition* [Minneapolis, Minn.: Fortress Press, 1991], 162). Although this is a devastating critique of the direct application of Lindbeck's formal work within a Roman Catholic context, I do not want to neglect or minimize the insights about theology Lindbeck has developed. His work can be mined for insights and adapted for use in Catholic theology (as the present book does), but it cannot be simply applied as a "method" for Catholic theology because of the status of institutional authorities within the Catholic tradition.

[5] Avery Dulles, S. J., *Models of Revelation*, 2d ed. (Maryknoll, N.Y.: Orbis Books, 1992), 155.

can be construed *essentially* as necessary for the endurance of a practice; materially, practices of authority emerge *contingently* as responsive to developments within and without the communities that carry the practice. The conclusion of the chapter reflects on the practice of Christian theology as a service to communities whose identity is the people of God, the body of Christ, the community of disciples.

Truth in a Practical Theology of Tradition

The purpose of this section is not to develop a full-fledged theory of knowledge or religious knowledge. Rather, it makes one crucial point: An epistemological constructivism is compatible with a metaphysical realism. The argument goes as follows. First, many postmodern epistemologists assume and sometimes argue that we construct what we know.[6] This thoroughly constructivist account of knowledge is a position that grows out of the focus on practices in the present work. Properly understood, I agree with it. Second, many postmodern thinkers assume that if we construct what we know, then we must be anti-realists. That is, the "objects" of our knowing, from stars to God to lead to maple trees, are fabrications or fictions. They claim that our knowing cannot or need not match or mirror or reflect reality, that is, be epistemologically "realistic." I disagree with this. Thus, my third point is to show that a "realistic" option is available even to a radically constructivist approach. Hence, a practical theology can show how a tradition can be both thoroughly constructed and epistemologically "realistic," and therefore can be true in a realist, not a fabricated or fictitious anti-realist sense.

It is a commonplace among social theorists and many philosophers that our truths are constructs. One argument for this commonplace might go something like this: Animals engage in communicative performances. The more both developed and social the species and the more developed the communicative performances in which its members engage, the more complex the forms of communication they have

---

[6] For a cogent and useful analysis of (and alternative to) contemporary patterns in epistemology, see Susan Haack, *Evidence and Inquiry: Towards Reconstruction in Epistemology* (Oxford: Basil Blackwell, 1993). Haack argues against what she calls a "vulgar" form of anti-realist pragmatism in favor of her own "foundherentist" approach. While my own view shares much with Haack's (despite her arbitrary rejection of religious experience in her understanding of what counts as evidence [214]), the argument here against anti-realism is rather different from hers.

invented. Some mammalian species, such as dolphins and whales, generate sounds to facilitate communication. More advanced mammals, such as humans, construct or invent the more complex communicative systems we call languages. These sign systems can be used for both simple and complex communicative performances. Some human cultures develop a written language to preserve the information in the oral communications. Of these, some cultures invent ways to mass produce that information from letterpress printing to electronic storage. Even if the potential for language use is somehow innate in some species, actual languages and their uses are constructs or inventions. Linguistic acts (whether verbal or graphic) are possible only because humans have developed (invented, constructed) complex semiotic systems. We make claims in linguistic acts. Whatever claims we make are constructs, as performing the acts of saying or writing those claims is possible only because a constructed semiotic system makes those acts possible. If all claims are constructed, and some of them are true, then all true claims are constructed.

Religious claims arise in practices that are also constructs, as shown in chapter 3. They are uttered in a language that is a human construct. Thus, religious claims are instances of constructed claims. How, then, can we call them true? How can one make sense of Nathan Mitchell's seemingly odd claim that "religion and ritual are precisely *products* of culture. . . . It is because of that, ritual can make claims to truth."[7] To answer these sorts of questions requires exploring religious epistemology. As I have elsewhere[8] discussed these issues at length, here I will only sketch a constructivist-realist position and show how it can be applied to understand the status of truth in a tradition construed as a practice or set of practices.

Over the past few decades, a philosophical tradition of anti-realism has developed.[9] Anti-realists are constructivists regarding the "source" of our language: We construct our language. Anti-realists see reality-

---

[7] Nathan D. Mitchell, *Liturgy and the Social Sciences* (Collegeville, Minn.: Liturgical Press, 1999), 92.

[8] See *The Wisdom of Religious Commitment*, 58-101, and, for an appraisal account of truth, there labeled an "assessment account" of religious stories, *Story Theology* (Collegeville, Minn.: Liturgical Press, 1991 <1985>), 182-214.

[9] One very influential version of anti-realism is found in Richard Rorty, *Philosophy and the Mirror of Nature* (Princeton, N.J.: Princeton University Press, 1979). The presentation of anti-realism here is a rough sketch of Rorty's position; other anti-realist positions can be found in the work of Jacques Derrida, Michel Foucault, and their followers. Rorty also suggests that much of American pragmatic philosophy, especially the work of John Dewey, is best understood as anti-realist.

independent-of-our-concepts-of-it (if there be such a thing) as irrelevant to the meanings of our concepts or the truth and falsity of our claims. Anti-realists have argued that the *criteria* for truth of claims, insofar as there is any such thing as truth, are to be found within a linguistic community and the language it uses. We can say a claim is true by its acceptance by members of that community who recognize that it "fits" within their use of language. Hence, their "anti-realism" consists in their finding "reality" irrelevant to meaning and truth.

For example, a claim an engineer makes is "true" just in case it is well formed in a language engineers use and is accepted by other engineers. There is no need for a "realistic" theory of truth that assumes a claim is true if the claim matches or mirrors or refers to what there is in the real world. Philosophers from Plato to the present have construed a foundational-realist theory of truth, in which our knowledge is grounded in the "fact" that our true claims mirror the-world-as-it-is-in-itself (realism) and the "fact" that the-way-the world-is-in-itself is just what makes our claims true (foundationalism); and they have been confused, the constructivist anti-realists claim. The actual way we warrant our claims is to have them accepted by other speakers when they accept the "facts" we construct.

How do these anti-realists warrant such a claim? An example shows one way of supporting their view. Consider someone making a claim, "That tree is a sugar maple." The criterion for "that tree is a sugar maple" being true is not the tree that the speaker refers to in uttering the sentence (as a realist might say), but whether one uses the term *sugar maple* in a way that passes muster with one's interlocutors who have decided to call *sugar maples* only a few species of the many maples that people tap for sap to boil into syrup and sugar.[10] Sugar maples do not exist in the real world somehow independent of our concept of them. Indeed, we literally cannot say what exists in the real world independent of our concepts. What could that be? How could we conceptualize and communicate what-there-is-independent-of-concepts without concepts of some sort, however vague? The "world beyond our concepts" is literally inconceivable, incommunicable, unthinkable. It is a myth to say that it is in any useful way "given"

---

[10] That coming to know something requires participating in a practice, technically, a doxastic (belief-forming) practice, is one of the strengths of recent work in epistemology that looks beyond the tradition of individualism in much modern epistemology (see above, chap. 2, footnote 27; and Tilley, *The Wisdom of Religious Commitment*, esp. 77-92, and the literature cited there).

independent of our concepts.[11] "It" or "they" may be in some sense "here" or "there," but even to say so little is to conceptualize the world. Since our concepts are constructed and their uses are given in a constructed linguistic system, reference-to-things-as-they-are-outside-our-concepts-of-them is useless as a foundation for or a criterion for truth. To think that rightness of reference to or correct mirroring of being makes a claim true is a philosophical delusion, some anti-realists suggest, that wants the comfort of "reality" being what we think it is (a delusion if there ever was one). And just as *sugar maple* is not a thing-in-the-world-independent-of-language but rather a concept that people can and do use for certain purposes, so *God* is not a thing-in-the-world-independent-of-language but rather a concept that people can use or avoid—and which anti-realists, following Freud and other masters of suspicion, tend to avoid as simply expressing a wish or delusion about the constitution of the world. *God,* like *sugar maple,* is a human construct, a fiction, or a fabrication; neither the reality nor unreality of *God* or certain trees gives these concepts meaning. Neither the reality or unreality of *God* or certain trees makes claims using these concepts true or false.

Such a bald sketch fails to convey the attraction of constructivist anti-realism. Nonetheless, many philosophers and some theologians have come to accept its basic outline and its "intra systematic," constructivist, non-referential, anti-realist view of truth.[12] They find such a position insightful. Early forms of it generated the discipline of the sociology of knowledge and the notion of the social construction of reality.[13] Constructivist anti-realists like Michel Foucault have explored the relationships between power and knowledge and accounted for the construction of what counts as knowledge, sometimes

---

[11] Wilfrid Sellars discusses "the myth of the given" in his classic article, "Empiricism and the Philosophy of Mind," in his *Science, Perception, and Reality* (New York: Humanities Press, 1963), 127-96.

[12] Paul Feyerabend and, at least in some of his work, Thomas S. Kuhn are philosophers who take positions like this. Literary critic Barbara Herrnstein Smith has proffered a spirited defense of an anti-realist position in *Contingencies of Value: Alternative Perspectives for Critical Theory* (Cambridge, Mass.: Harvard University Press, 1988). Christian theologian Gordon Kaufmann is a constructivist who sometimes seems to take an anti-realist position. Postmodern theologians like Thomas J. J. Altizer, Mark C. Taylor, and Edith Wyschogrod are also anti-realists of various stripes. That there are, at least to my knowledge, no Catholic theologians or philosophers firmly committed to an anti-realist position is, in my judgment, very significant.

[13] See Thomas Luckman and Peter Berger, *The Social Construction of Reality* (Garden City, N.Y.; Doubleday, 1966).

by powerful elites. Foucault and others have also shown how our linguistic patterns shape and reproduce social relationships. Constructivist analyses, such as those developed above regarding eucharistic theology, have explained the shifts in language and concepts over time, especially the fact that at least a few concepts are practically untranslatable from one cultural-linguistic system to another.

Yet does one have to pay the price of anti-realism to get the theoretical benefits and insights of cultural-linguistic constructivism? Must constructivists be anti-realists? My answer is no. Following the lead of American philosopher Wilfrid Sellars, I argue that one can (and should) separate constructivism from anti-realism.

Richard Rorty, in *Philosophy and the Mirror of Nature*, argued that Western philosophy, at least since Plato, has been afflicted with the wrong Idea: that our ideas, concepts and claims are true *because* they reflect the "real" world. His is a prime example of a constructivist, anti-realist epistemology. At a symposium devoted to a discussion of Rorty's manifesto, Sellars suggested, roughly, that Rorty—and by extension, constructivists in general—had not considered the possibility that the key realist concept of *accuracy of reference,* the "mirroring" relationship of realistic philosophy that Rorty had rejected, might not be a *criterion* for judging the truth of a claim but rather an *effect* of our getting our claims right.[14] Accuracy of reference may indeed be what *makes* the content of claims true, but that fact (if it is a fact) is not something that we can use to *judge* whether claims are true or not. This form of realism is *not* defeated by constructivist arguments, for it is not a form of foundationalist realism; it can be called a consequential realism.

An example will help make this important point clear. I may be able unerringly to pick out sugar maples from other trees in a grove. What makes my claim, "This is a sugar maple," reliable is the skill I have developed at identifying sugar maples. It is a skill in practical forestry that I have learned and apply in the practice of "sugaring." Exercising the skill of identifying sugar maples presumes that I can use concepts that we have constructed in the course of horticultural and scientific practices, for example, *sugar maple.* A practical account

---

[14] The symposium was part of the 1980 Annual Meeting of the Eastern Division of the American Philosophical Association, Boston, Mass., December 1980. The following material expands on points sketched in my essay "Practicing History, Practicing Theology," in *Theology and the New Histories,* ed. Gary Macy, The Forty-fourth Annual Volume of the College Theology Society (Maryknoll, N.Y.: Orbis Books, 1999), 14.

of how I acquire this ability to use a concept makes sense of this ability I have developed. A constructivist account of the concept will make sense of the concept.

However, assume you want to tap all the sugar maples in a grove for their sap. You ask me how many sugar maples are in the grove (so you can figure out how many taps to buy and how much tubing to get to collect the sap). I take the time to examine the grove and then reply, "There are 237 mature, tappable sugar maples in this grove." This claim is *reliable* just in case I have the skill of identifying sugar maples and I have exercised that skill, that is, engaged in the practice of identifying sugar maples, properly.[15] This claim is precisely *true* just in case that there are 237 mature, tappable trees we call sugar maples in the grove (but notice, this claim cannot be called "true of the world independent of the concept 'sugar maple,'" but "true of the world as conceptualized to include certain trees we call 'sugar maples'"). This claim is *acceptable* (as true) if those who can recognize tappable sugar maples agree on finding 237 sugar maples in the grove should they check that claim.

But notice that there are significant differences between a claim being reliably produced, being true, and being accepted as true. This is the key difference overlooked by those who infer anti-realism is a necessary implication of constructivism. Would you say the claim is false if someone else finds 239 mature sugar maples in the grove? Or

---

[15] This point harvests the claim of reliability theorists in epistemology, such as Alvin Plantinga. Roughly, these philosophers construe knowledge as warranted, true belief. They argue that if our appropriate faculties are working in an appropriate environment to generate a claim, this *warrants* the belief as *reliable* unless there are "defeater-arguments" lurking in the vicinity that would undermine or overwhelm our warrants. There is a wide variety of "defeater arguments." For example, someone might impugn my faculties ("He was drunk when he counted.") or show that I really am not well-versed in identifying maple trees, and so on. Obviously, each of these "defeaters" is context specific—and if I can find a "defeater defeater," I can, perhaps, warrant my claim despite the counterargument.

For a discussion of Plantinga's work, see Tilley, *The Wisdom of Religious Commitment*, 70-72, and the literature cited there. Plantinga's work is a form of "entitlement" epistemology: one is "entitled" to hold a belief just in case it is reliably formed in appropriate circumstances; but one's "entitlement" to a belief is sufficient to have that belief be acceptable in a community of inquirers, as the example in the text suggests. In Plantinga's theory, one property of a belief is that it is warranted (if it is) and another property is that it is true (if it is). In the present view, if a belief is warranted (reliably produced), that is at least a prima facie indicator that there is reason to appraise the belief as "true" in a community of inquirers.

235? Or 517? Clearly, if one of us finds 517 tappable sugar maples and the other finds 237, one of us (at least) is wildly unreliable. One of us doesn't know what he or she is doing. If two others check the grove, and they find 235 and 239 sugar maples to be tapped, that is good reason to think that the person who found 517 is unreliable, even if we cannot precisely identify what makes that person unreliable. That claim is not even "in the running" to be accepted as true (unless some wildly odd circumstances obtain, such as three of us conspiring to deceive the farmer; but we can leave these deviant cases aside here). But what of the persons who find 235 or 239? We come out close enough in our counts to suggest that we are reliable in our practice and have exercised it well. If the fact that there are XXX sugar maples in the grove makes one of these claims true, and the others false, how can we tell? We simply don't have access to "the facts" independent of our constructed concepts and practical investigations. *Facts independent of our concepts are not criteria for the reliability or acceptability of a claim.* This is the insight of constructivism. Mirroring states of affairs or things in the world does not constitute a claim's being true. This is the *false* implication many draw from constructivism that Sellars's remark has identified. There is no reason to think that mirroring what-there-is (including what we have constructed) cannot be a *result* of our claim being right; one could say, with appropriate qualifications, that such mirroring even *makes the claim true.* But "mirroring" is not a relation independent of our practices, nor is it a foundation for our practices, nor is it a criterion for truth. Thus, mirroring the world cannot provide a practice-independent criterion of a claim's being true. The error of much "realist" epistemology is to infer from the realist view that mirroring the world or part of it *makes* a claim true, that such mirroring can be used (1) to *show* whether a claim is true or false, or (2) to show whether a claim is *acceptable* as true in a community of inquirers.

The position adapted here is a "consequential realism." Being-realistically-true is neither a criterion for judging whether our claims are true nor a foundation for showing that our claims are true. Constructivists' analyses and arguments have undermined such foundational realism, but a "consequential realism" is left unscathed. Even if total constructivism of our knowledge is the best account we can give of our knowledge (and it is one that fits best with the practical account of tradition we have given here), this does not necessarily imply total anti-realism in epistemology. It leaves room for consequential realism, in which mirroring what-there-is is the result of our reliably produced claims, is what makes our claims true, but is not a criterion for judging or showing our claims to be true. There is no good reason that a constructivist cannot be a realist of this consequentialist variety.

So where does that leave us in relating a practical account of tradition to the issues of truth?

First, there can be no appeal to a practice-independent "cause" of our claims to be the "warrant" for our claims. As Terence Penelhum has noted, the world in which we live is *"intellectually ambiguous."*[16] Many practices make much sense, but rather different senses of the world, for many purposes. We cannot get into position to warrant our claims that our beliefs are true (and, perhaps, others' beliefs are false) on the basis of "the world." Penelhum finds this intellectual ambiguity of the world an embarrassment for believers. It need not be, as we shall see below. But the world does not simply validate our beliefs about it.

Second, the appeal to reliably formed beliefs common among contemporary philosophers of religion leaves participants in different practices in a situation of "epistemic parity." Participants in numerous practices may properly and reliably develop beliefs that are contradictory.[17] This generates a problem of pluralism: How are some reliably formed beliefs "acceptable" as true when other reliably-formed beliefs contradict them? Since appeal to the-world-independent-of-our-practice-formed-beliefs is foreclosed as a criterion of truth and appeal to beliefs-formed-reliably-in-practices is a criterion insufficient to show those beliefs acceptable as true, we must turn to an "appraisal account of truth."

Many practices include a practice of appraising. The content of appraisals are truth claims. Realtors appraise real estate; editors appraise writing; reviewers appraise arguments; consumers appraise merchandise; juries appraise guilt; athletic judges appraise performances. Each of these appraisals results in practical truth claims. "This real estate is worth $147,000." "This manuscript will never be a book we can sell." "This essayist has demonstrated her point convincingly." "This shirt is not worth $22.95." "He is guilty of involuntary manslaughter, not of murder." "Her floor exercise is worth 9.7 points." These claims may be formed by people well-trained in appraisals (and

---

[16] Terence Penelhum, *God and Skepticism* (Boston: Reidel, 1983), 156.

[17] William A. Christian Sr., *Oppositions of Religious Doctrines* (New York: Herder, 1969) has shown that doctrines of different religious communities can be contradictory. William P. Alston, *Perceiving God* (Ithaca, N.Y.: Cornell University Press, 1991), 177-80, claims that there is no "practice-independent" way to judge beliefs. Also see Alston, "Response to My Critics," *Religious Studies* 30/2 (1995): 171-80.

thus their appraisals should be reliably formed unless other factors interfere), but that alone does not make those appraisals acceptable. One can challenge appraisals by employing other real-estate appraisers, submitting one's manuscript to another publisher, highlighting points in an essay a reviewer may have discounted, discussing the prices of comparable shirts, appealing the verdict to a higher court, or "booing" the judges. Indeed, appraisals often require more than one expert (juries composed of twelve peers, panels of judges, multiple appraisals of the cost of repairing damaged automobiles) to be construed as valid. All of our explicit truth claims, from simple to complex, can be construed as the linguistic expression of practical appraisals, from "there are 237 tappable maple trees in the grove," to "this argument is valid," to "God's in his heaven—all's right with the world."

No single standard for appraisal can cover all cases. However, there are five adaptable standards that can guide appraisals of religious claims. Like all rules, they cannot show how to apply themselves. Nor can they show clearly which are to be applied when or to which claims they are relevant. Insofar as these standards adequately portray the actual way we use *true* in our practices, they are appropriate; that they may need revision or application to different contexts is obvious. That they are not and cannot be some "transcendental" perspective is also implied by the arguments in this book. The claim is that these five standards formulate appropriate rules of thumb that have been distilled from and can be used in many practices that involve appraising those life-shaping convictional claims that are developed in religious and quasi-religious practices.[18]

First, a claim can be appraised as true if it represents the world in which we live, or a part of it, in a revealing way. This rule captures the insight of Heidegger's claim that truth—in Greek *a-leitheia* (literally, "not covered")—is an uncovering. Examples of revelatory truth are parables (which, as chapter 3 suggested, can reveal that God's community is different from what was expected), the punch lines of incisive jokes, or the unraveling of mysterious plots from denouements in detective novels to the gypsy Azucena's closing line to Count de Luna (who has just had his rival, her "son," executed) in Verdi's *Il Trovatore*: "He was your brother." A revealing claim or performance rings true; an obscuring performance or claim is boring or hollow and thus fails to ring true.[19]

---

[18] The following five paragraphs adapt the standards first developed in Tilley, *Story Theology*, 187-211.

[19] A roughly similar claim is made by Francis Schüssler Fiorenza regarding "retroductive warrants" in *Foundational Theology: Jesus and the Church* (New York: Crossroad, 1985), 306-10.

Second, a claim that fits with other facts we recognize can be appraised as true; one that does not we find to be false. This standard applies primarily to ordinary, empirical claims. We can appraise the claim "There are 237 tappable sugar maples in this grove" as true (or, perhaps, roughly true, or approximately true, or close enough) if we can agree on the appraisal as fitting the facts "we" know. This rule utilizes the realist insight that true claims mirror the world not as a theory of truth but as a guide for appraisal. What is retrievable in realism is that, for most empirical claims, "looking and checking the world" is what we do to appraise claims: We count maple trees to find out if a person's claim is true. Realist *theories* of truth overextend this ordinary practice of checking as if it were the criterion of truth. However, as Nelson Goodman has shown, many different claims, possibly even contradictory ones, may accurately reflect the world or part of it.[20] A claim that "fits the world as we know it" is one we can appraise as true (always remembering that a claim that upsets "the world as we know it" is one we may find true because it is revelatory).

Third, a true story or claim or practice is one that enables communities or individuals to be "true to themselves."[21] Conversely, one that purchases self-identity (communal or individual) at the price of self-deception brings people to be (however odd it sounds) false to themselves. Perhaps the most humiliating example of such self-deception is the Christian tradition of anti-Semitism, captured in the accusation that "the Jews," in executing Jesus, were "Christ-killers." The obvious fact that the Romans executed Jesus (however much *some* members of the Jewish community in Roman-occupied Palestine may have helped to bring it about) should have made this view clearly unacceptable. That this belief became a determining conviction of the identity of Christian communities is a symptom of the folly of self-deception.[22] Repudiating that conviction and acting to rectify, insofar as

---

[20] Nelson Goodman, *Ways of Worldmaking* (Indianapolis, Ind.: Hackett, 1978).

[21] One advantage of an appraisal account of truth is that it goes beyond most epistemologies in noting that not only individual claims, but narratives as a whole and even belief-forming practices (science, phrenology, etc.) can be appraised for their truth and their truth-generating power.

[22] The best theological account of self-deception and its effects remains Stanley Hauerwas and David B. Burrell, "Self-Deception and Autobiography: Reflections on Speer's *Inside the Third Reich*," in *Truthfulness and Tragedy: Further Investigations in Christian Ethics* (Notre Dame, Ind.: University of Notre Dame Press, 1977), 82-98. The invocation of "folly" alludes to Barbara Tuchman, *The March of Folly: From Troy to Vietnam* (New York: Knopf, 1984). Tuchman does not invoke the concept of self-deception but argues that some policies chosen by authorities in political and religious communities have been self-destructive for the traditions and institutions that authorized the roles those leaders took.

possible, the horrible results of that view enable Christian communities to be more truly themselves.

Fourth, a claim, narrative or practice that enables one or shows one how to "be true to" others and to the tradition carried on in practice. can be appraised as "true." Obviously, fidelity and authenticity are closely linked for communities. A community that is faithful to its forbears, fellow-travelers, and future members is a community that carries an authentic tradition. This standard tends to be most obviously applicable to individuals and their stories. These folk are "models" of exemplary behavior in a community or exemplary standards of practice. As noted in chapter 4, recognizing exemplars is neither practice-independent nor easy; nor are such models necessarily constant among different contexts. Yet it is just stories of exploitation, of the perversion of practices like justice that show what fails to be model behavior or what kinds of practice instantiate infidelity. One pattern in the long series of espionage novels of John LeCarré is the exploration of practices, such as double-agency espionage, that make any definite sense of fidelity impossible for those who live in and live out the practice.[23] Learning how to be true to others may be far more important for human happiness than learning an assemblage of true claims.

Fifth, practices that enable their participants as individuals and a community to live in ways that propel them to develop revelatory insight, to utter fitting claims, to be authentically themselves, and to keep faith with others are true because they help create lives of truthfulness. This sort of appraisal of practices is very difficult and may be rather rare for an individual or a community. For some individuals or communities, it may be impossible, if circumstances make impossible any "stepping out" of a tradition, even imaginatively. I have devoted an entire book to this topic with regard to religious traditions.[24] To paraphrase an ancient Jewish sage, to learn how to know what is true is to engage in practices that free a person and community to live in truthful ways.

In sum, if foundational realism is false, if constructivism is true, if reliabilism may be necessary even though it is insufficient as a theory for showing what is true, and if a form of realism is compatible with constructivism, then such an appraisal account of "truth" becomes possible and credible. Of course, another option would be to reject or

---

[23] This is one constant theme in his novels; see, for instance, John LeCarré, *A Perfect Spy* (New York: Knopf, 1986).

[24] See Tilley, *The Wisdom of Religious Commitment*, esp. the epilogue,155-60.

ignore any possibility of epistemological realism, even consequential realism, and simply construe such realism as a "fifth wheel" that does nothing significant for one's epistemology.[25]

Doctrinaire anti-realism is compatible with constructivism. The arguments sketched here do not show that a constructivist must or should be a consequential realist, only that a constructivist can be a realist. However, anti-realism is not compatible with one of the insights of the Catholic Intellectual Tradition discussed in chapter 5, that we live in a sacramental universe. Indeed, it is hard to see how acceptance of a religious tradition is compatible with thoroughgoing anti-realism. For Catholics, the analogical imagination is, in some sense, a "realist" imagination. If the universe is sacramental, then it is no surprise that some like Penelhum find it "intellectually ambiguous," that there are many religious accounts that seem more or less to fit, to be compatible with, the world as we conceptualize it. Sacramental practices just are practices that can be construed in multiple ways.[26] The only construal evidently excluded is a monovalent one that reduces the practice to "merely" a natural one or "only" a supernatural Divine Gift. The only construal of the universe formally ruled out by a sacramental imagination is that it is only what it appears to be and is insignificant of any "more." Just as others can construe sacraments "monovalently," and the universe "flatly," so others can construe constructivism non-realistically. However, as it is a cornerstone of the Catholic Intellectual Tradition to construe the world as a multivalent sign of God, so a Catholic acceptance of epistemic constructivism carries along an acceptance of consequential realism. Consequential realism "fits" a sacramental universe.

For some foundational realists, this position will seem incredibly subjectivist and relativist. But appraisals, although personal, are *never* subjective in the sense that objectivism opposes. However contingent and disputable they may be, appraisals cannot be "purely" subjective in the sense of arbitrary, capricious, or subject to no standards. Appraisals are always subject to the standards of practices; and good appraisers are people well trained in the practice of appraising. Any fool can give an unwarranted opinion of any claim he knows nothing about. But such opinions are not appraisals in the

---

[25] If we followed Rorty and found that epistemology is dead, this would also apply to epistemology's "successor," whatever that may be once epistemology has eroded away under the constructivist deluge.

[26] See, for example, Gary Macy's retrieval of the multiple construals of the Eucharist in the medieval period, *Treasures from the Storeroom* (Collegeville, Minn.: Liturgical Press, 1999).

sense developed here. Just as people unfamiliar with maple trees or the real-estate market in a neighborhood may have opinions about property values or sugar bushes, so can people unfamiliar with religious practices have opinions about religion; such evaluations are of equal weight. Good appraisals of religious practice require qualified appraisers to make *reliable* claims and intersubjective acceptance to *show* that they are true.

Appraisals can change. What has been accepted as a tolerable practice in the past, such as just war-making and capital punishment, may no longer be appraised as tolerable in the present. A claim that is accepted as true today might not have been accepted or appraised as true in the past, such as the claim that religious freedom is based in the dignity of the human person created by God. As cultural contexts change and as traditions change in response to the contexts in which they are inculturated, appraisals can change; what might be good theology in the Huron Nation of the seventeenth century may not be good theology in Rome in the twenty-first century.

Constructivism does not mean that truth is all relative. Such a claim is either unobjectionable or empty. If it means that claims are formed in particular times and places and appraisals of them are equally contextual, it is unobjectionable. My shaving mirror, a polished piece of brass, the Hubble telescope, and the tiny mirrors in video projectors, all, if they are well constructed, reflect reality in different ways. But all are used for different purposes in different contexts. What we will count as a true reflection will vary in each case. Hence, if one protests against constructivism as developed here as an inappropriate "relativism," I would ask, "What can the alternative be?" A universal eye, God's point of view, and a mirror for all occasions are all inaccessible to us, just as concepts of reality independent of our concepts are, even if they can exist. And as the alternative, if one exists, is not within our reach, the objection against the form of contextualism developed here, a practical constructivism, is empty.

The foundational realist will also find such a view fragile, unguaranteed by God or the world. However, at the beginning of the twenty-first century, foundational realism has been shown to be untenable, at least in any form strong enough to support a metaphysical system necessary to guaranteed epistemic claims. Foundational realism provides no real support for religious claims. Living religious traditions *are* fragile. The Catholic analogical imagination is also fragile—it could be lost if it is not cultured in successor generations. Coping with that fragility, then, does not require better foundations, but good *traditio*—handing on the practice.

The "appraisal account" of truth also explains a fact that Lindbeck's cultural-linguistic theory and Schreiter's semiotic theory do not. While doctrinal rules may, as Lindbeck suggests, function to *guide* discourse, his inference that they do not also make truth claims is in error. If monotheism is not, in some sense, true, then a discourse system that includes a "monotheistic rule" is as silly, as systematically misleading, as phrenology or astrology. Of course, it is possible that any set of practices is systematically misleading, even the set of practices that constitutes science. What makes living religious traditions different from delusive or silly systems is that religious traditions' claims are subject to ongoing appraisal and modification. Freud's claim, as noted in chapter 1, that religions are not only illusions but also delusions because they are not self-correcting, may be true of religious and pseudo-religious traditions like astrology. However, the great living faith traditions change, at least in part in response to other intellectual practices in their culture.[27] That they do so shows not only that their central and distinctive doctrines (and the application of any "rules") are affected by and affect reliably formed claims. Not only can they not be isolated from the practice of appraisal as not making truth claims, but they are also subject to appraisal and change. Change may occur as a response to claims reliably formed by individuals in practices other than religious ones, claims that seem to contradict religious claims. If such claims formed in other practices are formally or informally appraised by the community that engages in both kinds of practice as true, consistency requires that one or the other change. Reliable resolutions of conflicts between the claims developed in astrophysics and those developed in Christian practice, for instance, are not to be resolved directly, but by appraisals conducted by those who carry both traditions by participating well in both kinds of practices.[28] But if there are seeming (or real) contradic-

---

[27] Michael Horace Barnes, *Stages of Thought:The Co-evolution of Religious Thought and Science* (New York: Oxford University Press, 2000), provides an extended argument that the great living faith traditions develop in similar ways. Even if one finds that Barnes's overarching thesis may not be proven beyond a reasonable doubt, the data Barnes collects and analyzes clearly support an argument against reducing religious traditions to "mythopoeic" irrationality.

[28] Participation in both religious and scientific practices is not sufficient, of course, to resolve these claims. But arguments from those who participate in only one of them are strikingly unconvincing to those who participate in the other. For example, Steven Weinberg's 1999 talk to the Conference on Cosmic Design of the American Association for the Advancement of Science in Washington, D.C., revised and published as "A Designer Universe?" *New York Review of*

tions, it is appropriate to appraise the claims and to modify one or the other or both.

Hence, insofar as the religious practices that humans construct and the claims that those practices generate *are* true, the result is that those practices and claims do reflect God's grandeur in practice and in truth—if the universe *is* sacramental. That the reflection is never perfect, and never will be perfect while we see through a glass darkly, seems obvious. Nonetheless, we have shown the compatibility of constructivism in epistemology with a form of realism in metaphysics. A profoundly contextual epistemological account that (1) begins with practices that give rise to constructed (and, one hopes, reliably formed) claims, (2) invokes an appraisal account of truth for accepting claims, and (3) incorporates a "consequential realism" rather than a "foundational realism," can avoid both the anti-realist implications many find in constructivism and the problems of a theory of "development" to account for change in religious practice and doctrine. The present account of tradition, therefore, has a place for truth.

Revelation in a Practical Theology of Tradition

In his introduction to the English translation of *Dei Verbum*, the *Dogmatic Constitution on Divine Revelation* of the Second Vatican Council, R. A. F. McKenzie, S.J., lays out one version of the elements of a doctrine of revelation. Revelation is a "manifestation by God—primarily of Himself; secondarily of His will and intentions." That manifestation is a communication that is "part of a larger pattern . . . destined ultimately for the good of all." This communication is public, not private, and "has to be made known to others by the testimony of its recipient. Passed on orally, it becomes tradition; recorded in writing, it becomes scripture." Hence, scripture and tradition *contain* revelation, but not all of scripture or tradition *is* revelation; however, the

---

Books 46/16 (21 October 1999): 46-48, presumes that belief in a designer requires "grounds" and "evidence" as if it were a scientific hypothesis. From the point of view of someone who lives in and lives out both practices, he misses the point precisely because he does not understand how to participate in religious practices; his examples of the bad influence of religion are all either a century old or drawn from zealots whose destructive actions are *repudiated* by a vast majority of members of their own traditions. Weinberg's practical knowledge of physics is unbalanced because his knowledge of religion is purely academic, not practical. He doesn't participate seriously in both types of practice.

relationship between revelation on the one hand, and scripture and tradition on the other, is not to be conceived as between a part and a whole, but as scripture and tradition in some way sacramentally bearing revelation.[29]

Avery Dulles, S.J., in his analysis of the Second Vatican Council's understanding of revelation claims further that the council "clearly taught that the Holy Spirit is active in continuing to communicate the revelation already given. . . . Granted that God addresses the Church through the scriptures and the sacraments, does God not speak also through creation and through secular history?"[30] Hence, revelation is God's "word," but not a communication narrowly limited to the formal structures and history of Judaism and Christianity and not fully contained in particular events and people of the past. McKenzie's comments and Dulles's theological claims clearly represent a contemporary, orthodox Catholic account of revelation.[31]

This section shows that the practical theory of tradition comfortably accommodates the fundamental theology of revelation articulated by Dulles in *Models of Revelation*. Like Dulles's view, the present position is postcritical and realist. It rejects the claim that revelation can be construed as the delivery of immutable divine propositions into the hands or ears of ancient writers (objectivism). It similarly rejects the view that revelation can be understood as the influence of pure internal light or feeling or focal awareness on the part of individuals (subjectivism). The present analysis cannot show the full richness of Dulles's reflections. A thorough conversation with his work might also reveal significant differences between us on specific areas within revelation theology. Such a conversation, however, would take

---

[29] R. A. F. McKenzie, S.J., "Revelation," *Documents of Vatican II*, ed. Walter M. Abbott, S.J., and Joseph Gallagher (New York: Guild Press, America Press, Association Press, 1966), 106. McKenzie also comments on the particularity of revelation—that it occurs at specific times and places to or for specific people. As a way of claiming that revelation is not some universally diffused background noise to which humans may or may not listen, this claim is unexceptionable. Yet it can be misleading in that it may open the door for the disputes about the "bearers" of revelation too quickly. The questions "Is this person, text, tradition, practice revelatory?" are questions for appraisal. They come only after (at least logically) one has come to at least tentative answers to questions about what revelation is and how it functions.

[30] Avery Dulles, S.J., *Models of Revelation*, 234-35. Subsequent references to this book will be given parenthetically in the text of this section.

[31] For a survey of more recent work on the theology of revelation, see the essays in Paul Avis, ed., *Divine Revelation* (Grand Rapids, Mich.: Eerdmans, 1997).

us far beyond the confines of the present book.[32] Here the point is to show that there is substantial convergence concerning the key issues of the fundamental theology of revelation (what revelation is and how it functions) between one orthodox, Catholic fundamental approach to revelation and the practical theory developed in this book.

Dulles writes explicitly as a Christian theologian. His approach, especially his understanding of symbols, is shaped by Christian convictions and the theological practice of faith seeking understanding—specifically, in this case, understanding of revelation. Dulles describes revelation as "the self-manifestation of God through a form of communication that could be termed, at least in a broad sense, symbolic" (266). Lest it be thought that Dulles's position is, in some sense, purely "symbolist" or "merely symbolic," Dulles affirms that God's symbolic communication should be understood as a sacramental symbol; such symbols "contain and mediate the reality they signify" (267). In this, Dulles is an epistemic realist: "Symbols give rise to true affirmations about what is antecedently real" (267). Nor is he in danger of reducing revelation to a human creation. Dulles claims that "revelatory symbols are not pure creations of the human imagination. The basic symbols of Christian revelation . . . are the persons, events, and other realities whereby God brings into existence the community of faith we call the Christian Church" (266). Dulles finds that "the figures of speech and the literary imagery are secondary to the real symbols out of which they emerge" (267).

Dulles firmly rejects emotivism and subjectivism. The claim that in some way humans create their own symbols arbitrarily and then dub them with the honorific *revelation* is anathema. For Dulles, true symbols must be reflective of the real, and specifically the real manifestation of God in "the interplay of nature and history" (266). Nonetheless, no "clear dichotomy can be drawn between the symbolic and the nonsymbolic" (132). For Dulles, God is the primary cause of revelation, but "revelation never occurs in a purely interior experience or an unmediated encounter with God. It is always mediated through symbol" (131).

Dulles also rejects the objectivist claim that revelation is initiated by God inserting "prefabricated propositions . . . into the human mind"

---

[32] For instance, in a review essay Dermot Lane raised questions about the context, forms, and content of revelation that would demand substantial development in Dulles's work in a number of areas ("Dulles on Revelation," *The Living Light* 21 [1984], 76-77), especially in ways indicated by European political and Latin American liberation theologies. Resolving these *quaestiones disputata* belongs to a fully developed theology of revelation.

(267). Dulles recognizes that the symbols we use to express and understand divine revelation are "given in a specific history" and mediated through scripture "read in the light of living and ongoing tradition" (268). Nonetheless, God's self-manifestation through and in symbolic communication "has cognitive value that can be expressed, to some extent in true propositions" (268). If a proposition is "authorized by revelation," it cannot be false in its own terms in any other context (268).

That a practical account of revelation would join Dulles in rejecting objectivism and subjectivism is obvious; we both reject the possibility of unmediated revelation, unmediated access to some world-as-it-is-in-itself, a presumption that is necessary for both objectivism and subjectivism. The remaining fundamental questions are twofold: Is Dulles's account of symbol sustainable in a constructivist context? Is his account of realism necessarily foundationalist, or can it be understood as a form of consequential realism?

Dulles's assertion that revelatory symbols are not pure human creations would seem to be incompatible with the constructivism of the present position. Yet such is not the case. That claims, beliefs, and symbols emerge from practices does not imply that they are "pure human creations." No constructions are so pure.[33] Each construction grows out of previous practices and beliefs. Just as there is no pure "given," as noted above in discussing "the myth of the given," neither is there a pure "taken." That there is a pure "taken" is as much a myth as there is a pure "given" as we form our concepts. This residual dichotomy still tends to structure the opposition between those who study and those who live in traditions, as noted in chapter 1. But that there is both "given" and "taken" is the insight that makes the theory of the development of doctrine discussed in chapter 4 so attractive; even the originating events and people of a tradition, like Jesus, are found within an already-existing stream of tradition, Judaism.[34] That

---

[33] The careful reader will note that in no place in this book are constructed practices, beliefs, or symbols said to be created. Although this fact is *not* the result of editing the earlier chapters to fit the present one, but of the original composition of those chapters, the theory proffered herein *before* explicitly theological considerations does not preclude God from being the primary cause and therefore primary creator of any of these practices or beliefs. This usage on the part of the author was not deliberate but certainly reflects nonetheless the author's theological presumptions.

[34] The significance of this point for understanding religious experience is explored in Terrence W. Tilley, "The Philosophy of Religion and the Concept of Religion: D. Z. Phillips on Religion and Superstition," *Journal of the American Academy of Religion* 68/2 (June 2000): 345-56.

practitioners develop the belief that the originating events and people are the result of the creative presence and action of God fits perfectly well in a practice in which the analogical imagination is a primary component. How God acts in self-manifestation and whether God's acts are the primary cause, secondary efficient cause, or occasion for a given person or event to be construed by a community as revelatory are questions that can be disputed by theologians working within the tradition. That human constructs can also be divine creations is an affirmation that is at the heart of a tradition that relies on and produces an analogical imagination. Hence, Dulles's account of symbols fits with a constructivist account as given here, although it clearly would not fit with *all* constructivist accounts.

Although much of Dulles's language sounds as though he would favor a foundationalist realism, his account of revelation is not foundationalist. His nuanced account deserves quotation:

> On the one hand, revelation precedes faith inasmuch as, before anyone can believe there must be symbols wherein God expresses what he is, and wills to be, for the world. These symbols, before their meaning is understood and accepted, are virtual revelation. When believers accept revelation, they allow their minds to be determined by the meaning they find in the symbols. Thus revelation shapes their faith.
>
> On the other hand, faith exists before revelation inasmuch as the symbols do not yield their meaning except to religious inquirers or believers who are actively committed to the search for truth. The quest itself involves a kind of implicit faith—a confidence that the search is not a futile one and that God's revelation, if it exists, can be recognized. When the search has succeeded, faith actively receives revelation and provides it, so to speak, with a dwelling place in the mind. Since revelation cannot exist as such outside a created mind, revelation may be said to presuppose faith (279-80).

Since symbols are symbols within communicative practices, revelation is possible in and through, and actual only in and through, semiotic systems in which symbols are available. Although events, people, or things may be virtually (potentially) revelatory outside of a practice, there is no way to identify or recognize them except through the exercises in a practice of faith.[35] For a practical account, it would be as senseless as accepting what Sellars has identified as "the myth of the given" in epistemology to make any claim about such "virtual" possibilities—except to say that they are not purely constructed out of a free-floating human imagination. As we can say that there is something "given" to be "taken" (to allude to the dilemma explored in chapter 1), a potentially revelatory event or person that can be taken in faith as revelation similarly is a claim that revelatory symbols are not constructed out of nothing. Hence, for Dulles, revelation is not a foundation for Christian faith and practice but the correlate of faith within a tradition of the practice of faith.[36] One might even say that the practice attentively seeking truth—a practice I have argued is a necessary component of a tradition worthy of commitment[37]—is the necessary context for both faith and revelation. Hence, Dulles's position is realist and yet does not require revelation as a foundation.

The questions that arise with regard to the symbols of revelation in a practical theory are analogous to the questions that arise with regard to truth in a constructivist account. Above we drew distinctions between what *makes* a claim true, what makes a claim *reliable*, and how we *appraise* claims. What *makes* a person, event, or other reality revelatory may well be that it is the self-manifestation of God in and through the communicative practice of faith. What makes a claim that a given person or event or other reality is revelatory *reliable* is that it is produced in a practice in which attentively seeking the truth is a constituent. Hence, some Christians may well reliably claim that revelation is found in the Bible, while some Muslims may reliably claim that God's revelation given to Mohammed is inscribed in the Qur'an. Some scientists may even find the revelations of scientific practice to be just that—revelatory. But if multiple reliably produced (or apparently reliably produced) claims are "on the table," in that all seem to have some good warrant to be reliably produced, the

---

[35] Dulles also claims that there are "real symbols" out of which the "figures of speech and literary imagery" of religious symbolism emerge (266). But apart from the practices of a tradition, the assertion of the existence of such "real symbols" can do no more work than the assertion that there is a "virtual revelation"—which is a materially empty set of items that can only do work in the context of acceptance in a "created mind."

[36] For a brief account of the history of the use of revelation as a foundational category in Catholic theology, see Francis Schüssler Fiorenza, *Foundational Theology,* 256-59, 266-67. His alternative hermeneutical approach is summarized therein, 285-311.

[37] See Tilley, *The Wisdom of Religious Commitment,* 131-53.

question is how we *appraise* them: Which of them can we appraise as true since they cannot all be true? Guides like those sketched in the previous section would then come into play, although the discussions within a family of traditions (like Christianity) would be shaped differently than conversations among members of different traditions. Once we distinguish (1) what *constitutes* revelation from (2) how claims that a person, event, or other reality is revelatory are *reliably* produced in religious practices, and both from (3) claims about how we are to *appraise* such claims, Dulles's account of revelation not only fits within a practical account of tradition, but also may even be clarified by construing it as a position that is best understood as consequentially, not foundationally, realist. Exploring Dulles's account as (epistemically) a non-foundational realism also clarifies the present approach by showing how the presumption of a sacramental universe, charged with the grandeur of God, is a necessary constituent if this account is to be adapted as a theology of tradition.

Dulles summarizes the relationship of revelation to theology in a developmental manner: "Revelation, rather than being presupposed as fully known from the start, is progressively elucidated as theology carries out its task" (283). That the task of the practice of theology is the elucidation of faith is unexceptionable. Dulles does not mean that theologians *progressively* elucidate the faith in the problematical ways we noted in chapters 3 and 4.[38] If we understand the work of theology in a practical theory of tradition, we cannot say that theologians progressively get clearer on what revelation is, but rather that they have the ongoing task of elucidating revelation as understood in the traditions again and again as the cultures in which the traditions flourish and the traditions that flourish change. This does not mean we fail to make progress because we fail to learn from our predecessors, but only that we do not get "closer to" the truth. Hence, we can fully agree with Dulles's conclusion that "revelation is the source and center, the beginning and end, of the theological enterprise" (283). For if theologians do their job well, they help the community to live in and live out the tradition better. The task of theologians, then, is not to supersede the past but to elucidate the living practice of faith in fidelity to our forbears and in responsibility to our present and our future fellow-travelers. And even if divine revelation is not available as

---

[38] Dulles's approach of "historical situationism" is explored especially in "Tradition as a Theological Source," in *The Craft of Theology* (New York: Crossroad, 1996), 87-104.

an external foundation of that tradition, perhaps the result of living out that tradition well is revelatory, perhaps even a light unto the peoples. Thus, the present approach acknowledges the place of the craft of theology without invoking the myth of theological progress.

Revelation, in Dulles's view, does not function as a source or norm of faith independent of the tradition to which the tradition can appeal. The appeal to revelation as a source is internal to the tradition. Revelation is not prior to faith but is the correlate of faith: "God, as encompassing cause, produces both the symbols that speak to faith and the faith that discerns the symbols" (280). This religious claim is completely compatible with constructivism for a tradition steeped in the analogical imagination—a tradition that produced a mind like Friedrich von Hügel's, as shown in chapter 5. Revelation is the norm of faith external to the community, but a norm, for theological purposes, immanent in the enduring community of communities that practice the faith and thus carry on the tradition in their practices.

When we consider the fundamental claims about the nature and function of revelation in the position of Catholic theologian Avery Dulles, S.J., and the practical theory of tradition developed here, we see that they are not only compatible but mutually elucidating. We have seen that Dulles's approach seems more compatible with a consequentialist than a foundationalist epistemic realism. My conclusion is that the practical, constructivist account of tradition offered here can rather easily account for what would, at first glance, seem to be a major difficulty: the place of revelation in the tradition, at least in the version of that fundamental doctrine by a distinguished American Catholic theologian. Insofar as Dulles's view is in line with the positions taken on revelation by the Second Vatican Council (and I believe it is), a constructivist, practical account of tradition can be used to develop a Catholic theology of revelation in line with Vatican II.

Authority in a Practical Theology of Tradition

The issue of "authority" in theology unfortunately tends to focus on "authorities." We seek to show who has and should have authority over whom, what text or rule is or should be normative, whether oversight in a tradition is bound to an office, or in what way past practices and belief should be authoritative over present practice and belief. Some scholars even criticize others for ignoring the role of authorities and their influence over individuals in community.[39] Chapters 1 and 2 showed that authorities may even have the power to invent new traditions deliberately and to impose them. Again, it is beyond the bounds of this chapter to develop a full-fledged practical theology of authority. However, we can sketch the places of authority in a practice and indicate what this means for a practical theology of tradition.[40]

The authority in a practice does not come from outside the practice, but arises in the relationships between the practitioners who seek the ends that the practice makes it possible to reach.[41] Partici-

---

[39] See, for example, comments in chapter 2 above, and Terrence W. Tilley, "The Institutional Element in Religious Experience," *Modern Theology* 10/2 (1994): 185-212; see also Katherine Tanner, *Theories of Culture: A New Agenda for Theology* (Minneapolis, Minn.: Fortress Press, 1997), in which she shows that anthropologists who observe and describe culture can miss "the power dimension of meaning. . . . Power is at stake in the interpretation of beliefs, values, or notions with a cultural currency. Struggles over power come to be enacted in struggles over meaning" (47).

[40] The present account is indebted to scholars who have applied Michel Foucault's work to religious discourse, especially Kathleen Boone, *The Bible Tells Them So: The Discourse of Protestant Fundamentalism* (Albany, N.Y.: SUNY Press, 1989); Rebecca Chopp, *The Power to Speak: Feminism, Language, God* (New York: Crossroad, 1989); Mary McClintock Fulkerson, *Changing the Subject: Women's Discourses and Feminist Theology* (Minneapolis, Minn.: Fortress Press, 1994); and Vincent J. Miller, "History or Geography? Gadamer, Foucault, and Theologies of Tradition," in Macy, *Theology and the New Histories,* 56-85. Some material in the next three paragraphs is based on a note in T. W. Tilley, *The Evils of Theodicy* (Washington, D.C.: Georgetown University Press, 1991), 31.

In addition to the historical work on differing forms of authority in the nineteenth- and twentieth-century Catholic traditions of J. Robert Dionne, S.M., *The Papacy and the Church: A Study of Praxis and Reception in Ecumenical Perspective* (New York: Philosophical Library, 1987), American theologians have recently developed nuanced, relational accounts of authority. A survey can be found in David Stagaman, S.J., *Authority in the Church* (Collegeville, Minn.: Liturgical Press, 1999), xi-xiv. David Stagaman and Charles E. Curran, *The Catholic Moral Tradition Today: A Synthesis* (Washington, D.C.: Georgetown University Press, 1999) both address the theme of the relationship of authority to dissent from authoritative teaching in the church. The essays in Catholic Common Ground Initiative, *Church Authority in American Culture* (New York: Crossroad, 1999) explore some of the challenges that occur (to use language developed below) when two differing practices occupy the same cultural space from theological (Avery Dulles, S.J., Joseph Komonchak), canon law (James Coriden), and sociological (Philip Selznick) perspectives. It is beyond the scope of the present text to engage in extensive exploration of these important discussions.

[41] Cf. Stagaman, *Authority in the Church,* 31. I am sympathetic with much of Stagaman's historical work and his analysis of authority. However, we have a rather different understanding of *practice,* so that he finds that *authority* is a

pants each have roles in the practice and enact the code or rules of the practice. In studying these relationships among practitioners and their roles, Kathleen Boone notes that "one confronts . . . a power which cannot be localized but is of one cloth, a power woven in and through every thread."[42] A person who enters a practice (for instance, is converted to a fundamentalist Christian group or becomes an intern in an American hospital) engages in a practice that accepts some rules as normative and beliefs as unquestionable. For instance, the former takes the Bible, usually the authorized version, as authoritative; the latter, medical textbooks currently endorsed by the "medical establishment." People within the practice also accept the purposes of the practice, as noted in chapter 2.

Within the practice, all participants are authoritative by their roles. Boone's analysis shows the powerful, nearly inerrant authority of the pastor of a fundamentalist congregation as the interpreter (reader) of an inerrant text. In a hospital, the attending physician is authoritative in medical matters over the intern. Yet the intern can (within limits) practice independently of the attending physician. The intern can also challenge the attending physician or other members of the medical staff on specific issues. Unlike the nurses' aides, also participants in the practice, interns have a status that allows their challenges not only to be heard but also to be made—for an orderly to question a physician's judgment or to proffer a diagnosis is simply "not done" in a hospital (although registered nurses are professionally required to question and sometimes disobey dubious orders from physicians).

No role carries an absolute authority. Fundamentalist congregations can turn the biblical text against a preacher or resort to other authorities, perhaps by joining another congregation. Denials of payment for specific services by insurance claims agents can be appealed within and without the insurance company. Patients can seek second opinions concerning proposed medical treatments (and good medical and insurance practice agree today that this is "good practice"). Practices have ways in which participants, including clients and patients,

---

practice (39-45), while I find it a constituent of practices created in large part by the social locations of the practitioners. Stagaman is also more influenced by postliberal theology than by critical theory, and thus he does not connect authority with power clearly or recognize clearly nonmagisterial authorities. This leads him to giving a major place to "dissent" from authority (61-63), rather than to recognize the way other authorities in the ecclesial community bring about changes in magisterial authority (a theme of Dionne, *The Papacy and the Church*).

[42] Boone, *The Bible Tells Them So*, 2-3.

can moderate the influence of and challenge specific exercises of authority. There are sites for resistance in every system of practices. These sites, although not always accessible to all participants in a practice, may provide even the oppressed with a place for authoritative resistance. Mary McClintock Fulkerson, for example, has described the ways in which women in a patriarchal society have positions of power in which they can utilize fundamentalist religious discourse in subversive ways.[43] Participants in a discourse can challenge specific actions of physicians in a hospital or pastors in a church (however difficult the proper paths to such challenge may be to find and to use). In extreme cases, persons can be removed from their authoritative roles (pastors defrocked, lawyers disbarred, physicians removed from practice).

Yet the authority of each of these *roles* can only be changed by a revolution that reconstitutes a practice or destroys the practice and begins a new practice (revolutions against monarchy could be construed as a reconstitution of political practice or as the destruction of monarchy as a political practice and the substitution of aristocracy or a republican form of government in its stead). Challenges to specific authoritative acts are not necessarily challenges to authoritative roles. People in positions of authority may be challenged in many ways, even a call to fidelity to the tradition that gives them authority. However, if persons in authority are challenged so often as to lose credibility, they may lose their authoritative roles: kings dethroned, politicians thrown out of office, gangster lords assassinated. But challenges to *authorities* are different from challenges of the *authority* of offices or roles (a distinction all too often overlooked).

In sum, authority in a practice is determined by the roles the practitioners have in a practice and is limited both by relationships and rules that shape the roles and relationships in a practice.

The authority of a practice is also limited by relationships and accommodations made with other practices in the same cultural "space." Because different practices can be undertaken in the same space, external limits on authority *of* a practice may also affect authority *in* a practice. Within the hospital, for instance, the physicians, the hospital administration, various examining committees, the government, and insurance companies also have authoritative positions. Just as authority in a practice is limited to certain spheres in which the authoritative role holds power, so authority is also limited where practices intersect. Insurance adjusters cannot give a diagnosis or prescribe

---

[43] Fulkerson, *Changing the Subject,* 239-98.

surgery because their practice is not medicine, but insurance; similarly, interns cannot authorize payment for services. In this sense, the hospital is a place wherein many practices come together to form a major node in the "health-care system." That there are role-specific conflicts between participants in the practices in the system (physicians and insurance adjustors, for instance) is a result not merely of "intrusion" or "obstinacy" on the part of practitioners of different practices, but on interpractice conflicts, conflicts that may become acute when roles constituted in different practices must be undertaken in one "location" and when role-specific duties and rights conflict.[44]

What do these observations about authority in a practice have to say concerning a theology of authority?

Authority in the Church does not have its foundation outside the Church but arises in the relationships between the communion of saints, the people who practice discipleship, seeking to live a holy life and die a holy death. The Church is not founded on an external authority, whether Jesus or the scriptures. Jesus does not function as an authority apart from the Church, but precisely as the one whose body the members of the Church form. The scriptures do not function as an authority outside the Church, but precisely as the first authoritative text within the community of Christian practice. This is not to deny that Christ or the scriptures are the foundation of the Church, any more than it is to deny that revelation is the foundation of faith. But just as the-way-things-are-in-themselves is not directly available as a foundation for our knowledge independent of our doxastic practices, and just as God-as-God is independent-of-the-world is not directly available as a foundation for our faithful response to and acceptance of revelation, so God or Christ or scripture as-they-are-in-themselves are not directly available as a foundation for the Church independent of faithful participation. Just as reflecting what there is can best be construed as a result of good doxastic practices, so fidelity to divine authority is best construed as the result of good religious practices.

Within the explicit community of disciples, the Church, all Christians have an authority appropriate to their roles. The *Dogmatic Consti-*

---

[44] One way of understanding the contribution of Michael Walzer's important *Spheres of Justice: A Defense of Pluralism and Equality* (New York: Basic Books, 1983) is that it shows good and bad ways of negotiating just compensation for harm and reward for difficulties and dangers among different practices in which we participate. The issue of "interpractice" justice is beyond the concerns of the present text.

tution on the Church of the Second Vatican Council, *Lumen Gentium*, lays out in chapters 3 through 5 the "offices" of the members of the Church. How these offices or roles are constituted is a contingent matter.[45] Other than by initiation into the Church through baptism, how one receives these roles is also a contingent matter.[46] One can argue that authority structures in the Church emerge in response to conflicts within and without the community of Christian practice.[47] Catholic teaching also recognizes the authority of conscience,[48] which may place one in disagreement with authoritative teaching. The creative work of theologians to challenge official doctrinal formulations, discussed especially in chapter 4, also exemplifies the role-specific duties and rights—and thus the authority—that theologians can exercise. As with all traditions, patterns of authority both are "made" and feel "found" within the practice.

An important distinction must be drawn when considering resistance to authority. That one "dissents from" an authoritative pronouncement does not entail that one must reject the authority that pronounces. These are two different claims, requiring different warrants in arguments to support them. An argument to support one's nonacceptance of the official condemnation of artificial contraception

---

[45] For instance, in "The Ordination of Women in the Early Middle Ages" (*Theological Studies* 61/3 [2000]), historian of theology Gary Macy argues that the very meaning of the concept of ordination has evolved so that what "constitutes" ordination to a role within the Church (and the correlated distinctions of clerical and laic roles) is not a constant but a contingent state of affairs. Macy's examples are primarily patristic and medieval.

[46] With regard to one authoritative role, that of bishop, Garrett Sweeney notes the different patterns for naming bishops and the centralization of a pattern of papal appointment in the nineteenth century (see *Bishops and Writers* [Wheathampstead, Herfordshire: Anthony Clarke Books, 1977], 199-231).

[47] The change of patterns in papal primacy provides an example of the contingency of patterns of authority. See Klaus Schatz, *Papal Primacy: From Its Origins to the Present*, trans. John A. Otto and Linda M. Maloney (Collegeville, Minn.: Liturgical Press, 1996). For a call for the reformation of the present pattern, see John R. Quinn, "The Exercise of the Primacy and the Costly Call to Unity," in *The Exercise of the Primacy*, ed. Phyllis Zagano and Terrence W. Tilley (New York: Crossroad/Herder, 1998), 1-28.

[48] In his commentary on Canon 752, which prescribes a "religious respect of intellect and will" for the teaching of the hierarchy, James Coriden notes that since teachings are included that are not infallible and can be erroneous, "the principles of the pursuit of truth and the primacy of conscience still come into play" (see *The Code of Canon Law: A Text and Commentary*, ed. James A. Coriden, Thomas J. Green, and Donald E. Heintschel [New York/Mahwah: Paulist Press, 1985], 548).

by Catholic authorities is very different from one to support one's nonacceptance of papal and magisterial authority *tout court*. One can accept the former argument without being required to accept the latter. One can accept magisterial authority in general but resist or argue against specific exercises of that authority.

The authority within and of the Church is also limited where religious practice intersects other practices. Such potential conflicts are ordinarily construed as oppositions of religious and political authority, or confrontations of the Church and the academy. Yet even the shape of such confrontations is contingent: the ways in which medieval popes and kings engaged in clashes of authority are different from the oppositions between the Church and doctrinaire, liberal regimes such as revolutionary France, or between the Church and pluralist, tolerant nations such as the United States. Like hospitals, cultural spaces in which multiple practices are found, inculturated religious practices take place in cultural spaces where other practices are also found.

More important are the conflicts initiated because Christians do not live exclusively "in" the community of practice that is the Church. A person's social location is not determined by religion alone. We also live in other communities of practice, for example, political communities, families, voluntary associations, professional societies, and so on. As James W. McClendon Jr. put it, the Church is not the world, but "the line between the church and world passes right through each Christian heart."[49] Conflicts affect the "selves" we become in practice because we are constituted in multiple roles given by multiple practices. These conflicts often seem most painful when our role-specific duties and rights collide.

A theology of authority growing out of a practical account of tradition must both recognize the constancies in practice and in authorities that conservatives recognize and also acknowledge the contingency and multiple sites of authority within a tradition that liberals valorize. That there can be no purely external foundation for authority may raise the suspicions of theological conservatives as much as the epistemological claims made above raise the suspicions of realists. What we can say is that divine authority is not a criterion by which we can judge the practices of authority, but that the authentic practices of authority can and will result in reflecting the authority of

---

[49] James Wm. McClendon Jr., *Systematic Theology*, vol. 1, *Ethics* (Nashville, Tenn.: Abingdon, 1986), 17.

God. That authoritative roles have a rightful and necessary place within a tradition and thereby limit, sometimes severely, participants' freedom to act to achieve the goals of that tradition may raise liberals' hackles, especially if they presume that all authority is external to individuals and that authority conflicts (at least potentially, and often in practice) with the freedom of a Christian. Yet if participants are shaped by practices and authority is internal to a practice, then authority is not necessarily external to the person. Moreover, authority patterns are characteristic of traditions, even liberal traditions. However "free" in an abstract metaphysical sense people may be, "independent" of practices, if they participate in no practices and live in no regimes of authority, that freedom is a practical delusion. For without participating in linguistic practices, they could not speak. Without participating in other social practices, they could not have a concrete identity. As our exploration of "following a rule" in chapter 4 showed, remarkable creativity is possible within practices. Moreover, one can abandon oppressive religious practices in a pluralistic society even if one cannot engage in revolution against them. Practical freedom, like all freedom save ideal and abstract freedom, is constrained. By recognizing that authority is as invented and reinvented within a practice, and yet is as internalized in various ways by participants as any other aspect of the practice, the desultory debates of "liberals" and "conservatives" can be recast and, perhaps, come to resolution of some issues concerning authority.

A practical approach to authority might even have the effect of providing a way to understand one of the most difficult and controversial themes in the Christian tradition. The paradox that runs through much theology since Augustine is that "true freedom is obedience to God." In a practical approach to tradition, this dark saying can be taken to mean that if our authoritative religious practices do result in reflecting God's will for humanity, then the result will be authentic human freedom. Like revelation and faith, authority and freedom are constituents of, not independent foundations for, our practices. As reflecting God's revelation accurately, then, can be a result of authentic fidelity, so embodying true freedom can be a result of authentic obedience—a freedom and obedience that is no respecter of rank or order in the community.

To work out a theology of authority would require substantial development beyond the present account. The point here is merely to sketch the lines on which such a theology could be developed and to show how a practical approach to freedom and authority might illumine longstanding theological disputes.

Conclusion

A practical theology of tradition, then, reshapes each of the theological topics with which tradition is typically related. It suggests ways to overcome arguments between liberals and conservatives about authority that have long been stalemated. It is enhanced by and illuminates a mainstream theology of revelation in the Catholic tradition. It provides ways not only to recognize the constructedness of our practices and traditions, but also to account for how we develop and warrant truth claims while avoiding the anti-realism typical of much postmodern thought.

Catholic traditions are invented and reinvented whenever and wherever they are inculturated. The Christian tradition is never not inculturated. Thus it always has been and always will be invented. As cultures change and as other practices develop in concert with, independent of, or even out of explicitly Christian practices, Christian practice changes. It is not that it *must* change or that it *should* change; it *does* change. If Christianity is to be the living faith of the dead, and not the dead faith of the living, to paraphrase Chesterton, its practices and the doctrines that are the grammar of its practices will change in response to internal and external changes.

Crucial for identity through change is *not* remembering *what* the past said or did. Remembering our forbears is a practice, one of the practices constituent in any living tradition. Fidelity to them and to those who will come after us is a virtue. To be faithful members of a religious tradition is to engage in *traditio* faithfully, the practice of passing to the future our inheritance from the past. We cannot and must not merely repeat the past or even its formulations or rubrics. Rote repetition may even be counterproductive to fidelity, a counterfeit of faithful remembering. As chapter 4 showed, fidelity may require even abandoning traditional formulations. The traitor may be the *traditor* who is the most "traditionalist"!

Our fidelity is constituted not by a "what" but by "how." Our faithful memories are not preserved in practices frozen in the past but in living performances that warm our hearts and enlighten our minds. Our communal memory, as Paul Connerton reminds us, is carried in our bodies shaped by our practices, especially those ritual practices that make and remake us, invent and reinvent us as a people.[50] The refrain to a popular liturgical song captures this:

---

[50] Paul Connerton, *How Societies Remember* (Cambridge: Cambridge University Press, 1989).

> We remember how you loved us to your death,
> and still we celebrate for you are with us here;
> and we believe that we will see you when you come
> in your glory, Lord.
> We remember, we celebrate, we believe.[51]

We may sing a different tune than our forbears, and our successors will sing yet differently. Not in spite of but because of those differences we can engage faithfully in *traditio*.

The Catholic tradition is constituted in the practices of prayer and discipleship: *Lex orandi, lex sequendi, lex credendi*. Faithfully transmitting our communal memory in fidelity to our past and our future is possible only in practice, only by engaging in the ongoing, ever-changing, and multilayered practice of *Inventing Catholic Tradition*.

---

[51] Marty Haugen, "We Remember," ©1980, G.I.A. Publications, Inc.

Bibliography

Abbott, Walter M., S.J., and Joseph Gallagher, eds. *The Documents of Vatican II.* New York: Guild Press, America Press, Association Press, 1966.

Ackrill, J. L. "Aristotle on Action." In *Essays on Aristotle's Ethics,* edited by Amélie Oksenberg Rorty, 93-101. Berkeley and Los Angeles: University of California Press, 1980.

Alston, William P. "A 'Doxastic Practice' Approach to Epistemology." In *Knowledge and Skepticism,* edited by M. Clay and K. Lehrer, 1-29. Boulder, Colo.: Westview, 1989.

———. *Perceiving God: The Epistemology of Religious Experience.* Ithaca, N.Y.: Cornell University Press, 1991.

———. "Response to My Critics." *Religious Studies* 30/2 (1995): 171-80.

Aquino, María Pilar. "Theological Method in U.S. Latino/a Theology: Toward an Intercultural Theology for the Third Millennium." In *From the Heart of Our People: Latino/a Explorations in Catholic Systematic Theology,* edited by Orlando O. Espín and Miguel H. Díaz, 6-48. Maryknoll, N.Y.: Orbis Books, 1999.

Asad, Talal. *Genealogies of Religion: Discipline and Reasons of Power in Christianity and Islam.* Baltimore, Md.: Johns Hopkins University Press, 1993.

Austin, John L. "A Plea for Excuses." In *Philosophical Papers,* edited by J. O. Urmson and G. J. Warnock, 123-52. Oxford: Clarendon Press, 1961.

Avis, Paul, ed. *Divine Revelation.* Grand Rapids, Mich.: Eerdmans, 1997.

Balthasar, Hans Urs von. *Dare We Hope "That All Men Be Saved"? With a Short Discourse on Hell.* Translated by David Kipp and Lothar Krauth. San Francisco: Ignatius Press, 1988.

Baltimore Catechism. < http://www.catholic.net/RCC/Catechism >.

Barbour, Ian G. *Issues in Science and Religion.* New York: Harper & Row, 1971.

Barnes, Michael Horace. *Stages of Thought: The Co-Evolution of Religious Thought and Science.* New York: Oxford University Press, 2000.

Barth, Karl. *The Humanity of God.* Richmond, Va.: John Knox Press, 1960.

Bell, Catherine. *Ritual: Perspectives and Dimensions.* New York and Oxford: Oxford University Press, 1997.

Bernstein, Richard. *Praxis and Action: Contemporary Philosophies of Human Activity.* Philadelphia: University of Pennsylvania Press, 1971.

Berry, Colman J., ed. *Readings in Church History.* 3 vols. New York: Newman Press, 1965.

Boeglin, Georges. *La question de la tradition dans la théologie catholique contemporaine.* Paris: Cerf, 1998.

Boone, Kathleen C. *The Bible Tells Them So: The Discourse of Protestant Fundamentalism.* Albany, N.Y.: SUNY Press, 1989.

Bracken, Joseph, S.J. *The Divine Matrix: Creativity as Link between East and West.* Maryknoll, N.Y.: Orbis Books, 1995.

———. *The Triune Symbol: Persons, Process and Community.* Lanham, Md.: University Press of America, 1985.

Breslin, John, S.J., ed. *The Substance of Things Hoped For: Fiction and Faith: Outstanding Modern Short Stories*. New York: Doubleday, 1987.

Buckley, Michael, S.J. *Papal Primacy and the Episcopate: Towards a Relational Understanding*. New York: Crossroad, 1998.

Burrell, David. *Exercises in Religious Understanding*. Notre Dame, Ind.: University of Notre Dame Press, 1974.

Catholic Common Ground Initiative. *Church Authority in American Culture*. New York: Crossroad, 1999.

Charlesworth, Max. *Religious Inventions: Four Essays*. Cambridge: Cambridge University Press, 1997.

Chopp, Rebecca. *The Power to Speak: Feminism, Language, God*. New York: Crossroad, 1989.

Christian, William A., Sr. *Oppositions of Religious Doctrines*. New York: Herder, 1969.

Clarkson, John F., S.J., et al. *The Church Teaches: Documents of the Church in English Translation*. St. Louis: B. Herder Book Company, 1955.

Clebsch, William A. *Christianity in European History*. New York: Oxford University Press, 1979.

Clifford, Richard J. "The Rocky Road to a New Lectionary." *America* 177/4 (16 August 1997): 18-22.

Code, Lorraine. *What Can She Know? Feminist Theory and the Construction of Knowledge*. Ithaca, N.Y.: Cornell University Press, 1991.

"Coma." < http://www.pbs.org/wgbh/nova/transcripts/2411coma.html >.

Comstock, Gary. "Two Types of Narrative Theology." *Journal of the American Academy of Religion* 55/4 (Winter 1987): 687-717.

Congar, Yves, O.P. "Church History as a Branch of Theology." *Church History in Future Perspective*. In Concilium 57, edited by Roger Aubert, 85-96. New York: Herder and Herder, 1970.

———. *Tradition and Traditions: An Historical and a Theological Essay*. Translated by Michael Naseby and Thomas Rainborough. New York: Macmillan, 1967.

Connerton, Paul. *How Societies Remember*. Cambridge: Cambridge University Press, 1989.

Coriden, James A., Thomas J. Green, and Donald E. Heintschel, eds. *The Code of Canon Law: A Text and Commentary*. Mahwah, N.J./New York: Paulist Press, 1985.

Cuneo, Michael. *The Smoke of Satan: Conservative and Traditionalist Dissent in Contemporary American Catholicism*. New York: Oxford University Press, 1997.

Cunningham, Lawrence S. *Catholic Prayer*. New York: Crossroad, 1989.

———. *The Catholic Experience*. New York: Crossroad, 1984.

———. *The Catholic Faith*. New York: Paulist Press, 1987.

———. *The Catholic Heritage*. New York: Crossroad, 1983.

Curran, Charles E. *The Catholic Moral Tradition Today: A Synthesis*. Washington, D.C.: Georgetown University Press, 1999.

D'Antonio, William V. "The American Catholic Laity in 1999." *National Catholic Reporter* (29 October 1999): 12.

Dalzell, Thomas G., S.M. "Lack of Social Drama in Balthasar's Theological Dramatics." *Theological Studies* 60/3 (September 1999): 457-75.

DeLillo, Don. *White Noise*. New York: Viking Penguin, 1985.

Derrida, Jacques. "Plato's Pharmacy." In *Disseminations*, translated by Barbara Johnson, 61-171. Chicago: University of Chicago Press, 1981.

Dillenberger, John, and Claude Welch. *Protestant Christianity: Interpreted through Its Development*. 2d ed. New York: Macmillan, 1988.

Dionne, J. Robert, S.M. *The Papacy and the Church: A Study of Praxis and Reception in Ecumenical Perspective*. New York: Philosophical Library, 1987.

Dolan, Jay P. *The American Catholic Experience: A History from Colonial Times to the Present*. Garden City, N.Y.: Doubleday, 1985.

Doyle, Dennis. "Journet, Congar and the Roots of Communion Ecclesiology." *Theological Studies* 58/3 (September 1997): 461-79.

Dulles, Avery, S.J. *Models of Revelation*. 2d ed. Maryknoll, N.Y.: Orbis Books, 1992.

———. *The Resilient Church: The Necessity and Limits of Adaptation*. Garden City, N.Y.: Doubleday, 1977.

———. "Tradition as a Theological Source." In *The Craft of Theology: From Symbol to System*, 87-104. New York. Crossroad, 1996.

Dybek, Stuart. "Hot Ice." In *The Substance of Things Hoped For*, edited by John B. Breslin, S.J., 85-111. Garden City, N.Y.: Doubleday, 1987.

Edwards, James C. *The Authority of Language: Heidegger, Wittgenstein, and the Threat of Philosophical Nihilism*. Tampa, Fla.: University of South Florida Press, 1990.

Edwards, Paul, ed. *The Encyclopedia of Philosophy*. New York: Macmillan, 1967. S.v. "Ramus, Peter," by Walter J. Ong, S.J.

Ellis, John Tracy, ed. *Documents of American Catholic History*. 2d ed. Milwaukee, Wis.: Bruce Publishing, 1962.

Espín, Orlando O. "Tradition and Popular Religion: An Understanding of the *Sensus Fidelium*." In *The Faith of the People: Theological Reflections on Popular Catholicism*, 63-90. Maryknoll, N.Y.: Orbis Books, 1997.

Evans, Helen C., and William D. Wixom, eds. *The Glory of Byzantium: Art and Culture of the Middle Byzantine Era, A.D. 843-1261*. New York: Metropolitan Museum of Art, 1997.

Fiorenza, Francis Schüssler. *Foundational Theology: Jesus and the Church*. New York: Crossroad, 1985.

Frei, Hans. *The Eclipse of the Biblical Narrative: A Study in Eighteenth and Nineteenth Century Hermeneutics*. New Haven, Conn.: Yale University Press, 1974.

Freud, Sigmund. *The Future of an Illusion*. Translated by James Strachey. New York: W. W. Norton and Co., 1961.

Fulkerson, Mary McClintock. *Changing the Subject: Women's Discourses and Feminist Theology*. Minneapolis, Minn.: Fortress Press, 1994.

Gadamer, Hans-Georg. *Truth and Method*. 2d. rev. ed. Translated by Joel Weinsheimer and Donald G. Marshall. New York: Continuum, 1989.

Geertz, Clifford. *The Interpretation of Cultures*. New York: Basic Books, 1973.

Geiselmann, Josef. *The Meaning of Tradition*. Translated by W. J. O'Hara. New York: Herder and Herder, 1966.

Gilman, Richard. *Faith Sex Mystery: A Memoir*. New York: Simon and Schuster, 1986.

Goizueta, Roberto S. *Caminemos con Jesús: Toward a Hispanic/Latino Theology of Accompaniment*. Maryknoll, N.Y.: Orbis Books, 1995.

Goodman, Nelson. *Ways of Worldmaking*. Indianapolis, Ind.: Hackett, 1978.

Grant, Robert M., and David Tracy. *A Short History of the Interpretation of the Bible*. 2d ed. Philadelphia: Fortress Press, 1984.

Greeley, Andrew M. *The Catholic Myth: The Behavior and Beliefs of American Catholics*. New York: Scribner's, 1990.

———. "Letter to the Editor." *America* 179/1 (4 July 1998): 29.

———. "Theology and Sociology: On Validating David Tracy." *Journal of the American Academy of Religion* 59/4 (Winter 1991): 643-52.

Grimes, Ronald. "Reinventing Ritual." *Soundings* 75/1 (1992): 21-41.

Gutiérrez, Gustavo. *A Theology of Liberation: History, Politics, and Salvation.* Translated and edited by Sister Caridad Inda and John Eagleson. Maryknoll, N.Y.: Orbis Books, 1973.

Haack, Susan. "Confessions of an Old-Fashioned Prig." In *Manifesto of a Passionate Moderate: Unfashionable Essays*, 7-30. Chicago: University of Chicago Press, 1998.

———. *Evidence and Inquiry: Towards Reconstruction in Epistemology.* Oxford: Basil Blackwell, 1993.

Harvey, Van A. *The Historian and the Believer.* New York: Macmillan, 1966.

Hauerwas, Stanley, and David Burrell. "Self-Deception and Autobiography: Reflections on Speer's *Inside the Third Reich.*" In *Truthfulness and Tragedy: Further Investigations in Christian Ethics*, 82-98. Notre Dame, Ind.: University of Notre Dame Press, 1977.

Haugen Marty. "We Remember." G.I.A. Publications, 1980.

Haught, John F. *Science and Religion: From Conflict to Conversation.* Mahway, N.J.: Paulist Press, 1995.

Henry, Patrick. "'And I Don't Care What It Is': The Tradition-History of a Civil Religion Proof-Text." *Journal of the American Academy of Religion* 49/1 (March 1981): 35-49.

Hick, John. *Death and Eternal Life.* New York: Harper & Row, 1980.

Hobsbawn, Eric, and Terence Ranger, eds. *The Invention of Tradition.* Cambridge: Cambridge University Press, 1983.

Hoffer, William, and Marilyn Mona Hoffer. *Freefall.* New York: St. Martin's Press, 1989.

Holmer, Paul. *The Grammar of Faith.* New York: Harper & Row, 1978.

Howell, Clifford. *Of Sacraments and Sacrifice.* Collegeville, Minn.: Liturgical Press, 1952.

Inglis, John. *Spheres of Philosophical Inquiry and the Historiography of Medieval Philosophy.* Leiden, Boston, Koln: Brill, 1998.

Jaenen, Cornelius J. *Friend or Foe: Aspects of French-Amerindian Cultural Contact in the Sixteenth and Seventeenth Centuries.* New York: Columbia University Press, 1976.

James, William. *The Varieties of Religious Experience.* New York: Collier Macmillan, 1961.

———. "The Will to Believe." In *The Will to Believe and Other Essays in Popular Philosophy*, 1-31. New York: Longmans, Green and Co., 1897; reprint New York: Dover Publications, 1956.

John Paul II. *Fides et Ratio.* < http://www.vatican.va/holy_father/john_paul_ii/encyclicals/index.htm >.

Johnson, Elizabeth A., C.S.J. *Friends of God and Prophets: A Feminist Theological Reading of the Communion of Saints.* New York: Continuum, 1998.

———. *She Who Is: The Mystery of God in Feminist Theological Discourse.* New York: Crossroad, 1992.

Jones, James H. *Bad Blood: The Tuskegee Syphilis Experiment.* New York: Free Press; London: Macmillan, 1981.

Jungmann, Joseph A., S.J. *The Mass of the Roman Rite: Its Origins and Development.* 2 vols. Translated by Francis A. Brunner, C.SS.R. New York: Benziger Brothers, 1951.

Kaufmann, Walter, ed. *Religion from Tolstoy to Camus.* New York: Harper & Row, 1961.

Kavanagh, Aidan. *Elements of Rite: A Handbook of Liturgical Style.* New York: Pueblo, 1982; Collegeville, Minn.: Liturgical Press, 1990.

Kennedy, Eugene. "Quiet Mover of the Catholic Church." *New York Times Magazine* (23 September 1979): 22-23, 64-74.

Komonchak, Joseph, Mary Collins, and Dermot Lane, eds. *The New Dictionary of Theology*. Wilmington, Del.: Michael Glazier, 1987. S.v. "Original Sin," by Gabriel Daly. S.v. "Tradition," by George H. Tavard.

Küng, Hans. *On Being a Christian*. Translated by Edward Quinn. Garden City, N.Y.: Doubleday, 1976.

LaCugna, Catherine M. *God for Us: The Trinity and Christian Life*. San Francisco: HarperSanFrancisco, 1991.

Landy, Thomas. "Catholic Studies at Catholic Colleges and Universities." *America* 178 (3 January 1998): 12-17.

Lane, Dermot. "David Tracy and the Debate about Praxis." In *Radical Pluralism and Truth: David Tracy and the Hermeneutics of Religion,* edited by Werner G. Jeanrond and Jennifer L. Rike, 18-37. New York: Crossroad, 1991.

———. "Dulles on Revelation." *The Living Light* 21 (1984): 76-77.

Lash, Nicholas. *Believing Three Ways in One God: A Reading of the Apostles' Creed*. London: SCM Press, 1992; Notre Dame, Ind.: University of Notre Dame Press, 1993.

LeCarré, John (pseud). *A Perfect Spy*. New York: Knopf, 1986.

Lindbeck, George. *The Nature of Doctrine*. Philadelphia: Fortress Press, 1984.

———. "The Problem of Doctrinal Development and Contemporary Protestant Theology." In *Man as Man and Believer*. Concilium 21, edited by Edward Schillebeeckx, 133-49. New York: Paulist Press, 1967.

Livingston, James C. *The Anatomy of the Sacred: An Introduction to Religion*. 3d ed. Upper Saddle River, N.J.: Prentice-Hall, 1998.

Lonergan, Bernard J.F., S.J. *Insight: A Study of Human Understanding*. New York: Philosophical Library, 1957.

Lourdeaux, Lee. *Italian and Irish Filmmakers in America: Ford, Capra, Coppola, and Scorsese*. Philadelphia: Temple University Press, 1990.

Luckman, Thomas, and Peter Berger. *The Social Construction of Reality*. Garden City, N.Y.: Doubleday, 1966.

MacIntyre, Alasdair. *After Virtue: A Study in Moral Theory*. Notre Dame, Ind.: University of Notre Dame Press, 1981.

———. *Three Rival Versions of Moral Inquiry: Encyclopedia, Genealogy, and Tradition*. Notre Dame, Ind.: University of Notre Dame Press, 1990.

———. *Whose Justice? Which Rationality?* Notre Dame, Ind.: University of Notre Dame Press, 1988.

Mackey, James P. *The Modern Theology of Tradition*. London: Darton, Longman & Todd, 1962.

Macy, Gary. "The Eucharist and Popular Religiosity." *Proceedings of the Annual Convention of the Catholic Theological Society of America* 52 (1997): 39-58.

———. "The Ordination of Women in the Early Middle Ages." *Theological Studies* 61/3 (2000).

———. *Treasures from the Storeroom: Medieval Religion and the Eucharist*. Collegeville, Minn.: Liturgical Press, 1999.

Mauriac, François. "A Christmas Tale." In *Substance of Things Hoped For*, edited by John B. Breslin, S.J., 20-29. Garden City, N.Y.: Doubleday, 1997.

McClendon, James Wm., Jr. *Biography as Theology: How Life Stories Can Remake Today's Theology*. Nashville, Tenn.: Abingdon, 1974. 2d ed., Philadelphia: Trinity Press, 1990.

———. *Systematic Theology*. Vol. 1, *Ethics*. Nashville, Tenn.: Abingdon, 1986. Vol. 2, *Doctrine*. Nashville, Tenn.: Abingdon, 1994. Vol. 3, *Witness*. Nashville, Tenn.: Abingdon, forthcoming.

McDannell, Colleen. *Material Christianity: Religion and Popular Culture in America.* New Haven, Conn.: Yale University Press, 1995.

McFague, Sallie. *Models of God: Theology for an Ecological, Nuclear Age.* Philadelphia: Fortress Press, 1987.

McKenzie, R. A. F., S.J. "Revelation." In *Documents of Vatican II*, edited by Walter M. Abbott, S.J., and Joseph Gallagher, 107-10. New York: Guild Press, America Press, Association Press, 1966.

Miller, Vincent J. "History or Geography? Gadamer, Foucault, and Theologies of Tradition." In *Theology and the New Histories,* edited by Gary Macy, 56-85. The Forty-fourth Annual Volume of the College Theology Society. Maryknoll, N.Y.: Orbis Books, 1999.

Mitchell, Nathan D. *Liturgy and the Social Sciences.* Collegeville, Minn.: Liturgical Press, 1999.

Mize, Sandra Yocum. "Dorothy Day's *Apologia* for Faith after Marx." *Horizons* 22/2 (Fall 1995): 198-213.

———. "On the Back Roads: Searching for American Catholic Intellectual Traditions." In *American Catholic Traditions: Resources for Renewal,* edited by Sandra Yocum Mize and William Portier, 3-23. The Forty-second Annual Volume of the College Theology Society. Maryknoll, N.Y.: Orbis Books, 1997.

Morris, Charles R. *American Catholic: The Saints and Sinners Who Built America's Most Powerful Church.* New York: Random House, 1997.

Morris, T. V. *The Logic of God Incarnate.* Ithaca, N.Y.: Cornell University Press, 1986.

Myerhoff, Barbara. *Number Our Days.* New York: Simon and Schuster, 1978.

New Catholic Encyclopedia. New York: McGraw Hill, 1967. S.v. "Pius X, Pope," by C. Ledré.

Newman, John Henry. *An Essay on the Development of Christian Doctrine.* 2d ed. London: James Toovey, 1846 (reprint of the 1845 edition); Westminster: Christian Classics, 1968 (reprint of the 1878 edition).

Orsi, Robert A. *Thank You, Saint Jude: Women's Devotion to the Patron Saint of Hopeless Causes.* New Haven, Conn.: Yale University Press, 1996.

Pelikan, Jaroslav. *Development of Christian Doctrine: Some Historical Prolegomena.* New Haven, Conn., and London: Yale University Press, 1969.

———. *Imago Dei: The Byzantine Apologia for Icons.* Princeton, N.J.: Princeton University Press, 1990.

Pelotte, Donald E., S.S.S. *John Courtney Murray: Theologian in Conflict.* New York: Paulist Press, 1976.

Penelhum, Terence. *God and Skepticism.* Boston: Reidel, 1983.

Pickstock, Catherine. *After Writing: On the Liturgical Consummation of Philosophy.* Oxford: Basil Blackwell, 1998.

Polanyi, Michael. *Personal Knowledge: Towards a Post-Critical Philosophy.* Chicago: University of Chicago Press, 1958.

Preus, J. Samuel. *Explaining Religion: Criticism and Theory from Bodin to Freud.* New Haven, Conn.: Yale University Press, 1987.

Quinn, John R. "The Exercise of the Primacy and the Costly Call to Unity." In *The Exercise of the Primacy: Continuing the Dialogue,* edited by Phyllis Zagano and Terrence W. Tilley, 1-28. New York: Crossroad/Herder, 1998.

Rahner, Hugo. *Greek Myths and Christian Mystery.* Translated by Brian Battershaw. London: Burns and Oates, 1963.

Rahner, Karl, S.J., and Joseph Ratzinger. *Revelation and Tradition.* Translated by W. J. O'Hara. New York: Herder and Herder, 1966.

Rappaport, Roy A. "The Obvious Aspects of Ritual." In *Ecology, Meaning, and Religion*, 173-221. Richmond, Calif.: North Atlantic Books, 1979.

Ricoeur, Paul. *Time and Narrative* I. Translated by Kathleen McLaughlin and David Pellauer. Chicago: University of Chicago Press, 1984.

Rorty, Richard. *Philosophy and the Mirror of Nature*. Princeton, N.J.: Princeton University Press, 1979.

Schaff, Philip, and Henry Wace, eds. *Nicene and Post-Nicene Fathers*. New York: Charles Scribner's Sons, 1900.

Schatz, Klaus. *Papal Primacy: From Its Origins to the Present*. Translated by John A. Otto and Linda M. Maloney. Collegeville, Minn.: Liturgical Press, 1996.

Schloesser, Stephen. "'When You Read Catholic Writers Everything Is Really, Really Dark': Twentieth Century Sacramental Modernism." Unpublished paper prepared for the Roman Catholic Studies Group of the American Academy of Religion, 22 November 1999.

Schreiter, Robert J., C.Pp.S. *Constructing Local Theologies*. Maryknoll, N.Y.: Orbis Books, 1985.

———. *The New Catholicity: Theology between the Global and the Local*. Maryknoll, N.Y.: Orbis Books, 1997.

Sellars, Wilfrid. "Empiricism and the Philosophy of Mind." In *Science, Perception, and Reality*, 127-96. New York: Humanities Press, 1963.

Shea, John. *Stories of God: An Unauthorized Biography*. Chicago: Thomas More Press, 1978.

Smith, Jonathan Z. *Drudgery Divine: On the Comparison of Early Christianities and the Religions of Late Antiquity*. Chicago: University of Chicago Press, 1990.

Smith, Barbara Herrnstein. *Contingencies of Value: Alternative Perspectives for Critical Theory*. Cambridge, Mass.: Harvard University Press, 1988.

Stagaman, David., S.J. *Authority in the Church*. Collegeville, Minn.: Liturgical Press, 1999.

Starr, Paul. *The Social Transformation of American Medicine*. New York: Basic Books, 1982.

Sullivan, Francis A., S.J., "Recent Theological Observations on Magisterial Documents and Public Dissent." *Theological Studies* 58/3 (September 1997): 509-15.

Sweeney, Garrett. *Bishops and Writers: Aspects of the Evolution of Modern English Catholicism*. Wheathampstead: Anthony Clarke Books, 1977.

Tanner, Kathryn. *Theories of Culture: A New Agenda for Theology*. Philadelphia: Fortress Press, 1997.

Thiel, John. *Imagination and Authority: Theological Authorship in the Modern Tradition*. Minneapolis, Minn.: Fortress Press, 1991.

Tilley, Terrence W. *The Evils of Theodicy*. Washington, D.C.: Georgetown University Press, 1991.

———. "The Institutional Element in Religious Experience." *Modern Theology* 10/2 (April 1994): 185-212.

———. "Incommensurability, Intratextuality, and Fideism." *Modern Theology* 5/2 (January 1989): 87-111.

———. "'Lord, I Believe: Help My Unbelief': Prayer without Belief." *Modern Theology* 7/3 (April 1991): 239-47.

———. "The Philosophy of Religion and the Concept of Religion: D. Z. Phillips on Religion and Superstition." *Journal of the American Academy of Religion* 68/2 (June 2000): 345-56.

———. "Polemics and Politics in Explaining Religion." *The Journal of Religion* 71/2 (April 1991): 242-54.

———. "Practicing History, Practicing Theology." In *Theology and the New Histories,* edited by Gary Macy, 1-20. The Forty-fourth Annual Volume of the College Theology Society. Maryknoll, N.Y.: Orbis Books, 1999.

———. "The Principle of Innocents' Immunity." *Horizons* 15/1 (Spring 1988): 43-63.

———. "A Recent Vatican Document on 'Christianity and the World Religions.'" *Theological Studies* 60/3 (June 1999): 318-37.

———. "Religious Pluralism as a Problem for 'Practical' Religious Epistemology." *Religious Studies* 30/2 (June 1994): 161-69.

———. *Story Theology.* Wilmington, Del.: Michael Glazier, 1985.

———. *The Wisdom of Religious Commitment.* Washington, D.C.: Georgetown University Press, 1995.

Tilley, Terrence, et al. *Postmodern Theologies: The Challenge of Religious Diversity.* Maryknoll, N.Y.: Orbis Books, 1995.

Tracy, David. *The Analogical Imagination: Christian Theology and the Culture of Pluralism.* New York: Crossroad, 1981.

———. *Plurality and Ambiguity: Hermeneutics, Religion, Hope.* San Francisco: Harper & Row, 1987.

Tuchman, Barbara. *The March of Folly: From Troy to Vietnam.* New York: Knopf, 1984.

Vidler, Alec R. *A Variety of Catholic Modernists.* Cambridge: Cambridge University Press, 1970.

Wainwright, Geoffrey. *Doxology: The Praise of God in Worship, Doctrine, and Life: A Systematic Theology.* New York: Oxford University Press, 1980.

Walzer, Michael. *Spheres of Justice: A Defense of Pluralism and Equality.* New York: Basic Books, 1983.

Weaver, Mary Jo, and R. Scott Appleby, eds. *Being Right: Conservative Catholics in America.* Bloomington, Ind.: Indiana University Press, 1995.

Weber, Max. *Max Weber on Charisma and Institution Building.* Edited by S. N. Eisenstadt. Chicago: University of Chicago Press, 1968.

Weinberg, Steven. "A Designer Universe?" *New York Review of Books* 46/16 (21 October 1999): 46-48.

Welch, Sharon. *A Feminist Ethic of Risk.* Minneapolis, Minn.: Fortress Press, 1989.

White, Andrew Dickson. *A History of the Warfare of Science with Theology in Christendom.* Gloucester, Mass.: Peter Smith, 1978.

Wiebe, Donald. *The Politics of Religious Studies: The Continuing Conflict with Theology in the Academy.* New York: St. Martin's Press, 1999.

Winch, Peter. "Discussion of Malcolm's Essay." In Norman Malcolm, *Wittgenstein: A Religious Point of View,* edited by Peter Winch, 95-135. London: Routledge, 1993.

Wittgenstein, Ludwig. *On Certainty.* Edited by G. E. M. Anscombe and G. H. von Wright. Translated by Denis Paul and G. E. M. Anscombe. Oxford: Basil Blackwell, 1969.

———. *Philosophical Investigations.* 3d ed. Translated by G. E. M. Anscombe. New York: Macmillan, 1958.

Wolterstorff, Nicholas. *Locke and the Ethics of Belief.* Cambridge: Cambridge University Press, 1996.

Wright, John Hickey, S.J. "Patristic Testimony on Women's Ordination in *Inter Insignores.*" *Theological Studies* 58/3 (September 1997): 516-26.

Wyschogrod, Edith. *Spirit in Ashes: Hegel, Heidegger, and Man-Made Mass Death.* New Haven, Conn.: Yale University Press, 1985.

Zagano, Phyllis, and Terrence W. Tilley, eds. *The Exercise of the Primacy: Continuing the Dialogue.* New York: Crossroad/Herder, 1998.

Index